The Two Syriac Versions of the Prayer of Manasseh

Gorgias Eastern Christian Studies

30

Series Editors

George Anton Kiraz

István Perczel

Lorenzo Perrone

Samuel Rubenson

Gorgias Eastern Christian Studies brings to the scholarly world the underrepresented field of Christianity as it developed in the Eastern hemisphere. This series consists of monographs, collections of essays, texts and translations of the documents of Eastern Christianity, and studies of topics relevant to the unique world of historic Orthodoxy and early Christianity.

The Two Syriac Versions of the Prayer of Manasseh

By

Ariel Gutman

Wido van Peursen

gorgias press

2011

Gorgias Press LLC, 954 River Road, Piscataway, NJ, 08854, USA

www.gorgiaspress.com

2011 ܫ

ISBN 978-1-4632-0050-3 **ISSN 1539-1507**

Cover Illustration: detail from Spencer Gr. 1 manuscript, New York public library (see p. 35).

Library of Congress Cataloging-in-Publication Data

Peursen, W. Th. van.
Two Syriac versions of the Prayer of Manasseh / by Wido van Peursen, by Ariel Gutman.
p. cm. -- (Gorgias Eastern Christian studies, ISSN 1539-1507 ; 30)
English and Syriac.
Includes bibliographical references (p.) and indexes.
1. Bible. O.T. Apocrypha. Prayer of Manasses. Syriac--Versions. I. Gutman, Ariel. II. Bible. O.T. Apocrypha. Prayer of Manasses. English & Syriac. III. Title.
BS1815.52.P48 2011
229'.6043--dc23

2011025531

Printed in the United States of America

To my parents,
Hélène and Per-Olof,
with love
(Ariel Gutman)

To the memory of my beloved father,
Willem Louis van Peursen
ܕܟܪܢܗ ܠܒܘܪܟܬܐ
(Wido van Peursen)

Contents

List of Tables

List of Illustrations

List of Figures

List of Glosses

1, 2, 3	1st, 2nd, 3rd person
SG	singular
PL	plural
M	masculine
F	feminine
CST	construct state
ABS	absolute state
EMPH	emphatic state
INT	intensive *binyan* (Paˁˁel or Etpaˁˁal)
CAUS	causative *binyan* (Apˁel or Ettaphˁal)
REFL	reflexive *binyan* (Etpˁel, Etpaˁˁal or Ettapˁal)
PRF	perfect tense/aspect
IMPF	imperfect tense/aspect
IMPT	imperative
INF	infinitive
AP	active participle
PP	passive participle
DEM	demonstrative pronoun
Q	interrogative pronoun
POSS	pronominal possessive suffix
OBJ	pronominal object suffix
LNK	linker particle (*d-* or *dil-*)
NEG	negation (*lā*)
EXP	existential particle (*ˀit* and its variants)

Notes:

- Glosses are given for the linguistic examples in chapters 2 and 3, following a vocalized transcription of the example. Punctuation marks are transcribed as well to an approximate counterpart.

- The elements of the glosses are separated by . except the verbal lexeme (the root together with the *binyan* markers), which is separated from the TAM (tense, aspect, mood) and pronominal morphemes by a : sign.

- The sign = precedes the enclitic personal pronoun (as well as the enclitic verbal form *(h)wā*). Other particles, whose status as enclitics is disputed (such as *dēn* or *gēr*), are not marked as such.

- In order to facilitate the reading of the glosses, the following conventional omissions are made:

  1. Verbs are in the Pˁal *binyan* unless marked otherwise.
  2. Free personal pronouns are glossed directly by a person marker.
  3. Nouns (and adjectives) without suffixes are in the emphatic state unless marked otherwise, while nouns with possessive suffixes are always in the construct state.
  4. Participles (predicative or not) are in the absolute state unless marked otherwise.
  5. Nouns, adjectives, and prounouns are singular unless indicated otherwise. Nonetheless, in some cases a SG gloss is given explicitly, to highlight a difference between the two versions.
  6. Adjectives and pronouns are masculine unless indicated otherwise (note that the 1st person pronouns are not marked for gender).
  7. Nouns are not glossed for gender, except the noun *biša* 'evil' which appears in both genders.

Preface

> *One of the finest pieces in the Apocrypha is the little classic of penitential devotion known as the Prayer of Manasseh. Constructed in accord with the best liturgical forms and full without being protracted, this beautiful prayer breathes throughout a spirit of deep and genuine religious feeling.*[1]

The research presented in this book is devoted to the comparison of two versions of one Syriac text, called 'The Prayer of Manasseh' (=PrMan), which is a short penitential prayer incorporated in the Syriac translation of the Bible, the *Peshiṭta.*

Like so many other texts from Antiquity, PrMan is attested in various manuscripts, which do not always agree as regards the text. When a scholarly edition is compiled, this variation has to be presented in a sensible way, be it in a diplomatic edition (one manuscript is selected as the main text; variants from other manuscripts are given in an apparatus) or in an eclectic edition (in which the main text consists of a scholarly reconstruction of 'the original', rather than the text of one manuscript). The Leiden Peshiṭta edition, especially in its first volumes (which include PrMan) most often follows the policy of a diplomatic edition. The basic manuscript for the Leiden edition is the Codex Ambrosianus (siglum: 7a1). For those books that are not found in this codex, to which PrMan also belongs, another manuscript is chosen. However, PrMan has the peculiarity that not one manuscript was selected as the main text, but rather two different manuscripts, which were presented in two parallel columns. The linguistic, philological and text-critical comparison of these two manuscripts is the central aim of this book.

[1] Metzger, *Apocrypha of the Old Testament*, 219.

Our research into PrMan forms part of a broader research project, which is carried out at the Peshiṭta Institute of Leiden University. This project, called 'Turgama: Computer-Assisted Analysis of the Peshiṭta and the Targum: Text, Language and Interpretation', has dealt so far mainly with the analysis of Syriac texts and their comparison to the Hebrew text in a computer-assisted analytical framework (see section 2.2). The two parallel texts of PrMan offered an ideal test ground for the extension of this framework to an inner-Syriac comparison. For this reason a pilot project was launched at the beginning of 2008; three years later, the results matured into this book.

As a first step in our research, both texts of PrMan were analysed according to the model of computational linguistic analysis developed in the Turgama project (and its predecessor CALAP – Computer-Assisted Linguistic Analysis of the Peshiṭta). The second step was the comparison itself. Since, however, the tools for the comparative analysis are still being developed, a great deal of this comparison was done manually, contributing to, rather than making use of the model and programs we are developing.

The book is divided into six chapters: Chapter 1 gives a historical and text-critical introduction regarding the Prayer of Manasseh and the milieu in which it originated. A survey of the different versions of the Prayer, in Syriac as well in other languages, is given, with a special emphasis on the two versions that concern us here. The chapter ends with a summary of the history of the Syriac language in relation to the Prayer of Manasseh for the non-specialist reader.

Chapter 2 forms the central axis of the research: in this chapter a detailed analysis of the grammatical differences between the two versions is given, covering three layers of grammar: morphology, phrase syntax and clause syntax. This chapter may be of special interest for those who are interested in Syriac linguistic research and its application.

Chapter 3 is concerned with the lexical profile of each version and the differences between them in this respect. This chapter combines a linear-based lexical comparison of the two texts with a non-linear quantitative approach to the lexeme inventory. As such, it may be of interest to those seeking different methods to compare texts.

Chapter 4 presents a comparison of the texts at the discourse level, using a hierarchical-analytical approach that has been developed in the CALAP project. In this chapter the main interest is not the separated linguistics units, as in the two previous chapters, but rather the relationship between the linguistic units, starting at the clause level. This chapter is also concerned with the question of the alignment of the two versions, and the status of various pluses or minuses (see especially section 4.6).

Although our main interest lies in the two versions as given by the two manuscripts that are used as the base text in the edition, we do not ignore the other Syriac manuscripts. Comments about these manuscripts are scattered throughout the book, and a more systematic examination of the variant readings is given in chapter 5.

Finally, chapter 6 contains a discussion of the relationship between the two manuscripts as well as the methodology used throughout the book. For the convenience of the reader, an appendix gives the full text of both versions together with an English translation.

Because of some fascinating characteristics of the Syriac language and because of the relevance of the interaction of linguistic analysis and text comparison beyond the field of Syriac studies, various readers of the pre-published manuscript of this book strongly encouraged us to add transliterations and glosses to the Syriac examples. Although we realize that for those who know Syriac this may be somewhat superfluous, we decided to do so in chapters 2 and 3 and to add a full transliterated and glossed text of the two versions of PrMan in an appendix. We hope that linguists and philologists who are not trained in Syriac may benefit from it and that our research into PrMan, combining a computational linguistic analysis and philological research, will contribute not only to the study of the textual history of the two versions of this Prayer and the relationship between them, but also to the broader field of Syriac linguistics and eventually to linguistic theory in general.

We would like to express our gratitude to the Netherlands Organization for Scientific Research (NWO) for its generous support to the Turgama research project, of which the present monograph is a deliverable. Furthermore, the cooperation between the two authors was made possible due to an exchange program between the Hebrew

University of Jerusalem and Leiden University, which we are also grateful for. We are also grateful to those colleagues who responded to our questions or gave feedback on earlier versions of the present volume, including Dr Konrad Jenner (section 1.5), Professor Jacques van der Vliet (section 1.5.2), Dr Uri Simonsohn (section 1.7), Dr Jan van Ginkel (section 1.7.3), Professor Paul Smith, Dr Julia C. Szirmai, and Dr Umar Ryad (section 1.7.4), Dr Pollet Samvelian and Dr Alain Desreumaux (chapters 2–6), and Professor Eep Talstra (chapter 4). This monograph also benefited much from the valuable input of other members of the Turgama project, viz. Dirk Bakker, Percy S.F. van Keulen, and Constantijn J. Sikkel.

We are grateful to those institutions that granted us permission to use the images of manuscripts included in the present volume, namely, London, British Library (illustrations 9–14, 19); New York, Public Library (illustration 15); Athens, National Library (illustration 17); Paris, Library Bibliothèque Nationale (illustrations 1–4, 16, 18); Florence, Biblioteca Mediceo-Laurenziana (illustration 5), Cambridge, University Library (illustrations 6–8); Monastery of Roussanou, Metéora, Thessaly, Greece (illustration 20). We are indebted to Dianne van der Zande, MA, for her assistance in collecting the images. Finally, we are thankful to Mrs Helen Richardson-Hewitt for her correction of the English.

We are thankful to Professor István Perczel, who kindly agreed to include this volume in the Gorgias Eastern Christian Studies series and who gave a valuable detailed review of an earlier version of this book.

The typesetting of this manuscript was done by the authors using XƎLaTeX and its various accompanying packages. The English text was typeset in the Junius-Unicode (Junicode) font. The authors are grateful to all the developers of these free software packages.

Ariel Gutman and Wido van Peursen
Paris and Leiden, May 2011

Chapter 1

Manasseh's Prayer and its place in the Syriac tradition

1.1 King Manasseh and his prayer

The Prayer of Manasseh (=PrMan) is a prayer of penitence attributed to the seventh-century B.C. king of Judah. According to 2 Chronicles 33:11–13, Manasseh, notorious for his wickedness and idolatry, humbled himself before God in captivity:

> Therefore the Lord brought against them the commanders of the army of the king of Assyria, who took Manasseh captive in manacles, bound him with fetters, and brought him to Babylon. While he was in distress he entreated the favor of the Lord his God and humbled himself greatly before the God of his ancestors. He prayed to him, and God received his entreaty, heard his plea, and restored him again to Jerusalem and to his kingdom. Then Manasseh knew that the Lord indeed was God. (NRSV)

Furthermore, the Chronicler tells that Manasseh's prayer is written in the 'Records of the Seers' (33:19), but he does not give the words of his prayer. PrMan seems an attempt to fill this gap.

In the present chapter we will investigate the sources in which PrMan is attested, starting with the source that has chronologically and text-historically priority over all other sources, the *Didascalia* (section 1.2). After that we will have a look at the other Greek and Latin sources, including biblical and liturgical manuscripts and an intriguing inscription found in Phrygian Hierapolis (section 1.3). This will be followed by some observations on the Hebrew version of the Prayer (section 1.4).

Most attention will be paid, however, to the focus of the present study, the Syriac textual witnesses, which include – in addition to manuscripts of the *Didascalia* – biblical manuscripts in which PrMan is part of the Odes or appended to Chronicles, and a number of Melkite Horologia (section 1.5). In these textual witnesses two Syriac versions can be discerned (section 1.6). The differences between the two versions concern not only the prayer itself, but also its introduction: Version B has a interesting superscription that speaks of a 'brazen bull' in which Manasseh uttered his prayer, after which it was broken into pieces and Manasseh was transposed back to Jerusalem. A separate paragraph is devoted to the background of this superscription and the traditions reflected in it (section 1.7). Our investigation into the textual witnesses of PrMan and the contexts in which they functioned is followed by a discussion about the religious milieu in which it originated (section 1.9).

For the benefit of the non-Syriac readership, we have included at the end of this chapter (section 1.10), a short introduction to the history of the Syriac language.

1.2 PrMan in the *Didascalia*

We can trace the existence of PrMan back into the early third century CE, as part of the Greek *Didascalia*, which was probably written in that century. The *Didascalia Apostolorum* or 'Teaching of the Holy Apostles' claims to have been written by the Apostles at the time of the Council of Jerusalem (Acts 15:1–29). It is a church order and contains instructions to various groups of people, including bishops, deacons, and widows. The Greek text of the *Didascalia* is no longer extant,[1] but it can be reconstructed on the basis of its Syriac translation and of the Greek text of the *Apostolic Constitutions*. Manuscripts of the Syriac *Didascalia* date from the 10th century and later,[2] but quotations of it in Aphrahat's *Demonstrations* suggest an early date

[1]Except for the fragments edited in Bartlet, 'Fragments of the Didascalia Apostolorum in Greek'.

[2]See below, section 1.5.1.

for this translation, perhaps in the first decades of the fourth century.[3] The *Apostolic Constitutions* were composed at the end of the fourth century CE. The first six books are based on the *Didascalia*. PrMan occurs in *Apostolic Constitutions* II, 22,12–14.[4]

The seventh chapter of the *Didascalia* opens with 'Therefore, O bishop, reach and rebuke and loose by forgiveness. And know your place – it is that of God Almighty, and that you have received authority to forgive sins.' What follows is an encouragement to the bishops to have a lenient, merciful attitude towards repentant sinners. In the third century CE, the question as to how to deal with repentant sinners was pertinent, because it had an immediate impact on the treatment of the *lapsi*, those who had denied their faith under the pressure of persecution, but afterwards returned to the Church. It has been argued that the instructions in this chapter imply a polemic against Novatianism, a movement that rejected the readmission to the communion of the *lapsi*.

A substantial part of this chapter of the *Didascalia* is devoted to Manasseh, who is put forward as an outstanding example of an extremely wicked sinner, who finally repented and thereupon received forgiveness from God.[5] The section on Manasseh draws upon material from Kings and Chronicles, but contains also four additions

[3]Thus Borbone, 'Preghiera di Manasseh', 540; Connolly, *Didascalia Apostolorum*, xviii. Connolly dates the Syriac translation of the *Didascalia* between 300 and 330 CE. Vööbus, *The Didascalia Apostolorum in Syriac*, I (Syr. 176), 26*–28*, is more hesitant to draw conclusions. He speaks of 'parallels' rather than 'quotations' and claims that it is impossible to say whether the Syriac version was prepared before or after the time of Aphrahat.

[4] Funk, *Didascalia et Constitutiones Apostolorum*, I, 84–88; Metzger, *Les Constitutions Apostoliques*, I, 216–220. For the Greek manuscripts of the *Apostolic Constitutions* see also Denis–Halewyck, *Introduction à la littérature religieuse judéo-hellénistique*, I, 665–666. PrMan 14b–15 has been preserved in the Latin translation of the *Didascalia* (Verona Fragments; Hauler, *Didascaliae Apostolorum Fragmenta Ueronensia Latina*, 33–34; Tidner, *Didascalia Apostolorum Canonum Ecclesiasticorum Traditionis Apostolicae Versiones Latinae*, 38) and in the Ethiopic version (Platt, *The Ethiopic Didascalia*, 49–51); for the Ethiopic version we have now also the excellent, but unfortunately unpublished edition of manuscript EMML 6533 in De Waard, *The Ethiopic Didascalia* (PrMan on pp. 45–48).

[5]On the function of PrMan in this chapter of the *Didascalia* see also Newman, 'Three Contexts for Reading Manasseh's Prayer in the Didascalia', 4–6; Newman, 'The Form and Settings of the Prayer of Manasseh', 122–124.

that do not have parallels in these books.[6] One of the additions is the Prayer of Manasseh, which is introduced by 'And when he was afflicted very greatly, he sought the face of the Lord his God, and humbled himself greatly before the God of his fathers. And he prayed before the Lord God and said: Prayer of Manasseh', after which the text of the prayer itself follows.

Since it is generally acknowledged that the text of PrMan in the Greek *Didascalia* has priority over all other extant versions,[7] it has been argued that the author of the *Didascalia* himself had composed PrMan.[8] Whether this is true or not depends on questions as to the date of origin of PrMan,[9] its religious background[10] and its original language,[11] and on the literary-critical analysis of the place of

---

[6] Cf. Newman, 'Three Contexts for Reading Manasseh's Prayer in the Didascalia', 6: 'Yet the tale does not accord with any single tradition, either the Hebrew or Greek of 2 Kgdms 21 or 2 Chr 33, but rather represents a paraphrastic account that draws on traditions found in the targums and shared by Samaritan and Greek sources'; see also Ryle, 'The Prayer of Manasses', 613; Vööbus, *The Didascalia Apostolorum in Syriac*, I (Syr. 175), 50–51.

[7] See below, section 1.3.

[8] Thus Nau, 'Un extrait de la *Didascalie*', 137; Nestle, *Septuagintastudien*, III, 12–13. Nau and Nestle attributed PrMan to the author of the *Didascalia*, rather then to that of the *Apostolic Constitutions* (*pace* Charlesworth, 'Prayer of Manasseh', 627 [Nau and Nestle]; Newman, 'The Form and Settings of the Prayer of Manasseh', 122, note 46 [Nau]). PrMan was attributed to the author of the *Apostolic Constitutions* by J.P. Migne (*Dictionnaire des Apocryphes*, 850). We had no access to *Libri Veteris Testamenti apocryphi* by J.A. Fabricius (1694), who, according to Charlesworth (ibid.), Nestle (ibid., 12, 17), Newman (ibid.) and others, also attributed PrMan to the author of the *Apostolic Constitutions.*

[9] A number of scholars have argued for a date in the first century CE, before the destruction of Jerusalem, or even earlier. For an overview see Charlesworth, 'Prayer of Manasseh', 627.

[10] If it is assumed that PrMan is a Jewish text and that the *Didascalia* is a Christian composition, the conclusion that the Christian author of the *Didascalia* used an existing Jewish source seems to be unavoidable. However, the arguments that have been put forward for a Jewish background of PrMan are not compelling (see below, section 1.9.3). There is a tendency to assume that the *Didascalia* is a reworked Jewish composition. Should that be the case, then the prayer may also be composed by the Jewish author of the original composition, but the arguments for a Jewish original of the *Didascalia* are not compelling either (cf. below, section 1.9.3).

[11] Some have advocated a Semitic original, others have argued that PrMan was composed in Greek. For details see Charlesworth, 'Prayer of Manasseh', 626. The

PrMan in the *Didascalia*. If one agrees with Pier G. Borbone that 'the most appropriate context is that of the *Didascalia*, of which it is an integral part of the story of the penitence of Manasseh',[12] one might be inclined to consider it as a composition by the author of the *Didascalia*,[13] but Judith H. Newman has argued that PrMan is an insertion in the *Didascalia*, rather than an original part of the composition, because the text of the prayer is preceded by the superscription, 'Prayer of Manasseh', which interrupts the flow of the narrative.[14] In our view, neither Borbone's nor Newman's argument is compelling. On the one hand, the relations between PrMan and the context do not prove its being composed by the author of the *Didascalia*. It is also possible that the author of the *Didascalia* used an existing source and was influenced by it when composing the surrounding text. On the other hand, the 'seemingly clumsy'[15] and 'puzzling'[16] superscription does not demonstrate that PrMan is an insertion in the *Didascalia*, because it is also possible that in the textual transmission the superscription entered the main text from the margins. This occurred also, for example, to some section titles such as 'The Vision of Eve', in manuscripts of the *Life of Adam and Eve*.[17]

Hebrew version of PrMan from the Cairo Genizah is a tenth-century translation from the Syriac (or Greek) and the Prayer of Manasseh in the Dead Sea Scrolls has no connection to the prayer under discussion. (see below, section 1.4).

[12]Borbone, 'Preghiera di Manasseh', 540: 'If we consider the locations of the Prayer of Manasseh in the manuscripts and in the works mentioned above [i.e. the *Didascalia* and the *Apostolic Constitutions*], it is not difficult to acknowledge that the most appropriate context is that of the *Didascalia*, of which it is an integral part of the story of the penitence of Manasseh. Moreover, it mentions the chains imposed on the king which are also mentioned in the Prayer. The *Didascalia* must, therefore be the original context of the Prayer.' (our translation).

[13]This is also suggested by Nickelsburg, 'Prayer of Manasseh', 770.

[14]Newman, 'Three Contexts for Reading Manasseh's Prayer in the Didascalia', 7; Van der Horst–Newman, *Early Jewish Prayers in Greek*, 135.

[15]Newman, 'The Form and Settings of the Prayer of Manasseh', 123.

[16]Newman, 'The Form and Settings of the Prayer of Manasseh', 124.

[17]See Tromp, *The Life of Adam and Eve in Greek*, 85–86.

1.3 OTHER GREEK AND LATIN WITNESSES TO PRMAN

PrMan occurs not only in textual witnesses to the *Didascalia* and the *Apostolic Constitutions* (above, section 1.2), but also in biblical manuscripts.[18] To these belong the Greek Codex Alexandrinus (5th c. CE) and the Psalterium Turicensis (7th c. CE), in which it is found among the Odes, following the book of Psalms, and the minuscule manuscript 55 (10th c. CE) and later minuscules.[19] It is generally acknowledged that the text of PrMan in the Greek biblical manuscripts derives from that in the *Apostolic Constitutions* or from the now lost text in the *Didascalia*.[20]

Another group of Greek witnesses consists of Byzantine Horologion manuscripts, in which PrMan occurs as part of the Great Compline. A Horologion (Ὡρολόγιον) or 'Book of Hours' is a service book containing a collection of texts, prayers and psalms that are used in the daily office in the Eastern Churches. The Great Compline is a penitential office that is performed on a number of special occasions (see below, section 1.5.3). We will come back to the role of PrMan in the Byzantine Horologion in our discussion of the Syriac Melkite Horologia.[21]

An enigmatic Greek witness was discovered in August 2004 by Italian archaeologists, who found an inscription from the fifth or sixth century CE containing the Greek text of PrMan during their excavations in Hierapolis of Phrygia (Turkey). The text of the Prayer was painted on the wall of an underground room of a private house. It has been suggested that this location indicates that the inscription

---

[18]By 'biblical manuscripts' we mean manuscripts that contain the running text of at least one book of the Bible, unlike manuscripts that contain only excerpts, such as the liturgical and masoretic manuscripts; see Van Peursen, 'La diffusion des manuscrits bibliques conservés'.

[19]The Greek text can be found in Rahlfs, *Psalmi cum Odis*, 361–363; cf. also p. 79. Rahlfs used the text of the Codex Alexandrinus as the basis. For the Greek manuscript evidence see also Denis–Halewyck, *Introduction à la littérature religieuse judéo-hellénistique*, I, 667–668.

[20]Thus e.g. Nau, 'Un extrait de la *Didascalie*'; Oßwald, 'Das Gebet Manasses', 17; Charlesworth, 'Prayer of Manasseh', 627.

[21]Below, section 1.5.3; see also Denis–Halewyck, *Introduction à la littérature religieuse judéo-hellénistique*, I, 668.

had some esoteric function, perhaps in a penitential ritual.[22]

Another interesting epigraphic source is a funeral stele from the Nile Valley, probably from Nubia,[23] the Epitaph of Kollouthos, which can be dated in the fourth quarter of the first millennium.[24] In this funeral inscription the prayer for the deceased contains a quotation from PrMan, verse 13. A. Łajtar assumes that the author of the inscription was inspired by the liturgical use of PrMan.[25] He refers to use of the same verse in the Greek Liturgy of St Mark as it is attested in the Kacmarcik Codex.[26]

In Latin PrMan was not preserved in Vulgate manuscripts until the 13th century, but in almost all manuscripts from the 13th century onwards, it occurs as an addition to 2 Chronicles 33:13, 19.[27]

1.4 THE HEBREW VERSION OF PRMAN

There are no strong reasons to assume that the extant Greek, Latin and Syriac versions of PrMan in the end go back to a Hebrew original. A Hebrew 'Prayer of Manasseh' is attested in the Dead Sea Scrolls (4Q381 fr. 33+35, lines 8–11), but this prayer has no connection with

[22] See the detailed analysis in the excavation report: D'Andria *et al.*, 'L'iscrizione dipinta con la Preghiera di Manasse a Hierapolis di Frigia (Turchia)'. For text-critical observations on this inscription see the discussion by G. B. Bazzana on pp. 434–442 of this report (=Bazzana, 'Osservazioni').

[23] Thus Łajtar, 'Épitaphe de Kollouthos', 258; Łajtar, 'Notes on Greek Christian Inscriptions from the Nile Valley', 140.

[24] Thus Łajtar, 'Épitaphe de Kollouthos', 258. Kubińska, 'Une pierre funéraire chrétienne au Musée National de Varsovie', 76, suggested an earlier date, in the fourth or fifth century; cf. Łajtar, ibid.

[25] Łajtar, 'Épitaphe de Kollouthos', 259: 'Tout porte à croire que le text de la messe entendue régulièrement à l'église est devenu une source directe d'inspiration pour l'auteur de l'inscription'.

[26] Cf. Macomber, 'The Anaphora of Saint Mark according to the Kacmarcik Codex'; quotation from PrMan 13 on p. 91; On this manuscript see also Macomber, 'The Kacmarcik Codex. A 14th Century Greek-Arabic Manuscript of the Coptic Mass'; Macomber, 'The Greek Text of the Coptic Mass and the Anaphoras of Basil and Gregory according to the Kacmarcik Codex'; and Khalil, 'Le codex Kacmarcik et sa version arabe de la liturgie alexandrine'.

[27] On the Latin version see also Denis–Halewyck, *Introduction à la littérature religieuse judéo-hellénistique*, I, 668–671; Schneider, 'Der Vulgata-Text der Oratio Manasseh'; Volz, 'Zur Überlieferung des Gebetes Manasse'.

the prayer under discussion.[28] Whereas the latter is characterized by key words and motifs that connect it with the Manasseh story in Chronicles,[29] such a connection is completely absent in the Qumran prayer. It has been argued that the Qumran prayer represents an early extra-biblical tradition, which predates the Chronicler's history, and was perhaps even part of the source to which the Chronicler refers,[30] but it is more likely that in this case the attribution to Manasseh is secondary.[31]

A Hebrew version of the prayer of Manasseh under discussion has been discovered, however, in a manuscript from the Cairo Genizah. In the extant folios of this manuscript[32] PrMan is surrounded by five other prayers, most of which have 'a mystico-magical character'.[33] Rather than the Hebrew original of the Greek or Syriac version of PrMan, this Hebrew version turns out to be a (re-)translation from the Syriac, and possibly also the Greek version. Thus according to Reimund Leicht, this Hebrew text of PrMan is a tenth-century translation from a Greek text close to the text of the Codex Turicensis, but reflects also unequivocal influence from the Syriac version. This is an interesting indirect witness to the spread of PrMan in the Syriac tradition and of the 'Jewish (re-)adaptation of a text from Christian sources'.[34]

There are reasons to assume that Christians who had converted to

---

[28]Cf. Schuller, '4Q380 and 4Q381: Non-Canonical Psalms from Qumran', 94–95; Schniedewind, 'A Qumran Fragment of the Ancient Prayer of Manasseh?'; Borbone, 'Preghiera di Manasseh', 542.

[29]See below, section 1.5.4.

[30]Thus Schniedewind, 'A Qumran Fragment of the Ancient Prayer of Manasseh?'.

[31]Thus e.g. Schuller, 'Non-Canonical Psalms', 123.

[32]Cambridge T.-S. K 1.144; T-S. K 21.95.T; T.-S. K 21.95.P. Edition: Schäfer–Shaked, *Magische Texte aus der Kairoer Geniza*, II, 27–78; PrMan on pp. 32 (text), 53 (translation).

[33]Leicht, 'A Newly Discovered Hebrew Version', 360.

[34]Leicht, 'A Newly Discovered Hebrew Version', 368. Other witnesses to acquaintance with Syriac liturgical texts from the Cairo Genizah include the fragments of a thirteenth- or fourteenth-century Syriac hymn book edited by Sebastian Brock; see Brock, 'East Syrian Liturgical Fragments from the Cario Genizah' and Brock, 'Some Further East Syrian Liturgical Fragments from the Cairo Genizah'; cf. Leicht, ibid.

Judaism were responsible for the (re-)adaptation of Christian sources, especially the translations from Greek sources.[35] These converts were acquainted with these sources and they knew their languages and scripts,[36] and they probably learned Hebrew at a later age, which may account for the fact that these sources are sometimes in poor Hebrew. Converts to Judaism from Christian backgrounds are frequently mentioned in the Genizah documents and it is conceivable that Cairo, outside the territory of the Christian Byzantine empire, was a safe place for them to take refuge.

1.5 THE SYRIAC TEXTUAL WITNESSES

1.5.1 General survey

The Syriac text of PrMan has been edited by W. Baars and H. Schneider in *The Old Testament in Syriac* 4/6 (Leiden 1972).[37] The textual basis of this edition includes biblical manuscripts, manuscripts of the *Didascalia*, marked with a D in the siglum, e.g. 10D1 and 13D1,[38] and Melkite Horologia, marked with an H in the siglum, e.g. 13H1.[39] The oldest biblical manuscript containing PrMan is

[35]This idea and the following considerations were suggested to us by Dr James K. Aitken.

[36]When Jews themselves wrote in Greek, they used Hebrew letters or the Greek majuscule script. It is doubtful, therefore, that they were acquainted with the Greek minuscule script.

[37]Baars–Schneider, 'Prayer of Manasseh'.

[38]10D1 (see illustrations 3–4) and 13D1 (see illustrations 6–8) are the main witnesses; cf. Vööbus, *The Didascalia Apostolorum in Syriac*, I (Syr. 175), 13*–16* (on 10D1); 40*–42* (on 13D1). For a detailed description of the contents of 10D1 see Zotenberg, *Catalogues des manuscrits syriaques*, 22–29. In addition to the *Didascalia*, which covers 90 out of 286 folio's, it contains excerpts from the *Apostolic Constitutions*, the *Doctrine of Addai*, the *Clementine Octateuch*, the canons of various councils, and many others. (Zotenberg's description of this manuscript contains 55 items.) In 13D1, too, the Didascalia occurs in 'a large Collection of Ecclesiastical Canons and extracts from various writers relating to Ecclesiastical Law'; see Wright–Cook, *Catalogue*, II, 600–628, esp. 600. For other D-manuscripts see table 1.1. See also the editions of the *Didascalia*: Lagarde, *Didascalia Apostolorum Syriace*, 29–30; Gibson, *The Didascalia Apostolorum in Syriac*, 60–61; Vööbus, *The Didascalia Apostolorum in Syriac*, I (Syr. 175), 89–91 (text); II (Syr. 176), 85–87 (translation).

[39]See illustrations 9–14. For other H-manuscripts see table 1.1; cf. *List of the Old Testament Peshiṭta Manuscripts*, 112, which only mentions 13H1, 15H1 and

9a1, in which PrMan is part of the Odes.[40] PrMan occurs also in the biblical manuscript 14/8a1 (a fourteenth-century supplement to 8a1), in which it is found between Wisdom and Isaiah; and in 17a6.7.8.9, four closely related seventeenth-century pandects, in which PrMan has been appended to Chronicles.[41] In addition, PrMan is attested in two other liturgical manuscripts. In 10t1 it occurs in an abbreviated Melkite Horologion[42] and in 16g7 in 'The Book of the Prayers of the Seven Hours'.[43] The full list of manuscripts is given in table 1.1 below.

The temporal gap between the Syriac translation of the *Didascalia* in the early fourth century, which is presumably the first appearance of PrMan in Syriac, and the oldest extant Syriac textual witness in the ninth century is considerable. If, however, we assume that 9a1 goes back to a sixth-century text-type, as a number of scholars have argued,[44] the gap becomes much smaller. Moreover, the occurrence of PrMan in 14/8a1 renders it likely that PrMan was originally also included in 8a1,[45] and this manuscript, too, seems to reflect text traditions that go back to an earlier period, perhaps also to the sixth century.[46] From a religious-historical perspective 14/8a1 is important because it is the sole East Syriac biblical manuscript containing PrMan.[47] However, even if these considerations are enough to

15H2. On Melkite liturgical manuscripts see Brock, 'Manuscrits liturgiques en syriaque', 278–280.

[40]See illustration 5. Cf. below, section 1.5.2.

[41]For the text of PrMan in 17a6 see illustrations 1–2. The text of PrMan in these manuscripts is almost identical with that in 9a1; cf. below, section 1.5.4.

[42]For a description of this manuscript see Pigoulewski, 'Manuscrits syriaques bibliques de Léningrad'. See further below, section 1.5.3.

[43]See below, section 1.5.6.

[44]See Jenner, 'A Review of the Methods', 262–264; Van Vliet, 'Deuteronomy', Introduction, G. xii; Lane, *The Peshitta of Leviticus*, 75–76. See further Walter, *Studies in the Peshitta of Kings*, 14–15.

[45]Compare the situation with the Nestorian Morning Prayer which appears to have been part of 8a1 and which was restored in the 14th-century supplement; cf. Jenner, *De perikopentitels van de geïllustreerde Syrische kanselbijbel van Parijs*, 10–11; Schneider, 'Canticles or Odes', Introduction, p. iv.

[46]Jenner, 'A Review of the Methods', 259–262.

[47]Thus Baars–Schneider, 'Prayer of Manasseh', Introduction, p. ii. On the clerical background of this manuscript see Jenner, *De perikopentitels van de geïllustreerde*

postulate the occurrence of PrMan in sixth-century Syriac biblical manuscripts, its absence in complete Bibles such as the sixth- or seventh-century manuscript 7a1 and the twelfth-century Buchanan Bible (12a1) and related manuscripts demonstrates that the fate of PrMan in biblical manuscripts, both regarding its inclusion and regarding its position in relation to other biblical books, shows considerable variation.

From our preceding discussion it follows that in the Syriac witnesses PrMan occurs in three different contexts: biblical manuscripts, manuscripts of the *Didascalia*, and Melkite Horologia. In the first group, that of the biblical manuscripts, there is a fundamental difference in its treatment as a liturgical composition (as part of the Odes) or as an appendix to the Chronicles narrative. The role of PrMan in the *Didascalia* has been discussed above, in section 1.2. We will now look at the place of PrMan as part of the Odes in 9a1 (section 1.5.2), its place in the Melkite Horologia (section 1.5.3) and its function as an appendix to Chronicles (section 1.5.4). In these various contexts, two versions of the Syriac PrMan can be discerned (section 1.6). The classification of the manuscripts into the various contexts and the two versions is given in table 1.2. The manuscripts which served as the basis for the Leiden critical edition are marked in bold-face.

Syrische kanselbijbel van Parijs, 10–11; Jenner, 'A Review of the Methods', 259–262. For a different view (namely that this manuscript is West Syriac rather than East Syriac), see Koster, *The Peshiṭta of Exodus*, 557, note 48.

Siglum	Manuscript	PrMan on fol.
9a1	Florence, Bibl. Medicea Laurenziana, Orient. 58	104b
10t1	St. Petersburg, M.E. Saltykov-Shchedrin State Public Libr., New Series 19	179a-180b
14/8a1	Paris, National Libr., Syr. 341	131a
16g7	Woodbrooke, Selly Oak Colleges Libr., Mingana Syr. 331	13b
17a6	Paris, National Libr., Syr. 7	182a-b
17a7	Rome, Casanatense Libr. 194	185b-186a
17a8	Rome, Vatican Libr., Syr. 7	206a-b
17a9	Rome, Vatican Libr., Syr. 8	176a
10D1	Paris, National Libr., Syr. 62	22b–23a[48]
13D1	Cambridge University Libr. Add. 2023	189b-190b
16D1	Rome, Vatican Libr., Borgian Syr. 148	17a-b
18D1	Rome, Vatican Libr., Borgian Syr. 68	23b-24a
19D1	Harvard, Houghton Libr., Semitic Accession 3971	25a-26b
19D2	Woodbrooke, Selly Oak Colleges Libr., Mingana Syr. 4	15b-16a
20D1	Rome, Vatican Libr., Syr 560B	20a-b
20D2	Montserrat, Abby Libr., Or. 31	48-49
13H1	London, British Museum Add. 14.716	70-72
13H2	Sinai, M. of St. Catherine, Syr. 151	124a-126b
13H3	Sinai, M. of St. Catherine, Syr. 116	81a-83a
13H4	Sinai, M. of St. Catherine, Syr. 158	95b-97b
13H5	Sinai, M. of St. Catherine, Syr. 166	175a-179a
13H6	Sinai, M. of St. Catherine, Syr. 169	128b-132a
15H1	Rome, Vatican Libr., Syr. 77	84b-86a
15H2	Rome, Vatican Libr., Syr. 565	122a-124b

Table 1.1: Syriac manuscripts containing PrMan and their sigla

[48]Thus the numbering scheme of the National Library. Baars–Schneider, 'Prayer of Manasseh' list this as 25b–26a.

Type of manuscripts	Sigla	Number of MSS
Biblical manuscripts		6
–Part of Odes	**9a1**	1
–Between Wisdom and Isaiah	14/8a1	1
–After Chronicles	17a6.7.8.9	4
Manuscripts of the *Didascalia*	10D1; 13D1; 16D1; 18D1; 19D1.2, 20D1.2	8
Liturgical manuscripts		1
–Part of 'The Book of the Prayers of the Seven Hours'	16g7	1
Melkite Horologia		9
–Following Psalms and Odes	**10t1**	1
–Other Horologion-Mss	13H1.2.3.4.5.6; 15H1.2	8

Table 1.2: Types of Syriac manuscripts containing PrMan

1.5.2 The Odes in 9a1

9a1 is the only biblical manuscript in which PrMan occurs as parts of the Odes following the Psalter. Even in liturgical Psalters – which, from the eight century onwards always have the Odes as an appendix to the Psalter – there are no other attestations of PrMan, except for 10t1, but there PrMan is in fact part of an abbreviated Horologion.

Most often the Odes in Syriac manuscripts, irrespective of the religious milieu in which they originated, consist of a series of nine canticles.[49] According to H. Schneider three Odes were appended to the Psalms before the fifth century, to which in the West Syriac tradition another six Odes were added on the model of the Greek

[49] Accordingly, the Leiden edition contains the following Odes: 1. First Canticle of Moses (= Ex 15:1–19/21); 2. Second Canticle of Moses (=Deut 32:1–43); 3. Canticle of Isaiah (=Isa 42:10–13, 45:8); 4. Canticle of Hannah (=1 Sam 2:1–10); 5. Canticle of Habakkuk (=Hab 3:2–19); 6. (Another) Canticle of Isaiah (=Isa 26:9–20); 7. Canticle of Jonah (=Jonah 2:3–10); 8. Canticle of the House of Hananiah (=Dan 3:26–56); 9. Prayer of the House of Hanaiah (=Dan 3:57–88); Appendices: Canticle of Hezekiah (=Isa 38:10–20); Canticle of David (=Ps 63:2–12).

tradition of nine Odes. The series is not completely identical to that in the Greek tradition and there is also some inner-Syriac variation regarding the Odes that are included and the order in which they occur. However, before the series of nine Odes became dominant in the Greek tradition, there existed an alternative list of fourteen Odes, which is attested, among other places, in the Greek Codex Alexandrinus, and which did include PrMan.[50] This alternative collection of fourteen Odes is reflected in 9a1.[51] The religious milieu in which 9a1 originated is a much debated issue,[52] which renders it difficult to evaluate the background of the occurrence of PrMan in 9a1. In any event, 9a1 is a lonely but interesting witness to the use of the fourteen-Odes series in the Syriac tradition.[53]

Not only is PrMan represented in the Greek and Syriac traditions, but the incorporation of PrMan into the Odes is also attested in Coptic Odes manuscripts from the sixth and seventh centuries onwards,[54] including the bilingual Greek-Coptic manuscript from the second half of the sixth century edited by Walter Till and Peter Sanz.[55] Furthermore, Georg Graf mentions the occurrences of

[50]Schneider, 'Die biblischen Oden im christlichen Altertum', 53: 'Tatsächlich hatte vor dem Sieg der endgültigen Neunodenreihe eine Vierzehnodenreihe weitere Verbreitung erlangt und sich da und dort bis ins 9. und 10. Jh. behauptet.' On the fourteen-Odes series in the Codex Alexandrinus see ibid. 52–57; it occurs also in the Codex Turicensis (see above, section 1.3), on which see ibid. 64.

[51]Cf. Schneider, 'Canticles or Odes', Introduction, p. v: 'Following the example of the Greek series of 14 Odes, 9a1 adds between Ode VII and VIII the Prayer of Hezekiah (= Is XXXVIII 10–20) and the Prayer of Manasseh'; cf. also Schneider, 'Die biblischen Oden seit dem sechsten Jahrhundert', 247.

[52]Cf. Jenner, 'A Review of the Methods', 262–264.

[53]Schneider, 'Die biblischen Oden seit dem sechsten Jahrhundert', 247: 'Der syrische Redaktor folgt also wohl liturgischem Einfluss und gibt uns damit Grund zu der Vermutung, dass die ganze Vierzehnodenreihe auch in syrischen Offizien verwendet wurde.'

[54]For details see Denis–Halewyck, *Introduction à la littérature religieuse judéo-hellénistique*, I, 673; *pace* Rahlfs, *Psalmi cum Odis*, 78, who claimed that the Odes do not occur in Boharic and Sahidic translations.

[55]Till–Sanz, *Eine griechisch-koptische Odenhandschrift*; on pp. 32–35 Till and Sanz discuss other Sahidic, Bohairic and Fayyumic Odes manuscripts. (We are indebted to Professor Jacques van der Vliet for this reference). See also above on the bilingual Greek-Arabic Kacmarcik Codex.

PrMan in an Arabic translation of the Psalms and the Odes.[56]

1.5.3 10t1 and other Melkite Horologia

When the series of nine Odes superseded the rival series of fourteen Odes, PrMan lost its prominent place among the Odes. That this apocryphal prayer did not survive in the new liturgical collection may be related to an increased awareness of the demarcation between canonical and apocryphal books.[57] Unlike all the other Odes, PrMan did not recur elsewhere in the canonical scriptures.[58] It received another place, however, in the Byzantine liturgy, as part of the Great Compline, a penitential office which is performed on a number of special occasions (in contrast to the Small Compline, which is performed most nights of the year). From there it also entered or re-entered Syriac liturgy,[59] due to the dominance of the rite of Constantinople in Syria and Palestine after the Byzantine reconquest of north Syria in the late tenth century. As a result, the old Antiochene rite was replaced by the rite of Constantinople.[60] PrMan was included in Melkite Horologia, in which it occupied the same position it has

[56]Graf, *Geschichte der christlichen arabischen Literatur*, I, 114–126 (on Arabic translations of the Psalms and the Odes), espeically 118 (reference to PrMan). The discussion of Arabic witnesses in Denis–Halewyck, *Introduction à la littérature religieuse judéo-hellénistique*, I, 674, mentions only translations of the *Didascalia*.

[57]Cf. Schneider, 'Die biblischen Oden im christlichen Altertum', 54. The nine-Odes series is an excerpt from the fourteen-Odes series, in which some Odes, including PrMan, have disappeared.

[58]For details see above, note 49.

[59]PrMan is also found in a Melkite Horologion in Christian Palestinian Aramaic; see Black, *A Christian Palestinian Syriac Horologion*, 294–298 (text of PrMan) and Black's comment on p. 13: 'The Prayer of Manasseh in its Palestinian Syriac form is of peculiar interest, for not only is it independent of the Greek text on more than one occasion, but in a number of places, particularly in several large additions and rearrangements of the text, it agrees with the Syriac text of the Prayer.'

[60]Cf. Brock, 'Manuscrits liturgiques en syriaque', 278 (on Melkite lectionaries): 'Les manuscripts melkites les plus anciens reflètent le rite antiochien authentique qui entretenait bien des liens avec celui des syro-orthodoxes. Mais à partir du Xe-XIe siècle, ce rite s'était adapté d'une manière radicale au rite de Constantinople, vraisemblablement suite à la reconquête Byzantine du nord de la Syrie (969–1084). See also Brock–Witakowski, *The Hidden Pearl III*, 34.

in Greek Horologia.[61] In 10t1, which is the oldest Melkite witness to the nine-Odes series[62] – the series excluding PrMan – the Psalms and Odes are followed by the Syriac translation of some other prayers from the Greek rite,[63] including PrMan.[64] Accordingly, although the siglum 10t1 marks this manuscript as a biblical manuscript, a liturgical Psalter, PrMan does not occur in its biblical section, but in an abbreviated Horologion.[65]

The liturgical use of PrMan is attested in other Eastern Christian traditions as well.[66] In the Ethiopic liturgy it is also part of Great Compline[67] and in the Armenian Church it is recited in the Vespers.[68]

1.5.4 An appendix to Chronicles in 17a6.7.8.9

That in some Syriac biblical manuscripts PrMan occurs as an appendix to Chronicles[69] will not come as a surprise. Manasseh's prayer is part of the narrative in 2 Chronicles 33 and the Chronicler mentions the 'Records of the Seers' as a source where this prayer has been recorded (above, section 1.1). The gap that is created by the fact that Chronicles itself does not contain the prayer has been filled by the

[61] Cf. Baars–Schneider, 'Prayer of Manasseh', Introduction, p. v; Borbone, 'Preghiera di Manasseh', 539, note 3.

[62] Schneider, 'Die biblischen Oden seit dem sechsten Jahrhundert', 257–258.

[63] Pigoulewski, 'Manuscrits syriaques bibliques de Léningrad', 89.

[64] The assumption that 9a1 is a Melkite manuscript, tentatively suggested by H. Schneider (Schneider, 'Canticles or Odes', Introduction, p. v; cf. Jenner, 'A Review of the Methods', 263), would raise the intriguing question of why in the same Melkite milieu a new translation was produced.

[65] Cf. Baars–Schneider, 'Prayer of Manasseh', Introduction, p. v: 'This peculiar recension of the OrM makes its first appearance in a biblical MS, a Melchite Psalter (10t1), though its later use is restricted to the Horologia. Actually even in this Psalter it does not form part of the Canticles as in 9a1 but of an abbreviated Horologion appended to the Psalter.' All extant Syriac Melkite Horologia up to the 13th century are in abbreviated form, which may be an indication of their dependence on the Greek liturgy (Dr Konrad Jenner, personal communication).

[66] Apart from its inclusion in the Odes in Coptic and Arabic sources, mentioned at the end of section 1.5.2.

[67] Raes, 'Les Complies dans les Rites orientaux', 144.

[68] Conybeare, *Rituale Aremenorum*, 480–481.

[69] Similarly in the Vulgate manuscripts from the 13th century onwards; see above, section 1.3.

composition under discussion. It seems likely that the attribution of this composition to Manasseh is original, that is to say, that it has been composed as a prayer of Manasseh, rather than that the attribution to Manasseh is secondary. Although there is in the prayer itself no direct connection to Manasseh by the use of, for example, a proper noun, the motifs that occur in it, including the emphasis on the sin of idolatry and the mentioning of chains, 'are most naturally interpreted on the assumption that the Prayer is put into the mouth of Manasseh, King of Judah'.[70] If it is composed as a prayer of Manasseh, this fits in well with the tendency to insert prayers into biblical stories, which is also attested in the additions to Daniel and Esther in the Greek version.[71]

Although the position of PrMan as an appendix to Chronicles is not surprising, it is interesting to note that this happens in the manuscripts 17a6.7.8.9, on which Baars and Schneider commented that '[e]xcept for some orthographic differences and one more conspicuous variant in vs. 5 (...) their text is identical with that of 9a1, from which they seem to have [been] copied either directly or indirectly.'[72] Accordingly, although the text of PrMan that appears in these seventeenth-century manuscripts is almost identical with that in 9a1, its position is completely different.

---

[70]Ryle, 'The Prayer of Manasses', 614. See also Ehrmann, *Klagephänome im zwischentestamentlicher Literatur*, 157: 'Deutlich ist der Versuch einer Anbindung der OrMan an 2 Chr 33 mittels Stichwortanknüpfung'; Charlesworth, 'Prayer of Manasseh', 628: 'Before translating the Prayer of Manasseh, I thought it may have been only eventually attributed to Manasseh, since his name does not appear in the prayer and since no clear statements in it demand attribution to this wicked king. But the abundant descriptions in the prayer are strikingly reminiscent of the Chronicler's account of him.' (contrast Charlesworth's more cautious remark on p. 625: 'Eventually, and perhaps originally, attributed to Manasseh').

[71]Cf. Charlesworth, 'Prayer of Manasseh', 631: 'It is now safe to say that this prayer is an expansion of Chronicles as Bel and the Dragon, Susanna, and the Prayer of Azariah and the Song of the Three Young Men are additions to Daniel.'

[72]Baars–Schneider, 'Prayer of Manasseh', Introduction, p. iii; cf. Nau, 'Un extrait de la *Didascalie*', 135: Between Paris no. 7 (=17a6) and the text in the *Didascalia* (Paris, 62; edited in 1854 in Lagarde, *Didascalia Apostolorum Syriace*) there are only orthographic differences. Similarly Wilkins, 'The Prayer of Manasseh', 168. These seventeenth-century manuscripts are copies of sixteenth-century manuscripts of 9a1; apparently the latter were produced when 9a1 was still much more legible (Dr Konrad Jenner, personal communication).

1.5.5 Preceding Isaiah in 14/8a1

PrMan takes a different position in 14/8a1, where it comes immediately before Isaiah. Perhaps this is due to the association between Isaiah (either the prophet or the book) and Manasseh. This association may have been enhanced by the fact that the Book of Isaiah contained the prayer of Manasseh's predecessor, Hezekiah (Isaiah 38:10–20), which immediately precedes PrMan in e.g. the Odes in 9a1.[73] Another source for the association between Manasseh and Isaiah may be the widespread tradition according to which Manasseh martyred Isaiah.[74] The gruesome details that are provided in some sources make the king's wickedness, and hence his repentance even more outstanding. In any event, it seems that in 14/8a1 PrMan was treated as a deutero-canonical or wisdom book, and does not appear in a liturgical context.

1.5.6 Another liturgical manuscript (16g7)

Although the manuscript 16g7 is included in the *List of Old Testament Peshiṭta Manuscripts* of the Peshiṭta Institute Leiden, it contains in reality a rich variety of texts. PrMan occurs in a section that is called 'The Book of the Prayers of the Seven Hours', in which it occurs alongside prayers of both biblical and patristic figures.[75] In a comment on the extract of Psalms of Solomon 16 in this manuscript, which immediately precedes PrMan, Wim Baars wrote the following: 'This manuscript contains among its various contents a collection of "Prayers of the Seven Hours." One of these prayers consists of (...)

[73] In the same manuscript PrMan is separated from the Book of Isaiah by only some portions from the Odes.

[74] Cf. below, section 1.7.2, for some reference to Syriac historiographical sources.

[75] Cf. Mingana, *Catalogue*, 610–616, esp. 610–611. Mingana gives the following list of 'authors mentioned by name in connection with some of the prayers': 1. Philoxenus; 2. The Prophet Jeremiah; 3. Solomon, son of David (=PsSal 16); 4. Manasseh, King of Israel (=PrMan); 5. John the seer of the Thebaid; 6. Isaac of Nineveh (five prayers); 7. Saba the Divine (=John of Daliatha); 8. Marcarius the Egyptian (two prayers); 9. Isaac of Nineveh (a treatise on mysticism in the form of a long prayer); 10. John Chrysostom (two prayers); 11. Basil of Caesarea; 12. Dionysius the Areopagite (eight prayers); 13. St. Ephrem (two prayers); 14. Philoxenus (three prayers); 15. Severus of Antioch; 16. The Prophet Isaiah.

[an] extract of the 16th Psalm of Solomon (...). From the context in which it occurs it seems that this extract had some liturgical function, but it is not clear (at least to me) which particular purpose it served.'[76] This remark applies *mutatis mutandis* to PrMan.

1.5.7 Contexts and functions

Looking at the distribution of PrMan in the Syriac sources, we can observe that it occurs in divergent contexts, which reflect different functions of the Prayer.[77]

1. Where PrMan occurs as an appendix to Chronicles, it figures in a narrative context. It is the prayer of Manasseh, king of Judah, and may be compared with, for example, Psalm 51, a penitential prayer ascribed to David, another Judean king. However, as J. H. Newman has argued, one could move on and consider PrMan in the Chronicles context not just as the prayer of an individual king, but also as a symbol of the people's repentance, because of the 'typological use of historical figures by the Chronicler to mirror the fate of the people in their exile to Babylon and their ultimate return and restoration'. In other words: Manasseh is not just a penitent king, but also the symbol of the people's exile and return and his repentance represents the repentance of the people.[78]

2. In the *Didascalia* PrMan appears in the context of instruction. The 'I' is still the Manasseh of Chronicles, as appears from the narrative elements surrounding the Prayer, but now he has become the prototype of the repentant sinner, rather than a leader or representative of the Judean people.

3. In a liturgical context the prayer has been more or less untied from the historical Manasseh and the 'I' has become the worshipper participating in the liturgy. The 'we' (plural) implied

[76]Baars, 'An Additional Fragment of the Syriac Version of the Psalms of Solomon', 222.

[77]Cf. Newman, 'The Form and Settings of the Prayer of Manasseh', 116–121.

[78]Cf. Newman, 'The Form and Settings of the Prayer of Manasseh', 120.

in the expression 'God of our fathers' in verse 1[79] (cf. section 1.9.3) becomes thus a reference to the liturgical community.[80]

1.6 Two Syriac versions (Versions A and B)

In the sources discussed in the preceding sections two versions of PrMan can be discerned, which Baars and Schneider presented in two parallel columns in the Leiden Peshiṭta edition. The first is found in the Syriac manuscripts of the *Didascalia* and the biblical manuscripts (except for 10t1). The text in the biblical manuscripts derived probably from the translation incorporated in the Syriac *Didascalia*.[81] The other version is found in 10t1 and the Melkite Horologia (and, as we commented above, even in 10t1 PrMan occurs in an abbreviated Horologion appended to the Psalter): 'Besides the translation deriving from the Didascalia Apostolorum, the Syriac Church, or more exactly the Melchite branch of Syriac Christianity, knew a second translation of the OrM (...) This peculiar recension of the OrM makes its first appearance in a biblical MS, a Melchite Psalter (10t1)'.[82]

Baars and Schneider comment on the version of 10t1: 'This translation, though not wholly independent, is largely different from the other'.[83] And according to Borbone, the recension from the Melchite Psalter goes back to a new translation from Greek. The independence appears from the phrases in verse 9 that have been preserved in 10t1 but not in 9a1.[84]

Table 1.3 summarizes the main witnesses to the two versions. The present study readdresses the question as to the relationship between the two versions of PrMan, i.e. the version represented by 9a1 (henceforth version A) and that of 10t1 (version B).

---

[79]But some manuscripts have 'the God of *my* fathers' instead.

[80]Cf. section 6.3.1 on liturgical phraseology shared by both versions of PrMan and section 6.3.2 on some other liturgical features in the B version.

[81]Cf. Nau, 'Un extrait de la *Didascalie*'.

[82]Baars–Schneider, 'Prayer of Manasseh', Introduction, p. v.

[83]Baars–Schneider, 'Prayer of Manasseh', Introduction, p. v.

[84]Borbone, 'Preghiera di Manasseh', 539, note 3; see below, section 4.6.

Version A (15 Mss)	Version B (9 Mss)
Basis for the main text in edition: –9a1	Basis for the main text in edition: –10t1
Other biblical manuscripts (5) –14/8a1; 17a6.7.8.9	Melkite Horologia (8) –13H1.2.3.4.5.6; 15H1.2
Manuscripts of the *Didascalia* (8) –10D1; 13D1; 16D1; 18D1; 19D1.2; 20D1.2	
Other liturgical manuscripts (1) –16g7	

Table 1.3: Textual witnesses to the two versions of PrMan

1.7 THE SUPERSCRIPTION IN VERSION B

1.7.1 Parallels in Jewish sources

Whereas version A has just the heading 'Prayer of Manasseh', version B has a more elaborate introduction, which reads as follows:[85]

> Prayer of Manasseh, king of the Israelites, when he was conducted in captivity in Babel, and they wanted to burn him: he felt sorry when he was inside the brazen bull, he prayed and the bull was broken into pieces, so that he found himself safe and sound in Jerusalem.

This introduction, especially the reference to the 'brazen bull' and the miraculous return to Jerusalem, has some interesting parallels in Jewish traditions. Thus we find in *Targum to 2 Chronicles* 33:12–13:

> Then the Chaldaeans made a brazen mule and bored many small holes in it. They shut him [i.e. Manasseh] up inside it and lit a fire all around it (...) [The Lord] shook the universe by his Memra, the mule was shattered, and he came out from there. Then there went forth a wind from between the wings

[85]We are grateful to our colleague Dr Uriel Simonsohn for some useful comments on an earlier version of section 1.7.

of the cherubim; it blew him by the degrees of the Memra of the Lord and he returned to Jerusalem to his kingdom.[86]

This passages shares with the superscription in PrManB the reference to a brazen animal in which Manasseh was held captive (which in the Targum is an interpretation of the נחשתים *nəḥuštayim* 'brazen vetters' in 33:11) and to his miraculous return to Jerusalem (which may have been motivated by וישיבהו ירושלם למלכותו *wayšiḇēhu yrušālayim lmalḵuto* 'He brought him back to Jerusalem to his kingdom' in 33:13).

The tradition that Manasseh was locked into a brazen bull is also found in *Targum Sheni to Esther* 5:14. The mule[87] of *Targum to Chronicles* reoccurs in a number of late Midrashim, including *Ruth Rabba*, *Devarim Rabba* and *Pesiqta de Rav Kahana*, and in the Palestinian Talmud.[88] *Apocalypse of Baruch* 64:8 speaks of a brazen horse.

In Jewish tradition the story of the captivity of Manasseh in an animal, in which he prayed a prayer of repentance, after which he was rescued from the animal, may also have been influenced by the story of Jonah, who likewise prayed when he was inside an animal, and who was also subsequently delivered from the animal.[89]

1.7.2 Parallels in Syriac sources

In Syriac sources the references to the animal in which Manasseh was held captive are rather scarce. Apart from the Melkite Horologia and

[86]Ed. Sperber, *The Bible in Aramaic*, IV/A, 64; translation adapted from McIvor, 'The Targum to Chronicles'.

[87]If that is the correct interpretation of the word מולתא *multā*; compare the discussion in Bacher, 'Le taureau de Phalaris dans l'Agada', 292–293; Bogaert, *Apocalypse de Baruch*, 315-316.

[88]For details see Bogaert, *Apocalypse de Baruch*, 316. For Rabbinic traditions about Manasseh's punishment see also Ginzberg, *The Legends of the Jews*, IV, 279–280; VI, 375–376.

[89]The book of Jonah is read on the Day of Atonement (*Yom Qippur*), as it is considered an exemplar of successful repentance, although Jonah's role towards the repentance of the people of Ninveveh is to say the least ambiguous and his prayer in chapter 2 cannot be characterized as a prayer of penitence (cf. e.g. Simon, *Jona*, 9–10). In the Christian-Syriac tradition, the canticle of Jonah was part of the canonical Odes (see footnote 49).

the Syriac *Apocalypse of Baruch*, we have found only one other Syriac reference, in Bar Hebraeus' *Chronicon*, which speaks of a ܙܘܕܝܘܢ ܕܢܚܫܐ *zāwdiwān da-nḥāšā* 'brazen *zodion*' (if ܙܘܕܝܘܢ indeed refers to an animal-shaped statue[90]). Other Syriac sources mention Manasseh's name – thus e.g. the eighth-century Zuqnin Chronicle (also known as Pseudo-Dionysius of Tell-Mahre),[91] the eleventh-century *Chronography* of Elias bar Sinaya (Elias of Nisibis)[92] as well as the thirteenth-century *Book of the Bee* (by Solomon of Akhlat)[93] – and others elaborate a bit more on his captivity and his repentance – thus e.g. the ninth-century commentary on Kings by Ishodad of Merv,[94] the twelfth-century Chronicle of Michael the Syrian,[95] and the Anonymous Chronicle of AD 1234[96] – but they usually do not add details that are not in Chronicles.[97] The only recurrent element in these sources that goes beyond the Chronicles story is the reference to Manasseh's role in Isaiah's martyrdom.[98]

1.7.3 Melkite and Byzantine parallels

According to P. G. Borbone, the parallels with Jewish traditions about Manasseh's punishment suggest that 10t1 was 'connected with environments in which a version of the legend of Manasseh was known, that was closer to the Jewish one, than to the one of the

---

[90]The Syriac word ܙܘܕܝܘܢ comes from Greek ζῴδιον *zōdion* and refers to a sign of the zodiac; the Greek word too is used for the object in which Manasseh was held captive, and has been interpreted as a designation of an animal-shaped statute; see below, section 1.7.3

[91]Ed. Chabot I, Text (CSCO 91), 15, 34, 35; I, Translation (CSCO 121), 10, 27, 28.

[92]Ed. Brooks I, Text (CSCO 62) 8*, 19*; I, Translation (CSCO 63) 2, 10.

[93]Ed. Wallis Budge, ܢܒ (text), 68–69 (translation).

[94]Ed. Van den Eynde, Text (Syr. 96), 146; Translation (Syr. 97), 173–174.

[95]Ed. Chabot IV, 53–54 (text); I, 87–88 (translation).

[96]Ed. Chabot I, Text (Syr. 36), 93–94; I, Translation (Syr. 56), 72.

[97]Note also the subscription in manuscript 17a7 which seems to be inspired by the Manasseh story in Chronicles (cf. Baars–Schneider, 'Prayer of Manasseh', Introduction, p. iii) and which speaks of the 'flame of fire' from which Manasseh was saved.

[98]This is twice mentioned in the *Book of the Bee* and further in the Zuqnin Chronicle, in the Anonymous 1234 Chronicle, and by Michael the Syrian.

Didascalia.'[99] It should be noted, however, that similar traditions are attested in Eastern Christian Melkite and Byzantine sources. A parallel for the ungulate motif is found in the *Annales* of the tenth-century Patriarch of Alexandria, Eutychius, where Manasseh is locked up in a brazen calf.[100] In the *Oratio in Sextum Psalmum* of Anastasius Sinaiticus (seventh century),[101] and in the *Annales* of Michael Glycas (twelfth century),[102] Manasseh is captured in a ζῴδιον χαλκοῦν *zōdion chalkoun*, which has also been interpreted as an animal-shaped statue.[103] Manasseh's captivity in a brazen statue (ἄγαλμα χαλκοῦν *agalma chalkoun*) is also reported in the *Chronography* of Georgius Syncellus (ninth century),[104] in which there is a correspondence between Manasseh's punishment and his sin, namely the fabrication of a four-faced idol (ἄγαλμα τεραπρόσωπον *agalma teraprosōpon*; compare the ܨܠܡܐ ܕܐܪܒܥ ܐܦܝܢ *ṣalmā dʾarbaʿ ʾapin* in *Peshiṭta to Chronicles* 33:7 and in Ephrem's *Hymns on Faith* 87:4[105]).[106]

How these traditions ended up in the various written sources mentioned above, cannot be reconstructed with any certainty. Per-

[99] Borbone, 'Preghiera di Manasseh', 547 note 1. On the story of Manasseh as reported in the *Didascalia* see above, section 1.2.

[100] Ed. Breydy I (Arab. 44), 25 (text); II (Arab. 45), 22 (translation). The text of Breydy's edition represents the Alexandrian version of Eutychius' *Annales*. Similarly in the later, Antiochean recension edited by L. Cheiko (section on Manasseh: I [Arab. 6], 69); see also B. Pirone's Italian translation (p. 119) and the Latin translation by J. Selden and E. Pococke in Patrologia Graeca 111 (p. 961). For the way in which Eutychius treated biblical stories and the sources he used for that see Simonsohn, 'The Biblical Narrative in the *Annales* of Saʿīd b. Baṭrīq'. Since Eutychius often follows Syriac traditions closely, his reference to these Manasseh stories may serve as an indication of the familiarity of these stories in Syriac circles (Dr Jan van Ginkel, personal communication). This provides an interesting addition to the scarce direct evidence in Syriac sources (see above).

[101] Patrologia Graeca 89, p. 1104.

[102] Ed. Bekker 367; similarly Patrologia Graeca 158, p. 372; ζῴδιον χαλκοῦν *zōdion chalkoun* occurs parallel to εἴδωλον *eidōlon*.

[103] Cf. Bogaert, *Apocalypse de Baruch*, 313–314; Gry, 'Le roi Manassé, d'après les légends midrashiques', 154.

[104] Ed. Mosshammer 254.

[105] Ed. Beck I (Syr. 73), 268 (text); II (Syr. 74), 228 (translation); cf. Phillips, 'The Reception of Peshitta Chronicles', 274; the 'four-faced idol' occurs also in Ishodad's Commentary on 2 Kings 21, which draws upon Chronicles (cf. above); see ed. Van den Eynde I (Syr. 96), 146 (text); II (Syr. 97), 174 (translation).

[106] Bogaert, *Apocalypse de Baruch*, 314.

haps they were first incorporated in Jewish sources and reached the Byzantine and Melkite chronicles via the early Christian historiographers such as Hippolyte of Rome (whom H. Achelis identified with 'Hippolyte, the interpreter of the Targum', who is quoted in an Arabic Catena collection to the Pentateuch that contains excerpts from early Christian authors such as Hippolyte to the twelfth-century Syriac scholar Dionysius Bar-Salibi[107]). These authors were on the one hand indebted to Jewish traditions[108] and on the other hand foundational for Christian historiography.[109] However, only fragments of the works of these early historiographers have been preserved, and any reconstruction of this 'missing link' between the extant Jewish and Christian sources remains tentative.

What we can say, however, is that the Melkite-Byzantine link discussed in the present section provides an alternative source for the traditions reflected in the superscription in the Syriac Melkite Horologia. It is not our aim to argue that the explanation in terms of a Jewish-Syriac connection should be replaced by one in terms of exclusively Byzantine influence, but rather to show that there are various ways in which these traditions may have ended up in the superscription in the Melkite Horologia and that the distribution of these traditions over both various early and late Jewish sources and Byzantine and Melkite Christian sources shows how widespread these traditions were. These stories were not related to certain theological-dogmatic positions, nor restricted to particular Jewish and Christian

[107] Achelis, *Hippolytstudien*, 113–120 (= 'IV. Hippolytus der Ausleger des Targums. Fragmente zum Pentateuch').

[108] Cf. Lagarde, *Materialien zur Kritik und Geschichte des Pentateuchs*, xi, on the Arabic Catena collection mentioned above: 'Sehr gern hätte ich dem zweiten hefte (...) einen kommentar beigegeben, ohne den weit aus die meisten leser gar nich wissen werden, was mit dem buche zu machen ist. dass ihnen ein midrasch völlig in der nationaljüdischen art vorliegt (...) dass der inhalt desselben zum theil auch in jüdischen büchern, zum theil in den ältesten christlichen vätern und in der christlichen volkslitteratur umläuft.' ('I would have liked very much to add a commentary to the second volume. Without it the majority of readers will not know what to make of the book. They will not realize that what they have before them is a Midrash completely in the Jewish national style (...), nor that its contents also circulate partly in Jewish books and partly in the oldest Christian Fathers and in Christian folk literature.')

[109] Thus Dr Uri Simonsohn, personal communication.

groups. They were part of a continuum of common narrative traditions, unhindered by any Jewish-Christian divisions.[110]

1.7.4 The animal motif

The enigmatic bull, mule or horse has puzzled many scholars, and has often been explained as the result of a scribal or translation error. S. Krauss assumed that it originated in a scribal error תורא *torā* 'bull' for תנורא *tannurā* 'furnace';[111] E. Nestle explained מולתא *multā* 'mule' as a scribal error for מזלתא *mazzālātā*, i.e. ζῴδιον; *simulacrum*;[112] L. Gry suggested that מולתא *multā* was an error for מולאיר *mulyār* 'caldron' and אתן *ʔatān* 'she-donkey' for אתון *ʔattun* 'furnace';[113] and Bogaert explained the unique reference to the 'horse' in the *Apocalypse of Baruch* as the result of a translation error: The Syriac translator misread the Greek ἰπνολέβης *ipnolebēs* 'boiler, cauldron' or perhaps ἰπνός *ipnos* 'oven' as ἵππος *hippos* 'horse'.[114]

We are not convinced, however, that we need a scribal error to explain the traditions under discussion. The motif of an animal as a torture instrument is not as enigmatic as it may seem to modern readers, as it was well-known in Antiquity, especially in the stories about Phalaris, the notoriously cruel tyran of Acragas in Sicily from the sixth century BC.[115] Various sources tell that he burned his victims in a brazen bull and ordered the fabrication of a horn sound system, so that he could hear their screams, representing the bellowing of the bull.[116] The bull and its use as a furnace to burn people is

[110]For a similar argument regarding the *Life of Adam and Eve*, see Tromp, 'The Story of our Lives', 221–222.

[111]Krauss, 'Die Legende des Königs Manasse', 330; similarly Borbone, 'Preghiera di Manasseh', 547, note 1; Bogaert, *Apocalypse de Baruch*, 313.

[112]Nestle, 'Miscellen', 309-312 (= '6. Das eherne Maultier des Manasse'); cf. Bacher, 'Le taureau de Phalaris dans l'Agada', 293–294; Krauss, 'Die Legende des Königs Manasse', 327–328; Bogaert, *Apocalypse de Baruch*, 313, note 4; compare ܒܙܘܕܝܘܢ ܕܢܚܫܐ *b-zāwdiwān da-nḥāšā* in the Manasseh story in the *Didascalia Apostolorum* (Vööbus, *The Didascalia Apostolorum in Syriac*, I (Syr. 175), 89, note 392) and in Bar Hebraeus' *Chronicon* (ed. Bedjan, 24 line 22).

[113]Gry, 'Le roi Manassé, d'après les légends midrashiques', 153–154. Compare to אתון נורא *ʔattun nurā* 'furnace of fire' in Daniel 3.

[114]Bogaert, *Apocalypse de Baruch*, 310.

[115]Phalaris' cruelty is also mentioned in 3 Maccabees 5:20.

[116]See Lenschau, 'Phalaris', 1650; see also Denis–Halewyck, *Introduction à la*

strikingly parallel to the Manasseh traditions, and the holes in Manasseh's bull (cf. *Targum to Chronicles*, quoted above[117]) have perhaps the same function as Phalaris' sound system: to make the victims' screams audible.

The attestations of this motif predating the Manasseh traditions in which it occurs provide a plausible background for its appearance in the Manasseh stories, so we do not have to resort to postulating of a scribal or translation error. But even if we were to postulate a scribal error to explain this appearance, we would still have to account for the variation regarding the animal in question (bull, mule, horse, calf). There are many parallels to such a variation in all kind of folk and fairy tales. If we look, for example, at the way in which fables developed over the centuries – from Aesop to Jean de la Fontaine – there is much variation in the identity of the animals that figure in the same stories. In the fable of Jupiter and the frogs – the frogs shout to Jupiter that they want a king who can control their dissolute habits; first, Jupiter gives them a small piece of wood, which they treat with scorn. When they ask Jupiter for another king, he sends them an animal – the animal that the godhead sends to the frogs to be their new king appears in the various versions as a water snake, a serpent, a stork, or a heron. Likewise, the fable about the tortoise and the eagle – the eagle takes up the tortoise who wants to learn to fly, but suddenly let it go; the tortoise falls and its shell is dashed to pieces – is also known in versions with a snail instead of a tortoise. And the story about the monkey that used the leg of a sleeping dog to pull the chestnuts out of the fire occurs also in a version in which the monkey uses a cat's leg (cf. the archaic English idiom 'a cat's paw').

Sometimes the variation seems to be arbitrary, due to the association of certain animals with others, which possess the same characteristics, such as the tortoise and the snail in the example above (both slowly carrying their home). Other examples of this kind are the variation between the dragon and the snake (both poisonous),

littérature religieuse judéo-hellénistique, I, 660.

[117]The holes also appear in Pseudo-Jerome, *Quaestiones hebraicae in libros Regum et Paralipomenon*, 1466–1467 (on 2 Chronicles 33:13), which speaks of a *vas aeneum perforatum* (without reference to any animal-like shape of it might have); cf. Bogaert, *Apocalypse de Baruch*, 314–315.

the stork, the heron and the crane (all three fish- and frog-eaters), and the cat and the weasel (both mouse-eaters). Sometimes there are zoological factors that account for the variation. Thus in some fables the European fox has been transformed into the African or Asian jackal. Sometimes the variation can be explained on the basis of linguistic factors.[118] Thus the change from the dog to the cat used by the monkey probably resulted from confusion of Latin *catellus* 'puppy' and *catulus* 'cat'.[119] Similar examples are attested in which a buzzard (*buteo*) becomes a bittern (*buttion*), a deer (*cervus*) becomes a slave (*servus*), or a magpie (*pica*) becomes a woodpecker (*picus*).[120] Occasionally the variation itself gave rise to new versions in which some of the animals of the existing versions were combined.[121]

In a different cultural environment, we came across another interesting case. Surah 3 (verse 49) and 5 (verse 110) of the Quran tell the story that Jesus fashioned birds out of clay, breathed into them, after which they became living birds, a story which is also found in the Apocryphal Gospels.[122] The fifteenth-century Ottoman author Ahmed Bican Yazıcıoğlu repeats the story in his *Dürr-i Meknûn* ('The Hidden Pearl'), but in his version the 'bird' has been replaced by a 'bat'.[123]

---

[118] Compare the suggestion that the animal motif entered the Manasseh stories due to a scribal error discussed at the beginning of this section, which, however, we did not consider compelling. We are not aware of any attempt to explain the variation regarding the animal in question (bull, mule, horse, calf) on the basis of linguistic factors. There is no formal similarity or another linguistic motivation for the change from e.g. 'bull' to 'horse' or the other way round, and the hypothesis that each animal entered the traditions independently, e.g. the bull from a scribal error and the horse from a translation error, completely ignores the paradigmatic relationship between these animals within the traditions and the phenomena of transmission and change discussed in the present section.

[119] Cf. Geirnaert–Smith, '*De warachtighe fabulen der dieren*', 31.

[120] Cf. Smith, 'Arnold Freitag's *Mythologia Ethica*', 188–189 and Smith, 'Het dronken hert'.

[121] An early modern example is the fable *The Viper and the File*, which divides the original viper into two or three different animals (a cat, a snake and/or a dragon) and the file into two characters: an anvil and a file; see Smith, 'The Viper and the File'.

[122] Cf. Elliot, *A Synopsis of the Apocryphal Nativity and Infancy Narratives*, 135–140.

[123] Ed. Kaptein 133 (§ 3.11); see also Kaptein's discussion on p. 56, where also

Taking into account the comparative material from other narrative traditions, we can consider the dispersion of the traditions about Manasseh's captivity in an animal and the variation regarding the animal in question as the tangible witnesses to widespread oral narrative traditions, which occasionally found their way into written sources.

We can only tentatively reconstruct how the motif of the ungulate was transmitted and changed in oral traditions. In different circles and situations, these animals may have enhanced varying associations to the specific audiences. The bull seems to have been a good candidate to be the animal in which the Judean king was tortured for those groups, Jewish or Christian, that were familiar with Phalaris' torture instrument. Since, however, Phalaris' bull was well known in Antiquity as well as in later periods, we cannot pinpoint the association of this bull with Manasseh's captivity to a certain time or place. The bull may also have been associated with idolatry, because of its widespread use as the representation of a deity.[124] The calf was for both Jews and Christians probably even more an outstanding symbol of idolatry because of the golden calf of the Israelites in the desert and the two golden calves that king Jeroboam had made. It must have been only a small step from Manasseh, the king who was notorious for his idolatry, to this symbol of idolatry. Perhaps the association was suggested by a correlation between Manasseh's sin (idolatry) and his punishment (captivity).[125] The association of a calf with idolatry may also have been common to Eutychius' potential Muslim readership, who were familiar with 'the calf with a hollow sound' in the Quran.[126] In a Jewish context the mule was perhaps also associated with idolatry, because it is said to have been worshipped by the Sepharvites, the people whom, according to 1 Kings 17:24, the king

earlier sources for this variation of 'bird' and 'bat' are given.

[124]For this use in various cultures from Western Europe, over the Mediterranean world and the Middle East to India, see Duchaussoy, *Le bestiaire divin ou la symbolique des animaux*, 56–75 (We are indebted to Dr Julia C. Szirmai for this reference.).

[125]See above on Georgius Syncellus; but Georgius does not say that the statue that Manasseh built and the statue in which he was held captive had the shape of a bull.

[126]On the 'calf with a hollow sound' in the Quran see Albayrak, 'The Calf with a Hollow Sound' (we are indebted to Dr Umar Ryad for this reference). Eutychius' account of Manasseh and the Quran stories both have Arabic عِجْل, *ʿiğl*.

of Assur brought from Mesopotamia to Samaria.[127] The mule may also have had a negative connotation because it was considered to be the result of the unnatural union between the horse and the ass.[128]

For the Christian Syriac audience and readership, some other parallels to Manasseh's bull may have been even more significant, namely the references to a similar torture device in Christian martyr stories, in which several saints are said to have been roasted in a brazen bull, for example the martyrs Eustace,[129] Antipas of Pergamum[130] and Pelagia of Tarsus.[131] The use of a similar motif in the Manasseh story attracted people who were familiar with the martyr stories and provided a context to this story. The role that the motifs played as narrative codes or literary sign posts may also have enhanced the reference to the bull (which occurs also in the martyr stories) rather than a mule or a horse.

Other parallels, such as the *equuleus* as a torture instrument (cf. the horse in the *Apocalypse of Baruch*)[132] or child sacrifices in the Phoenician and Punic Molech cult[133] are less obvious. Nevertheless, they all seem to attest to the wide distribution of various motifs that come together in the stories of Manasseh's brazen bull and they support our suggestion that we are dealing with a rich variety of oral narrative traditions that incorporated motifs that were well known in Antiquity, rather than with enigmatic elements that require a philological explanation in terms of scribal or translation errors.

1.7.5 Manasseh's transportation to Jerusalem

The expression 'and the bull was broken into pieces, so that he found himself safe and sound in Jerusalem', suggests acquaintance with an-

[127] Babylonian Talmud Sanhedrin 63b; see further Ginzberg, *The Legends of the Jews*, IV, 266; VI, 361.

[128] Cf. Ginzberg, *The Legends of the Jews*, I, 424; V, 322–323.

[129] Cf. Patrologia Graeca 105, p. 413; see also Bogaert, *Apocalypse de Baruch*, 317; Krauss, 'Die Legende des Königs Manasse', 332.

[130] Stadler–Ginal, *Völlständiges Heiligen-Lexicon*, I, 246.

[131] Stadler–Ginal, *Völlständiges Heiligen-Lexicon*, IV, 756.

[132] Krauss, 'Die Legende des Königs Manasse', 336; cf. Marquardt, *Das Privatleben der Römer*, I, 183, note 7.

[133] Cf. Bogaert, *Apocalypse de Baruch*, 317; Krauss, 'Die Legende des Königs Manasse', 335.

other tradition related to Manasseh's deliverance from his Babylonian captivity, namely his miraculous transportation to Jerusalem, which is well-attested, for example, in the Jewish sources mentioned in section 1.7.1 and in the Melkite and Byzantine historiographical sources mentioned in section 1.7.3. The narrative motif of a miraculous transportation is reminiscent of Ezekiel 8:3 (also from Babel to Jerusalem!), 11:24 (back from Jerusalem to Babel), Acts 8:39–40 (also with 'and he found himself in...'; Peshiṭta: ܐܫܬܟܚ *ʔeštkaḥ*); Bel and the Dragon 33–39. It is also a well-known motif in lives of saints. In Islam this motif has found a place in the stories about Mohammad's miraculous transport from Mecca to Jerusalem, from which he ascended to heaven (الإسراء والمعراج *al-ʔisrāʔ w-al-miʕrāǧ*).[134]

1.7.6 Narrative and liturgical traditions

In section 1.5.3 we discussed the liturgical use of PrMan in the Syriac-Melkite and Byzantine realm. We concluded that PrMan was probably reintroduced into Syriac liturgy due to Byzantine influence. In the present section we have seen that in the same realm historiographical and narrative traditions circulated about King Manasseh's captivity in a brazen bull, although the dispersion of these traditions seems to have been more widespread, and also included Jewish circles. To what extent these two streams of traditions are related, and whether both should be ascribed to the same Byzantine influence is hard to decide, but it is interesting to note that in the Syriac Melkite Horologion manuscripts the two come together.

1.8 Byzantine manuscript illustrations

1.8.1 New York, Public Library, Spencer Gr. 1

In section 1.7.3 we observed that some Melkite and Byzantine chronicles include the tradition about Manasseh being held captive in a bull. Fascinating additional evidence for acquaintance with this tradition in the Byzantine realm comes from a twelfth- or thirteenth-

[134]The Quran does not mention Jerusalem as the destination of Mohammad's travel, but rather 'the farthest mosque' (المسجد الأقصى *al-masǧid al-ʔaqṣā*), which the tradition (Hadith) located in Jerusalem.

century Byzantine Psalter in the so-called Aristocratic recension, New York, Public Library, Spencer, Gr. 1. On folio 395v of the manuscript there is a picture of Manasseh prostrating himself inside a bull, which serves as an illustration to the Prayer of Manasseh in the Odes (illustration 15 on page 69).[135] This illustration is unique because it is, to our best knowledge, the only picture of Manasseh inside the bull.[136] Art historians who dealt with this picture, including K. Weitzmann and S. Gardner, related it to the passage in the Apocalypse of Baruch dealing with Manasseh's captivity in a brazen horse,[137] but in our investigation we found closer literary parallels, in which the animal is a bull, just as in this illustration, rather than a horse, and which come from the same Byzantine milieu in which this manuscript was produced.

1.8.2 Paris, Bibliothèque nationale, Gr. 510

S. Gardner sees a relationship between the picture of Manasseh inside a bull in the New York manuscript and two other representations of Manasseh, which depict him standing before a bull, in Paris, Bibliothèque nationale Gr. 510, fol. 435v (illustration 16) and Athens, National Library, Cod. 7, fol. 256v (illustration 17, discussed below, in section 1.8.3).[138] The manuscript from Paris is a ninth-century Byzantine manuscript containing the Homilies of Gregory of Nazianzus. The other illustrations on folio 435v depict Daniel in the lion's den, the Three Young Men in the burning furnace, and Hezekiah who has fallen ill and is visited by Isaiah. The relationship between the four pictures on this page as well as their connection to the text of the manuscript is unclear, although scattered over the text of the Homilies references to Daniel, the Three Young Men,

[135] Cf. Cutler, *The Aristocratic Psalters in Byzantium*, 58.

[136] Similarly Gardner, 'Psalter', 170.

[137] Cf. above section 1.7.2. See Weitzmann, 'The Ode Pictures of the Aristocratic Psalter Recension', 83: 'The enclosing of Manasseh within the bull may well have been inspired by, though it is not a literal illustration of, an apocryphal story told in the Syriac Apocalypse of Baruch (...) Although we deal here with a horse, not a bull, it is obviously another variant of the same episode.' Similarly Gardner, 'Psalter', 170.

[138] Gardner, 'Psalter', 170.

Hezekiah and Manasseh do occur.[139] The association of the four pictures is hard to explain in their present context, but probably the illustration as a whole was copied from another source, most likely a Psalter in which each of the four scenes was attached to an Ode.[140] The four stories reflect the theme of God's deliverance for those who trust in Him or who repent of their sins, whereas the Three Young Men, Hezekiah, and Manasseh are connected through the various Odes ascribed to them. A similar combination of Daniel in the lion's den, the Three Young Man in the burning furnace, and Manasseh's repentance is reflected in the frescoes in the Santa Maria Antiqua.[141]

The interpretation of the picture of Manasseh itself is a debated issue. According to Weitzmann it shows Manasseh worshipping an idol, for which the artist adapted an image of the Golden Calf.[142] This interpretation agrees with the correlation between Manasseh's sin (an idol in the shape of a bull) and his punishment (in a brazen bull) discussed in section 1.7.3, and the association of a calf and idolatry mentioned in section 1.7.4. However, J. David has proposed an alternative interpretation, namely that the bull is a burnt offering that Manasseh sacrifices to God. Thus it depicts his restoration of the worship of the true God after his repentance.[143] This interpretation justifies the connection with the other three pictures of the same illustration, which seem to cover the common theme of deliverance (see above).

[139] For details see Weitzmann, *Illustrations in Roll and Codex*, 149, note 57.

[140] Thus Weitzmann, *Illustrations in Roll and Codex*, 149.

[141] David, 'L'église Sainte-Marie-Antique dans son état originaire', 488.

[142] Cf. Weitzmann, 'The Ode Pictures of the Aristocratic Psalter Recension', 82: 'In his early life Manasseh was a worshipper of idols, and so we see him in a miniature in the Paris Gregory, gr. 510, in orant posture behind the idol whose shape is not described in the Bible text. Thus the artist had to seek his own solution and apparently adapted the image of Aaron's Golden Calf.' Cf. Omont *Miniatures des plus anciens manuscripts grecs*, 30: 'Il faut sans doute voir dans cette composition une allusion à l'impiété de Manassès, qui avait relevé les idoles.'

[143] David, 'L'église Sainte-Marie-Antique dans son état originaire', 488; similarly Leclercq, 'Manassé'.

1.8.3 Athens, National Library, Cod. 7

The manuscript from Athens is a Byzantine Psalter from the second half of the twelfth century, in which the picture of Manasseh serves as an illustration to the Odes.[144] Here, too, we find Manasseh standing before a bull, just as in Paris, Bibl. nat. Gr. 510, but there are two differences.[145] First, there is an altar with flames below the bull and, second, in the upper right corner of the image the hand of God appears. Here the same question arises regarding the interpretation of the picture as in the case of the Paris manuscript: does it depict Manasseh's idolatry or his repentance? Weitzmann, who opts for the first interpretation, assumes that the bull, which in the Paris manuscript could still be interpreted as an idol, should here be interpreted as a burnt offering that was made to an idol, and that the hand of God in the upper right corner shows that in this picture 'Manasseh is represented in the dual role of worshipping the idol as well as the Lord after his change of heart', which 'clearly speaks for a conflation of two scenes, leading to a contradictory solution'.[146] However, such a complicated interpretation can be avoided if we opt for the second interpretation, namely that the picture depicts Manasseh offering a sacrifice to God after his repentance.[147] An additional advantage to this interpretation is that it implies a more logical connection with the Ode it illustrates: Manasseh's prayer to God is accompanied by an illustration in which he offers a sacrifice to God. Because of the similarity between the Athens miniature and the illustration in the Paris manuscript, our analysis of the latter as representing Manasseh worshipping God gives further support to J. David's analysis of the illustration in the Paris manuscript discussed above.

[144] For a description of this picture see Buberl, *Die Minaturenhandschriften der Nationalbibliothek in Athen*, 15 (Buberl erroneously calls this an illustration to the Prayer of Hezekiah); Cutler, *The Aristocratic Psalters in Byzantium*, 16.

[145] Weitzmann, 'The Ode Pictures of the Aristocratic Psalter Recension', 82.

[146] Weitzmann, 'The Ode Pictures of the Aristocratic Psalter Recension', 82.

[147] Compare, for example, the penitent David prostrating himself before the hand of God in Rome, Vat. Lib., Gr. 333, fol. 50v.

1.8.4 Paris, Bibliothèque nationale, Gr. 923

Paris, Bibliothèque nationale, Gr. 923 (illustration 18) is a ninth-century manuscript containing the *Sacra Parallela* ascribed to John of Damascus, which is a collection of sentences and excerpts drawn from the Scriptures and the Church Fathers on various topics such as virtues and vices, faith and discipline. There is a picture of Manasseh on folio 231v. Both in the text and in the pictures Manasseh occurs together with other penitent kings. In the miniature he is depicted prostrate, partly concealing the figure of King David, who is standing behind.[148] In the accompanying text four examples of penitent sinners are given: Judah (Genesis 38:26), David (2 Samuel 12:11–13), Ahab (1 Kings 21:27–29), and Manasseh (PrMan 7). After these biblical quotations follow a number of other citations on the theme of penitence from the Writings (Job, Proverbs) and the Prophets (Hosea, Joel, Isaiah, Jeremiah, and Ezekiel).[149] According to Weitzmann, 'Manasseh in proskynesis is typical of the early marginal Psalters which show the white-haired king in a similar position of complete prostration'.[150] He also points out that not only the text, but also the illustrations in this manuscript are selected from various other sources.[151]

Just as PrMan figured in various contexts (see section 1.5.7), so did the illustrations depicting Manasseh, partly with the same functions as the Prayer. In some cases the picture serves as an illustration to the Odes and occurs alongside pictures of other kings to whom Odes were ascribed, including David and Hezekiah; in Paris Gr. 510, where it occurs alongside Daniel in the lion's den, the Three Young

[148]In 2 Samuel 12:16 it is David who lay upon the ground all night, whereas here he is standing upright. For this reason Weitzmann assumes that the illustration relates to 2 Samuel 12:20 'Then David arose from the earth, and washed, and anointed himself, and changed his clothes; and he went into the house of the LORD, and worshipped', rather than to 12:16; cf. Weitzmann, *The Miniatures of the Sacra Parallela*, 108.

[149]Patrologia Graeca, 96, pp. 104–108.

[150]Weitzmann, *The Miniatures of the Sacra Parallela*, 108.

[151]Weitzmann, 'The Study of Byzantine Book Illumination', 16: 'A unique position is taken by the ninth-century codex of the *Sacra Parallela* in Paris, cod. Gr. 923, because it has, as is the nature of a florilegium, neither an original text nor original picture'.

Men in the furnace, and Hezekiah's illness, it serves mainly as an example of deliverance (especially if we follow J. David's interpretation); and in Paris Gr. 923 it figures as an example of penitence.

1.8.5 London, B.M. Add. 11870 (Eustace) and Monastery of Rousanou, Meteora (Antipas)

At the end of section 1.7.4 we mentioned Christian martyr stories in which several saints are said to have been roasted in a brazen bull. These stories have inspired quite a number of sculptures, wall paintings, manuscript illustrations and other works of art, spread over many art traditions or styles, including Gothic and Byzantine manuscript illuminations, ivories, sculptures and frescoes.[152]

In particular the stories of Saint Eustace are reflected in many works of art in both Western and Eastern Christianity. Places where depictions of his life and martyrdom can be found include the windows of the Cathedral of Chartres as well as a sculpture at one of the portals (which shows the bull in which he was martyred) and a wall painting in Canterbury Cathedral. Furthermore, the famous Church of Saint Eustace in Paris is dedicated to this martyr.

It is beyond the scope of the present study to deal with all these works of art, or, more generally, with the veneration of Eustace and other saints in the various Christian churches. However, to illustrate how the stories of the martyrs who were roasted in a brazen bull have found their way into various cultural expressions, we have added two pictures.

Illustration 19 comes from a Byzantine illuminated manuscript from the last quarter of the eleventh century, London, B.M. Add. 11870, folio 151r. The illumination contains four illustrations from Eustace's life: his vision, his baptism, his standing before Hadrian, and his martyrdom, in which he is depicted in a brazen bull above fire, together with his three fellow-martyrs Theopiste, Tehopistus and Agapius.[153]

Whereas Eustace played a prominent role in both the Western

[152]See, for example, the items listed in the Princeton Index of Christian Art (`http://ica.princeton.edu`).

[153]For a description see Princeton Index of Christian Art, Record 000046837.

and the Eastern churches, Antipas of Pergamum seems to be especially venerated in the Eastern Churches. A number of pictures depicting his martyrdom can be found in Byzantine sources. Illustration 20 shows a fresco in the Rousanou monastery in the Meteora region in Greece, depicting his martyrdom. It occurs in a series of martyrdom scenes in the narthex of the dome of the monastery. The picture dates from 1560. The decoration of the dome is 'a large-scale example of the work of the Cretan School at its peak'.[154]

1.9 The milieu in which PrMan originated

1.9.1 A Jewish prayer in a Christian Church Order?

Before starting our comparative analysis of the two Syriac versions of PrMan, let us readdress the question as to the milieu in which PrMan originated. In section 1.2 we saw that Nau, Nestle and others thought that PrMan was composed by the author of the *Didascalia*. This view is precluded if we take the *Didascalia* as a Christian document and PrMan as a Jewish composition. The assumption of the Jewish provenance of PrMan seems to be widely accepted nowadays.[155] M. Ehrmann even calls this assumption unchallenged.[156] About the precise Jewish milieu in which PrMan might have originated and about its date of origin there is less consensus. Some have argued for a Jewish composition from the pre-Christian Era, or, even more precisely, from the Maccabean period;[157] others have claimed that PrMan is a Jewish composition from the first centuries of the Chris-

[154]The Cretan School, also known as the Post-Byzantine School, flourished while Crete was under Venetian rule during the late Middle Ages and reached its climax after the Fall of Constantinople. Cf. Nikonanos, *Meteora*, 71.

[155]Exceptions are Davila, 'Is the Prayer of Manasseh a Jewish Work?' and Nickelsburg, 'Prayer of Manasseh', 771 (according to the latter the question as to whether the prayer is a Jewish or a Christian composition is disputed).

[156]Ehrmann, *Klagephänome im zwischentestamentlicher Literatur*, 157: 'Daß die Or Man jüdischer Herkunft ist, is unbestritten'.

[157]Cf. Ryssel, 'Das Gebet Manasse', 167: 'Vielleicht wurde der Bußpsalm, gleich zahlreichen anderen apokryphischen Stücken, in der Makkabäerzeit verfaßt, zu den Zweck, um den Juden den Gedanken nahe zu legen, daß Buße auch das jüdische Volk aus seiner schweren, wenngleich wohlverdienten Not befreien könne.'

tian Era.[158]

If one assumes a Jewish origin for PrMan in the first centuries of the Common Era, the assumption that it was composed by the author of the *Didascalia* can still be maintained, if one follows the claim, made by a number of scholars, that the *Didascalia* is a reworked Jewish composition.[159] In that case one could argue that PrMan is a Jewish composition that was created by the author of the Jewish work underlying the *Didascalia*.

It follows that the general consensus is that PrMan is a Jewish composition, which either was later on included by the author of the *Didascalia*, or composed by the author of a Jewish work underlying the *Didascalia*. However, before immediately accepting the claim that PrMan or the *Didascalia* are Jewish compositions, let us first have a careful look at the arguments that have been put forward to support these claims.[160]

[158]Thus e.g. Van der Horst–Newman, *Early Jewish Prayers in Greek*, 135 ('Although some scholars have suggested a date as early as the second century B.C.E., it seems a tentative dating in the first or second centuries C.E. may be more likely'); Eissfeldt, *Einleitung in das Alte Testament unter Einschluß der Apokryphen und Pseudepigraphen*, 644 ('eine jüdische Dichtung in griechischer Sprache aus ziemlich späte, wohl schon christlicher Zeit'); Bertholdt, *Historischkritische Einleitung*, 2619 (Bertholdt argues, among other things, that 'God of the repenters' [verse 13b] belongs 'in die Terminologie der spätern jüdischen Theologie'.)

[159]See above, footnote 10. Cf. Kohler, 'Didascalia', 588: 'Claiming to have been written by the Apostles, the work [= The Apostolic Constitutions] proves on closer examination to be based, like the Didache, upon an original Jewish work, transformed by extensive interpolations and slight alterations into a Christian document of great authority'. But Kohler's view about the relationship between the *Didascalia* and the *Apostolic Constitutions* is now outdated. Thus he continues with: 'There exists another version, bearing the name "Didascalia", in Syriac, Coptic, Ethiopic, Arabic, and (incomplete) in Latin, which, since the appearance of Lagarde's edition of the Syriac "Didascalia" in 1854, most modern scholars consider to be the original work. On the other hand, Bickell (...) has given convincing proofs that the "Apostolic Constitutions" is the original work, and the so-called "Didascalia" a mere condensation. In the latter the Jewish elements are to a large extent eliminated, and the Christian character is more pronounced.' However, it is now generally acknowledged that the first six books of the Apostolic Constitutions are based on the *Didascalia* rather than the other way round.

[160]In the following discussion we will not deal with the complexities of describing the Jewish-Christian spectrum in the first centuries of the Common Era. We have argued elsewhere that this spectrum is a continuum and that a bipartite division of

1.9.2 The supposed Jewish origin of Pseudepigrapha

The idea that PrMan must be a Jewish composition, as well as the idea that the *Didascalia* contains much Jewish material, or that it is a reworked version of an originally Jewish document, can be related to a trend that seems to have an undisputed hegemony in the study of the Pseudepigrapic and Early Christian literature since the nineteenth century, namely the tendency to underline the Jewish background of Christianity and hence to declare many Pseudepigraphic sources as originally Jewish, even if they have been transmitted only in Christian sources. This tendency, however, can be challenged. Thus for the *Testaments of the Twelve Patriarchs*, M. de Jonge has argued for the unity of the book as against attempts by R.H. Charles and others to distinguish between an originally Jewish work and later Christian interpolations.[161] In a similar way, the alleged Jewish background of *4 Baruch* and of the *Life of Adam and Eve* can be challenged.[162]

The same tendency to declare Pseudepigraphic material to be originally Jewish is also detectable in studies on two sources that are related to the contexts in which PrMan has been preserved: some prayers that have been preserved in the *Apostolic Constitutions* and the Odes. The prayers that occur in the seventh and eighth books of the *Apostolic Constitutions* are presented as 'Hellenistic Synagogal Prayers' in Charlesworth, *The Old Testament Pseudepigrapha*.[163] Even though these prayers have only been preserved in a Christian source and contain unequivocal Christian elements, they have been celebrated as precious documentation of ancient Jewish liturgy, used

this continuum into 'Jewish' and 'Christian' is an oversimplification; cf. Van Peursen, 'The Peshitta of Ben Sira: Jewish and/or Christian?', 260–262.

[161] De Jonge, *The Testament of the Twelve Patriarchs*; see also Hollander, 'The Testaments of the Twelve Patriarchs', 73–74; Hollander–De Jonge, *The Testaments of the Twelve Patriarchs*, 83–85.

[162] Cf. Tromp, Review of Herzer, *4 Baruch*, 105; Tromp, 'The Story of our Lives'; Tromp, *Het Leven van Adam en Eva*, 10–11. For the methodological questions involved see further De Jonge, *Pseudepigrapha of the Old Testament as Part of Christian Literature*; Kraft, 'The Pseudepigrapha in Christianity', 60–63; Davila, *The Provenance of the Pseudepigrapha*.

[163] Fiensy–Darnell, 'Hellenistic Synagogal Prayers', esp. 671–673; similarly Van der Horst–Newman, *Early Jewish Prayers in Greek*, 1–93 (restricted to *Apostolic Constitutions* VII, 33–38).

in the service of the Synagogue. Obviously, the Jewish character of the prayer could be maintained because the Christian elements were played down as 'the light veneer of a somewhat superficial Christian revision'.[164] Also the Odes, the collection of psalms and hymns from both the Old and the New Testaments (the latter including the *Magnificat* from Luke 1:46–55, the *Benedictus* from Luke 1:68–79, and the Beatitudes from Matthew 5:1–12), and which sometimes contains PrMan (cf. above, section 1.5.2) have been claimed to be an originally Jewish collection, to which later on the New Testament hymns have been added.[165] The assumption that these liturgical texts had a Jewish background agreed with the attempts 'to trace the origins of every aspect of early Christian liturgical practice back to Jewish antecedents'.[166]

1.9.3 PrMan as a Jewish composition

In the case of PrMan the main argument to consider it a Jewish composition seems to be the assumption that a Christian author would not use the formula 'God of our fathers, (God) of Abraham, Isaac and Jacob and their righteous seed' (verse 1), nor say that these patriarchs did not need repentance because they had not sinned (verse 8).[167]

---

[164] Baumstark, *Comparative Liturgy*, 11 ('Under the light veneer of a somewhat superficial Christian revision we have here [i.e. in Chapters 33–38 of the seventh book of the *Apostolic Constitutions*] a complete Graeco-Jewish ritual for the Morning Service of the Sabbath and feast days.') For a critical assessment of the validity of this claim and the methodology used by Baumstark and others advocates of a Jewish background of these prayers, see Fiensy, *Prayers Alleged to Be Jewish: An Examination of the Constitutiones Apostolorum*; see also Van der Horst–Newman, *Early Jewish Prayers in Greek*, 3–29.

[165] Thus Ehrmann, *Klagephänome im zwischentestamentlicher Literatur*, 157, following Schneider, 'Die biblischen Oden im christlichen Altertum', 30–34; cf. Van der Horst–Newman, *Early Jewish Prayers in Greek*, 157.

[166] Alikin, *The Earliest History of the Christian Gathering*, 10; and see his discussion of the history of research on the earliest history of the Christian gathering on pp. 8–13 for further references.

[167] Thus e.g. Wilkins, 'The Prayer of Manasseh', 170 (referring to verse 8); Oßwald, 'Das Gebet Manasses', 19–20 (referring to verses 1 and 8); Bertholdt, *Historischkritische Einleitung*, 2619; Von Stemm, *Der betende Sünder vor Gott*, 106; Denis–Halewyck, *Introduction à la littérature religieuse judéo-hellénistique*, I, 676–677; Charlesworth, 'Prayer of Manasseh', 628 ('The author was obviously a Jew, as almost

It is true that the expressions 'the God of Abraham, Isaac and Jacob' and 'the God of our fathers' are well-attested in the Hebrew Bible and Jewish sources. Their combination – in the Bible attested in Exodus 3:6, 15 (with 'your' instead of 'our'); 4:5 (with 'their' instead of 'our') and, in the context of a prayer, in 1 Chronicles 29:18 (with 'Israel' instead of 'Jacob') – is common in Jewish prayers and occurs, for example, in the first blessing of the *Amida*.

There are, however, also parallels to this formula in early Christian sources. The expression 'God of our fathers' occurs several times in the book of Acts (5:30; 22:14; 24:14) and the full phrase 'The God of Abraham, Isaac and Jacob, the God of our fathers' occurs in Acts 3:13 and 7:32 (in 7:32 with 'your' instead of 'our'). Other Christian sources refer to 'Abraham, our father' (Romans 4:12; James 2:21; 1 Clement 31:2) and 'Jacob, our father' (1 Clement 4:8).[168]

The references to the righteousness and blamelessness of the patriarchs, which at first sight also seem typically Jewish, have parallels in Christian sources as well. We could compare, for example, the way in which Justin Martyr in his *Dialogue with Trypho*, speaks of 'the holy Patriarchs' (120:5), 'the Patriarchs, the Prophets, and every just descendant of Jacob' (26:1), and 'their righteous forefathers, Noah, Enoch, Jacob', and others (45:4).[169]

Accordingly, even though the opening lines of PrMan may sound Jewish, especially to one who is acquainted with the *Amida* and other Jewish prayers, the parallels with Jewish literature and liturgy are not compelling evidence for a Jewish background to PrMan.[170] The assumption that a prayer containing these formula cannot have been composed by a Christian in the first centuries of the Common Era is untenable in the light of parallels in other Christian sources.[171]

---

all specialists today recognize').

[168]Cf. Bauer, *Griechisch-deutsches Wörterbuch zu den Schriften des Neuen Testaments und der frühchristlichen Literatur*, 1282 ('*d. großen Frommen des ATs*, d. auch für d. Heidenchristen, das "wahre Israel", Väter sind'); Bauer refers also to Justin, *Dialogue with Trypho*, 101:1.

[169]Ed. Bobichon I, 506 (120:5); 247 (26:1), 294 (45:4). Compare also the Islamic concept 'infallibility of the prophets' (عصمة الأنبياء, *ʿiṣmat al-ʾanbiyāʾ*).

[170]Nor is it compelling to assume that the superscription in version B reflects a Jewish background; see above, section 1.7.3.

[171]It should also be noted that the Christian scribes who transmitted the text ap-

The portrayal of Manasseh as the prototype of the repentant sinner does not argue either against a Jewish or against a Christian origin for PrMan, but it is worth observing that it perfectly fits a Christian context,[172] whereas in Jewish sources there is more often ambiguity regarding the evaluation of Manasseh as well as regarding the question as to whether God accepted his prayer. Some sources tell of his repentance, but in others he is 'an anti-exemplar, distinctly not worthy of emulation',[173] and he remains the godless idolater of the Book of Kings,[174] rather than the repentant sinner of Chronicles. At the end of the first century CE Josephus (*Antiquities* 10.3) follows the Chronicler's positive evaluation of Manasseh's repentance and restoration, but according to the author of the *Apocalypse of Baruch*,[175] Manasseh's prayer was rejected and the brazen horse (above, section 1.7) was a sign of his future judgement.[176] In the Mishnah and the Tosephta there are discussions as to whether Manasseh's prayer was accepted and whether he will have share in the World to Come.[177] In the Hebrew version of PrMan from the Cairo Genizah (above, section 1.4) Manasseh asks for forgiveness not only in this world but

parently did not feel uneasy or unfamiliar with the expressions and views in PrMan, since they did not attempt to adapt the Prayer to render it acceptable to a Christian audience.

[172]For references to Manasseh's repentance and his prayer in patristic literature, see Denis–Halewyck, *Introduction à la littérature religieuse judéo-hellénistique*, I, 662–664.

[173]Newman, 'Three Contexts for Reading Manasseh's Prayer in the Didascalia', 10.

[174]Cf. Van Keulen, *Manasseh through the Eyes of the Deuteronomists*.

[175]For arguments for a Jewish background of the *Apocalypse of Baruch*, including the author's attitude towards the Mosaic Law, his emphasis on the observance of the Sabbath and circumcision, and his expression of a 'robust national identity', see Davila, *The Provenance of the Pseudepigrapha*, 126–131; *pace* Nir, *The Destruction of Jerusalem*.

[176]*Apocalypse of Baruch* 64:9; cf. Bogaert, *Apocalypse de Baruch*, 300–303; Newman, 'Three Contexts for Reading Manasseh's Prayer in the Didascalia', 9–10; Borbone, 'Preghiera di Manasseh', 542; Denis–Halewyck, *Introduction à la littérature religieuse judéo-hellénistique*, I, 662.

[177]For details see Bogaert, *Apocalypse de Baruch*, 298–300; cf. Gry, 'Le roi Manassé, d'après les légends midrashiques', 155. Cf. Ginzberg, *The Legends of the Jews*, VI, 376, note 108: 'The prevalent opinion in rabbinic literature is that Manasseh is one of the few Jews who lost their portion in the world to come'.

also in the World to Come. Apparently the Hebrew translator was aware of the dispute as to whether Manasseh's repentance would be accepted in the World to Come.[178]

1.9.4 PrMan as a Christian document

If we start from the other assumption, and read PrMan as a Christian document, it is remarkable that it shares many motifs with the New Testament, even some of the motifs that have been called typically Jewish, such as the view that repentance is granted or withheld by God (PrMan 8; cf. Acts 11:18)[179] and the idea that repentance is the way to salvation (PrMan 8; cf. 2 Corinthians 7:9–10)[180]; the idea that the righteous do not need repentance (PrMan 8) is also reflected in Luke 5:32 and 15:7[181]; the 'repentance of forgiveness' (PrManB 7) is reminiscent of the 'repentance leading to the forgiveness of sins' in Luke 3:3[182]; Luke 18:13, about the tax collector 'who would not even look unto heaven' is reminiscent of PrMan 9 and the words 'I am not worthy' (PrMan 14; also in PrManB 10) are also uttered by the prodigal son in Luke 15:19, 21. In the invocation of God at the beginning of the Prayer, 'who held the Abyss, and sealed it' (PrMan 3) is reminiscent of Revelation 20:3 (where the Syriac translation has ܬܗܘܡܐ *thomā* and ܐܚܕ *ʔeḥad*, just as in PrManA,B 3).[183]

It is not our intention to argue that these parallels are exclusively Christian motifs and that they prove a Christian background. The point we want to make is that the text of PrMan does not contain compelling evidence of either a Jewish or a Christian origin and that the suggestion that PrMan is 'unquestionably' of Jewish origin is unfounded.

The parallels with Christian sources not only help us modify our view on the origin of PrMan, but also on its transmission and reception history. They indicate how PrMan may have been received

[178] Leicht, 'A Newly Discovered Hebrew Version', 367, 367.

[179] Compare also Vegas Montaner, 'Oración de Manasés', 116, note 8, who refers to some passages in the *Shepherd of Hermas*.

[180] Cf. footnote 10 on page 145.

[181] Even if the Luke passages are ironical; cf. below, footnote 11 on page 146.

[182] Cf. footnote 7 on page 144.

[183] Cf. Connolly, *Didascalia Apostolorum*, 72.

in Christian contexts and what biblical passages may have resounded when PrMan served as part of Christian liturgies. These resonances may even have been stronger in the Syriac than in the Greek tradition, because some lexical correspondences between PrMan and New Testament passages are even stronger in the Syriac versions than in the Greek versions.[184] Furthermore, it seems safe to conclude that the Christian recipients and tradents of PrMan could live with the text as it stands and apparently did not feel the need to change the allegedly Jewish idioms or to introduce typically Christian elements.

1.10 PRMAN IN ITS SYRIAC CONTEXT

The present volume focuses on the Syriac versions of PrMan. For this reason we will give in this section a short summary of the history of the Syriac language and tradition and the place of PrMan within it.[185]

The Syriac language is one of several languages which together constitute the 'Aramaic' group of languages. This group, in turn, is one of the sub-branches of the North-West Semitic languages. While other Aramaic languages were used long before the beginning of the Christian Era throughout the Middle-East and Mesopotamia, the first Syriac inscriptions, found in the neighbourhood of Edessa (nowadays the Turkish city of Urfa, or Şanlıurfa), date from the first century.[186] In this section we will not address the typical linguistic features of Semitic languages in general or Syriac in particular, but a number of these features will be introduced in our comparative analysis of the two versions of PrMan in the subsequent chapters.

Soon after its emergence, Syriac became an important language of Christian liturgy and literature, written with its own variant of the Semitic abjad (=consonantic alphabet), known as the Syriac alphabet. The most important book in the formative period of Syriac writing is unquestionably the Syriac translation of the Bible, known as the *Peshiṭta* ܦܫܝܛܬܐ ('the simple'). Promoted by the success of

---

[184] See the footnotes to section 3.1.

[185] This summary is mainly based on Costaz, *Grammaire syriaque*, 230–236; Muraoka, *Classical Syriac*, 2nd edition, 1–2; Brock, *A Brief Outline of Syriac Literature*; and Brock, *An Introduction to Syriac Studies*.

[186] Cf. Healey, 'The Edessan Milieu and the Birth of Syriac', §2.

Christianity, the Syriac language was propagated from Edessa to the north-west of Syria and later to the whole of Mesopotamia. This first period, from the third till the seventh centuries, is the 'Golden Age' of Syriac literature. To the authors of this period belong the famous fourth-century writers Ephrem and Aphrahat. In this formative period we can also postulate the origin of the Syriac translation of the Manasseh stories in the books of Chronicles, probably translated into Syriac around 200 CE,[187] and the appearance of PrMan in the Syriac translation of the *Didascalia* in the fourth century,[188] even though in both cases the extant manuscripts are from a later date.[189]

The Christological controversies about the relationship between the human and the divine in Christ, which culminated in the Councils of Ephesus (431 CE) and Chalcedon (451 CE), led to a gradual separation of the Syriac churches from the Greek-speaking Imperial Church.

- The East Syrians (sometimes called by the misnomer 'Nestorians'[190]) rejected both these councils since they supported Nestorius, who was condemned in Ephesus. Nestorius stressed the division between the divine and the human natures in Christ and hence rejected the designation 'Mother of God' for Mary. At the end of the fifth century the Church of the East separated from the Imperial Church. Unlike other Syriac churches, the Syriac Church of the East did not live under Roman rule.

- The West Syrians accepted the Council of Ephesus, but not that of Chalcedon, because they adhered to the view, rejected in Chalcedon, that Christ had only one nature.[191] The West

[187] Cf. Weitzman, *The Syriac Version of the Old Testament*, 258, 261.

[188] Cf. above, section 1.2.

[189] For Chronicles see Phillips, 'The Reception of Peshitta Chronicles', 260–265; for the *Didascalia* see above, section 1.2.

[190] Because of its origin as a debased and misleading epithet, designating the East Syrians as heretics (i.e. followers of Nestorius, the heretic), this term should be avoided.

[191] However, the Eutychian Monophysitism that was rejected in Chalcedon is not exactly the same as the Syriac Orthodox Monophysitism; see Brock, *An Introduction to Syriac Studies*, 69.

Syrians established their own church, which is known as the Syriac Orthodox Church. Jacob Baradaeus (after whom the West Syrians are sometimes unfortunately called 'Jacobites') played a vital role in the formation of this church and the organization of its hierarchy in the sixth century.

- Those who supported the Chalcedonian Creed were called the Melkites (i.e. 'those who adhered to the king'). They lived mainly in the west of the Levant and Egypt.

The biblical manuscripts in which PrMan has been preserved are from a West Syriac provenance, except for 14/8a1, which has an East Syriac origin (see above, section 1.5.1). Although the inclusion of PrMan in the Odes may reflect a liturgical use of it in the Syriac churches (cf. section 1.5.2), it is only among the Melkites that we find concrete evidence for its liturgical use as part of the Book of Hours. This use is an indication of the Greek influence on the Melkite liturgy. This influence can be accounted for by religious factors (because the Melkites backed the Byzantine emperor after the Council of Chalcedon) and by political and military developments (especially the Byzantine reconquest of North Syria in the late tenth century; cf. section 1.5.3). The Melkite-Byzantine link also provides a plausible explanation for the narrative traditions that are reflected in the superscription to PrMan in the Melkite Horologia (cf. 1.7.3).

The various branches of Syriac Christianity continued and developed their own dialects and scribal traditions. The dialectal variation is reflected, for example, in different pronunciations of the Syriac vowels; the various scribal traditions resulted, for example, in different vocalization systems. The two main vocalization systems are (1) a system based on Greek letters which became dominant in the West Syriac tradition and (2) a system with various combinations of dots which became common in the East Syriac tradition. However, the system with dots was also used by the West Syrians and there are also manuscripts containing a mixture of systems. In the transliteration in the present study we use the East Syriac system, since phonologically it is more detailed and more archaic than the West Syriac system.[192]

[192] Even though almost all Syriac manuscripts containing PrMan are of a West

The various branches of Syriac Christianity also developed their own variants of the Syriac alphabet. In addition to the original style of writing, the Esṭrangela (or Esṭrangelo) script,[193] the Serṭa (or Serṭo) script[194] came into common use among the West Syrians.[195] In the East a distinct East Syriac script (sometimes called 'Nestorian') was developed. E. Khalifeh has also identified a Melkite script, which he calls 'the Syriac Chacedonian Script that began to appear in the 10th–11th centuries'.[196]

From the eighth century onwards the Syriac language gradually lost its central position to Arabic and the Golden Age of Syriac literature came to an end. The loss was the strongest in the Melkite and Maronite communities and much less strong in the Church of the East. However, the use of Syriac as a liturgical language remained in these churches for much longer, as the Syriac Melkite manuscripts from the tenth, thirteenth and fifteenth century containing PrMan (see sections 1.5.1 and 1.5.3) confirm.

The eighth to the thirteenth centuries marked a period of consolidation and compilation, which reached its peak in the thirteenth century in the encyclopaedic work of Bar Hebraeus. The earliest manuscript containing PrMan (the ninth-century biblical manuscript 9a1) dates from this period (see section 1.5.1). It is also in this period

---

Syriac provenance (see above).

[193]This script is still in use today. In this book we use a font called 'Estrangelo Edessa' based on this script, developed by Paul Nelson and George Kiraz.

[194]For examples see illustrations 5–14 on pages 59–68.

[195]However, in recent years the traditional view according to which the Serṭa script developed from the earlier Esṭrangela has been challenged. F. Briquel Chatonnet and J. Healey have argued that in the first centuries of the Common Era a formal script, rather similar to what is later known as Esṭrangela, and a cursive script, which developed into Serṭa, existed side by side; see Van Peursen, 'La diffusion des manuscrits bibliques conservés', 206, with further references.

[196]Cf. Khalifeh, 'Antiochian Chalcedonian Orthodox Manuscripts', 4. In this article Khalifeh does not provide a characterization of this script. On the basis of his own observations, Professor Istvan Perczel (personal communication) describes it as follows: 'The script seems to be a development from the Esṭrangela script, including Serṭa elements. Later it started to resemble the East Syriac script, but I wonder whether it was influenced by the latter or this was a more or less independent development from the Esṭrangela. The Serṭa elements remain strong in that phase, too.'

that PrMan entered the Melkite liturgy as part of the Great Compline, illustrating the Greek influence on the Melkite liturgy following the Byzantine reconquest of North Syria in the late tenth century (see above), and that the first textual witness to this liturgy (the tenth-century manuscript 10t1) was composed (see section 1.5.3).

The conversion of the Mongols to Islam around 1300 posed a new threat to Syriac creative writing and many modern Western studies indeed give the impression that the literary (unlike the liturgical) use of Classical Syriac ended with Bar Hebraeus (1226–86) in the West Syriac tradition and with Abdisho of Nisibis (d. 1318) in the East Syriac tradition.[197] However, as S. P. Brock has emphasized in various publications, creative writing in Syriac continued after the death of these scholars and we can even observe a remarkable revival of writing in Classical Syriac since the end of the nineteenth century.[198]

In addition to this continued use of Syriac for creative writing, the heritage of the previous periods was transmitted and new manuscripts were produced. The *List of the Old Testament Peshiṭta Manuscripts* (with the addenda that were published in the Peshiṭta Institute Communications) lists more than 176 biblical manuscripts from the thirteenth to the twentieth century, including 21 complete Bibles,[199] some of which, as we have seen, include PrMan. A number of the *Didascalia* manuscripts and the Melkite Horologia that contain PrMan also stem from this period (see table 1.1 on page 16).

From its standardization in the formative period up to its use in modern times, the Syriac language has remained remarkably stable, especially in its morphology. In the field of phonology some developments can be discerned, including the emergence of the two systems

[197] Cf. Muraoka, *Classical Syriac for Hebraists*, §1 (p. 2): 'The advance of Islam dealt a virtual death blow to Syriac as a viable spoken idiom, although it managed to maintain some lingering existence even down to the thirteenth century, as is eloquently testified to by that well-known prolific polymath, Barhebraeus (1226–86).' The same impression is given in Wright, *A Short History of Syriac Literature*, which, too, ends with Bar Hebraeus and Abdisho.

[198] See Brock, 'Some Observations on the Use of Classical Syriac in the Late Twentieth Century'; Brock–Witakowski, *The Hidden Pearl III*, 129–153 (=Chapter 6, 'Twentieth-Century Writing in Syriac'); Brock, *An Introduction to Syriac Studies*, 8.

[199] Cf. Van Peursen, 'La diffusion des manuscrits bibliques conservés', 195.

of pronunciation discussed above. Syntactic changes can be observed as well, and we will refer to some of them in our linguistic analysis of PrMan and in our conclusions, when we address the question as to whether the two versions of PrMan reflect two different linguistic profiles (section 6.3.2). Since the diachronic study of Syriac syntax is still in its infancy,[200] our conclusions about the diachronic and typological classification of the two versions of PrMan remain preliminary.

Some of the communities that continued to use Syriac as a literary and liturgical language employed modern Aramaic vernaculars (dubbed Neo-Aramaic and sometimes Neo-Syriac) as their daily language. Even though these communities had a rich oral literature, only at the end of the sixteenth century do we see a development of a written literature in these vernaculars.[201] While these modern Aramaic varieties are sometimes written in the Syriac alphabet,[202] and share some linguistic traits with the classical language, from a linguistic point of view they are not direct descendants of the literary Syriac language.

[200]Cf. Van Peursen, 'Language Variation and Textual History'.

[201]See Brock–Witakowski, *The Hidden Pearl III*, 132; Murre-van den Berg, 'Classical Syriac, Neo-Aramaic, and Arabic'.

[202]The Jewish varieties of Neo-Aramaic were put into writing using the square Aramaic script (used also for Hebrew) and not the Syriac script, which was never used for liturgical purposes. An example of such a Jewish text was published in Sabar, *Pəšaṭ Wayəhî Bəšallaḥ: A Neo-Aramaic Midrash on Beshallaḥ*.

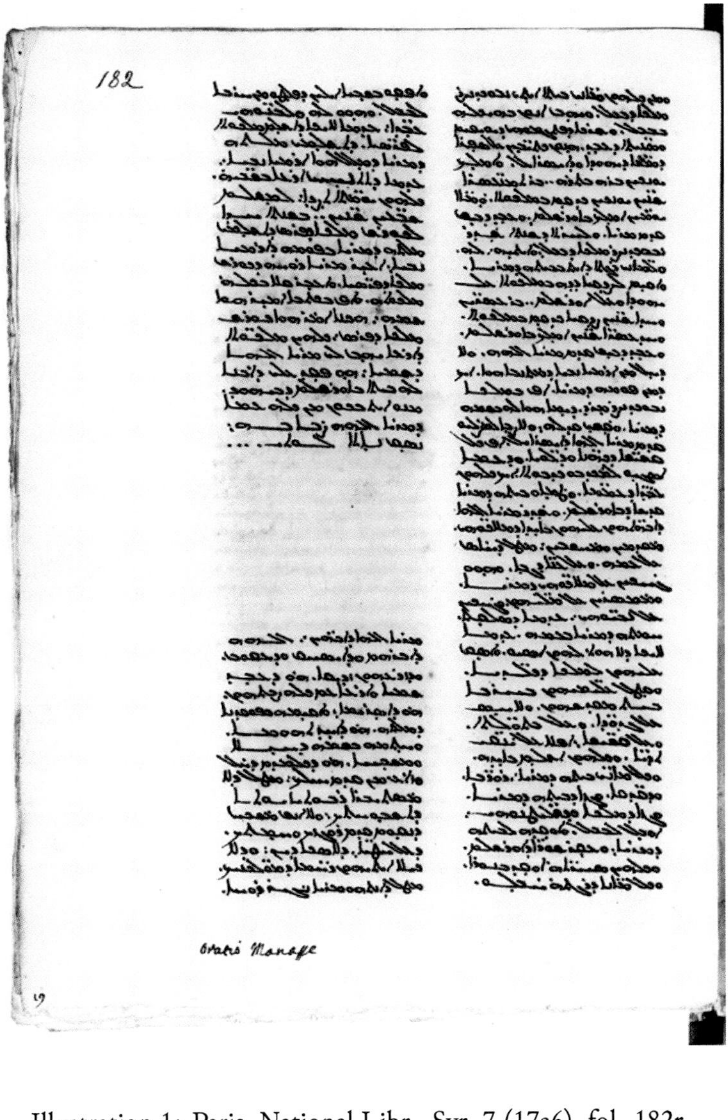

Illustration 1: Paris, National Libr., Syr. 7 (17a6), fol. 182r

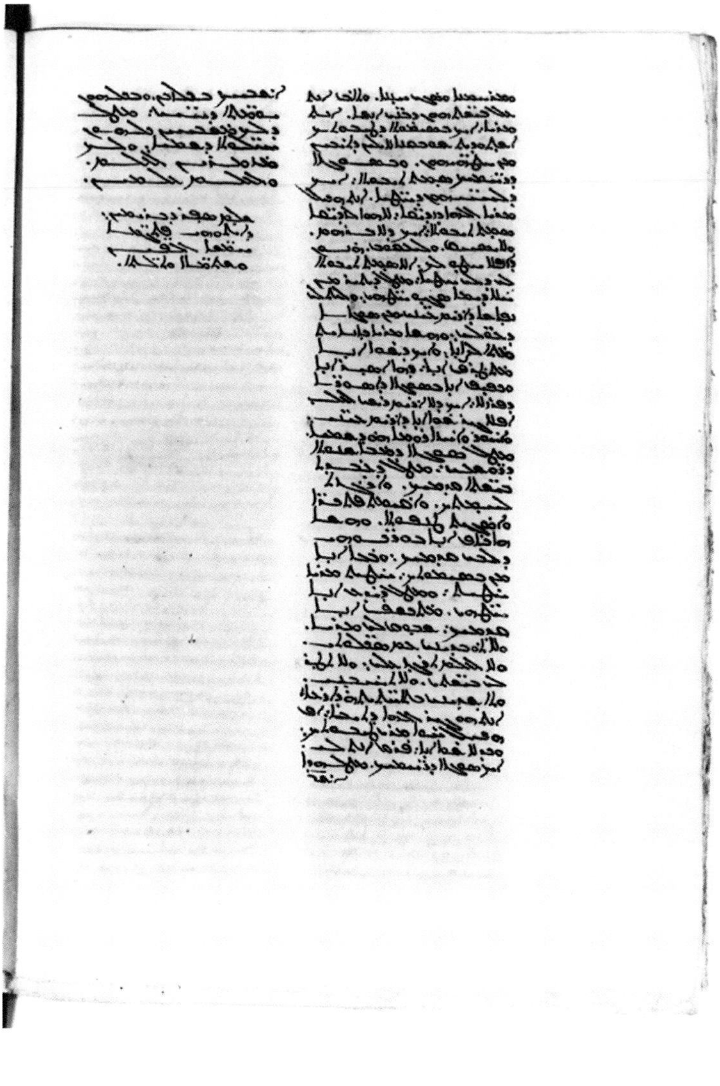

Illustration 2: Paris, National Libr., Syr. 7 (17a6), fol. 182v

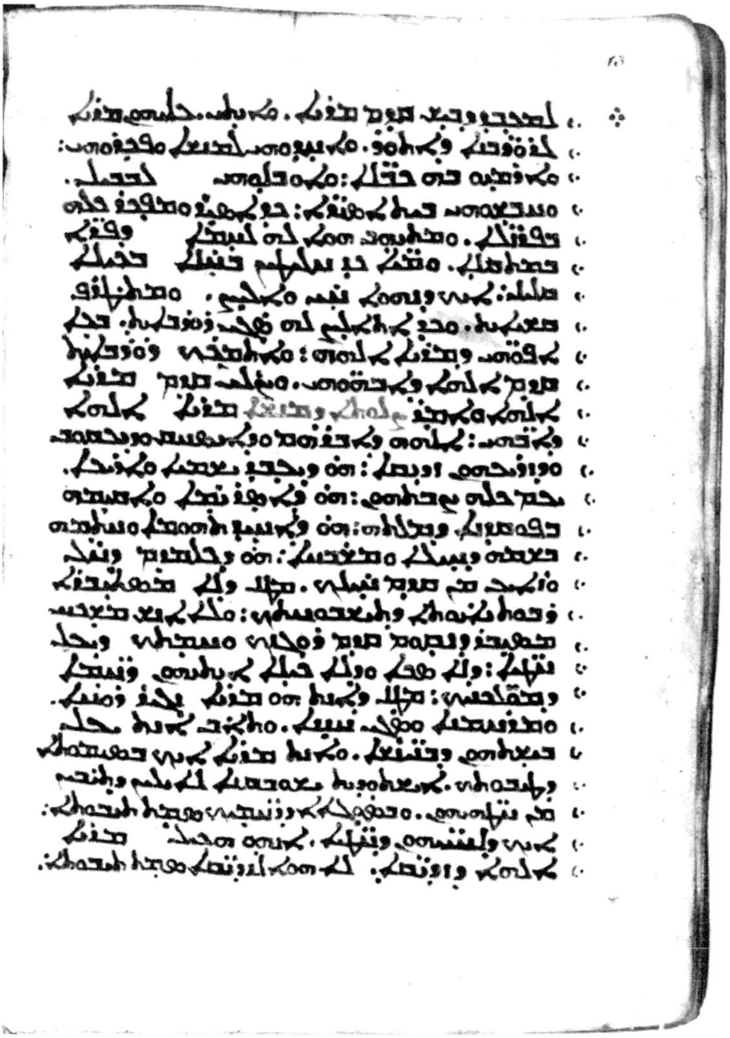

Illustration 3: Paris, National Libr., Syr. 62 (10D1), fol. 22v

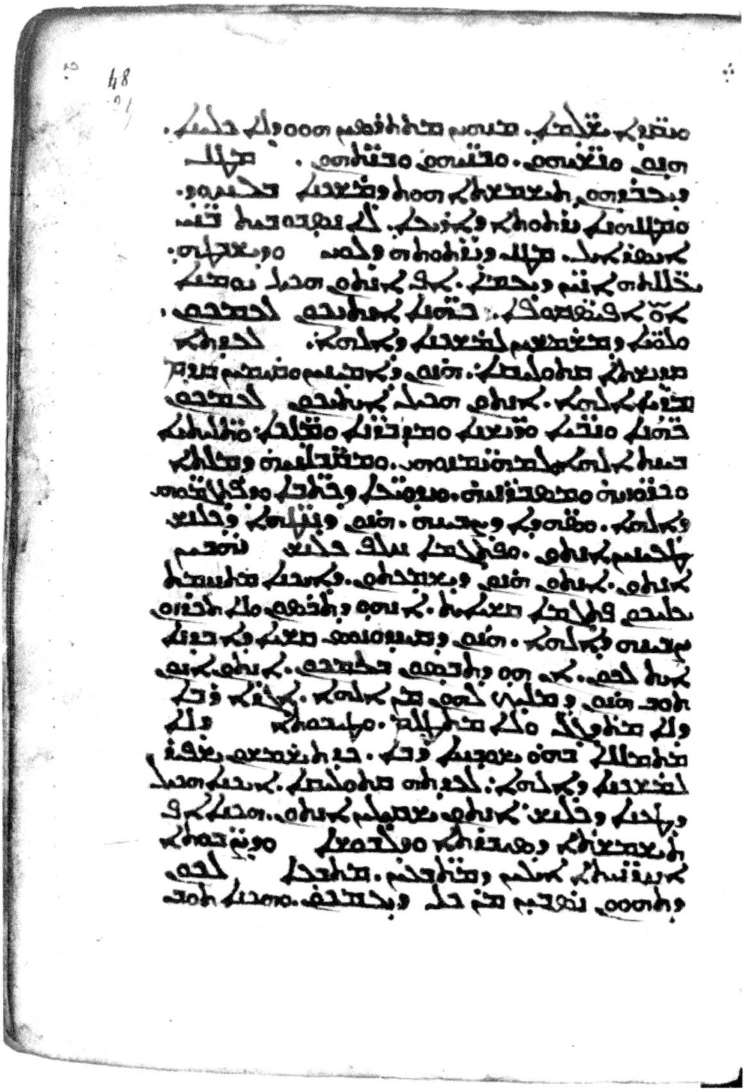

Illustration 4: Paris, National Libr., Syr. 62 (10D1), fol. 23r

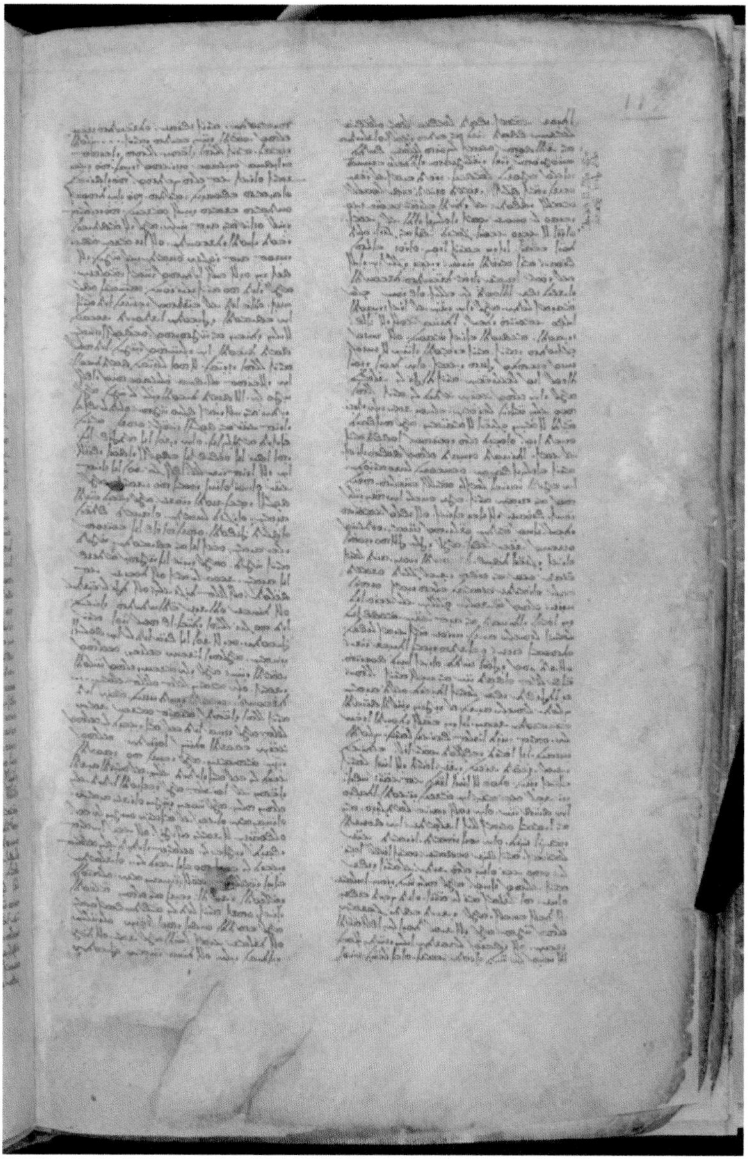

Illustration 5: Florence, Bibl. Med. Laur., Or. 58 (9a1), fol. 104v

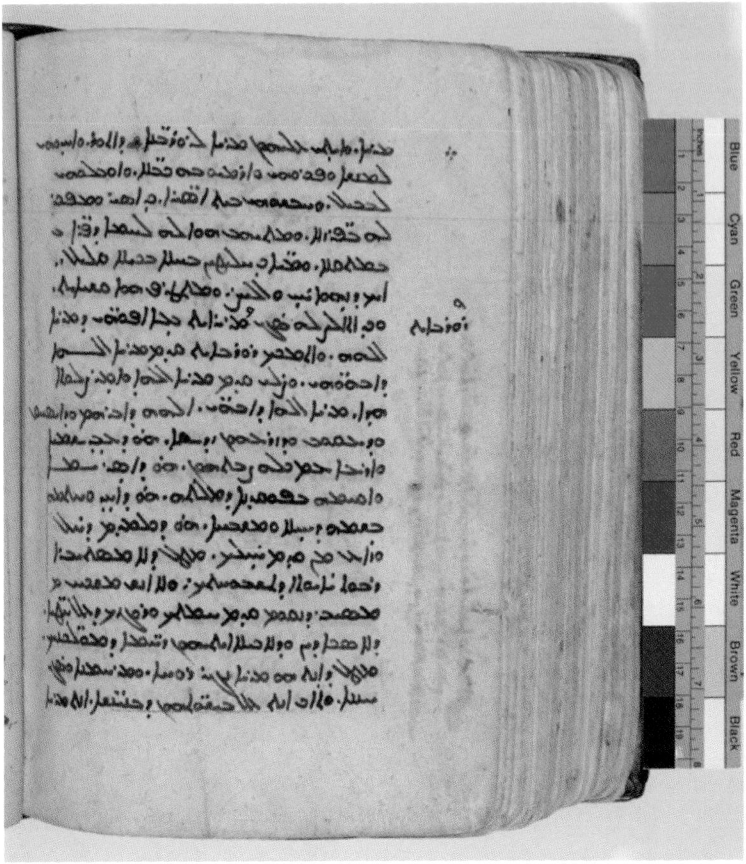

Illustration 6: Cambridge, Univ. Libr., Add. 2023 (13D1), fol. 189v

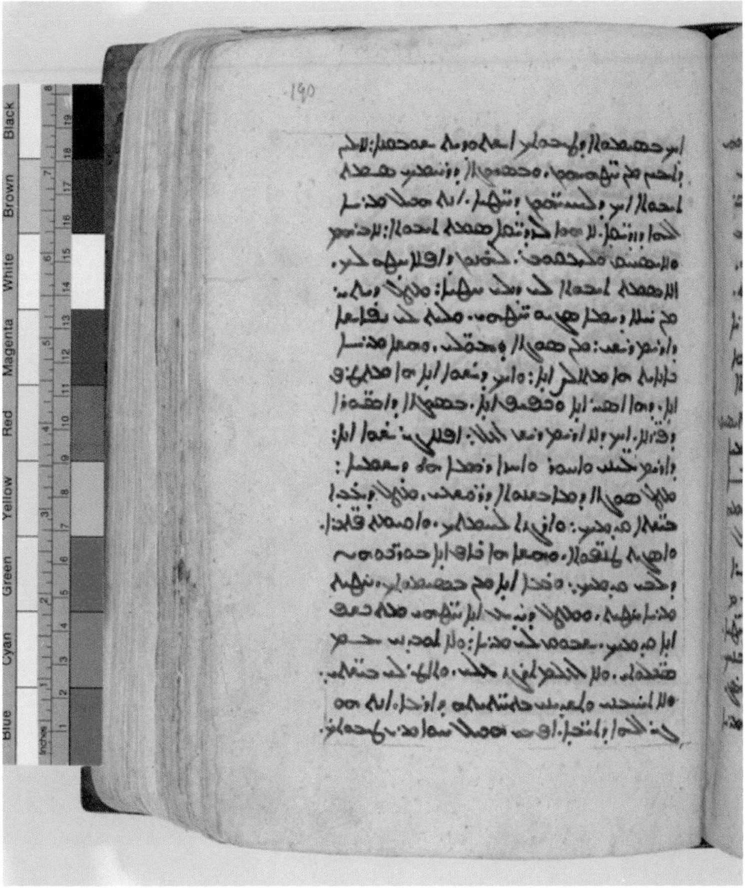

Illustration 7: Cambridge, Univ. Libr., Add. 2023 (13D1), fol 190r

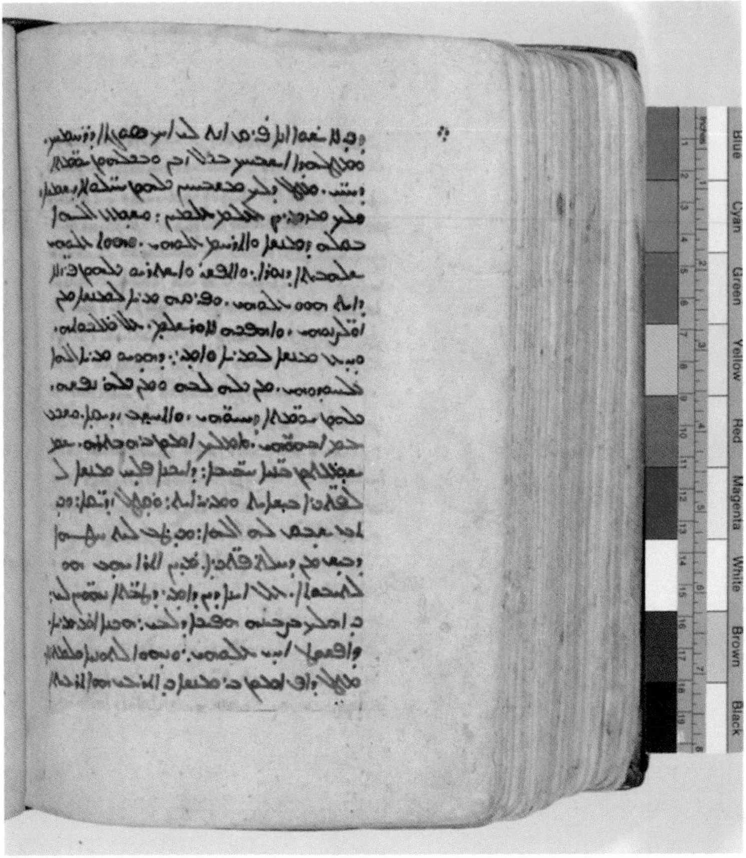

Illustration 8: Cambridge, Univ. Libr., Add. 2023 (13D1), fol. 190v

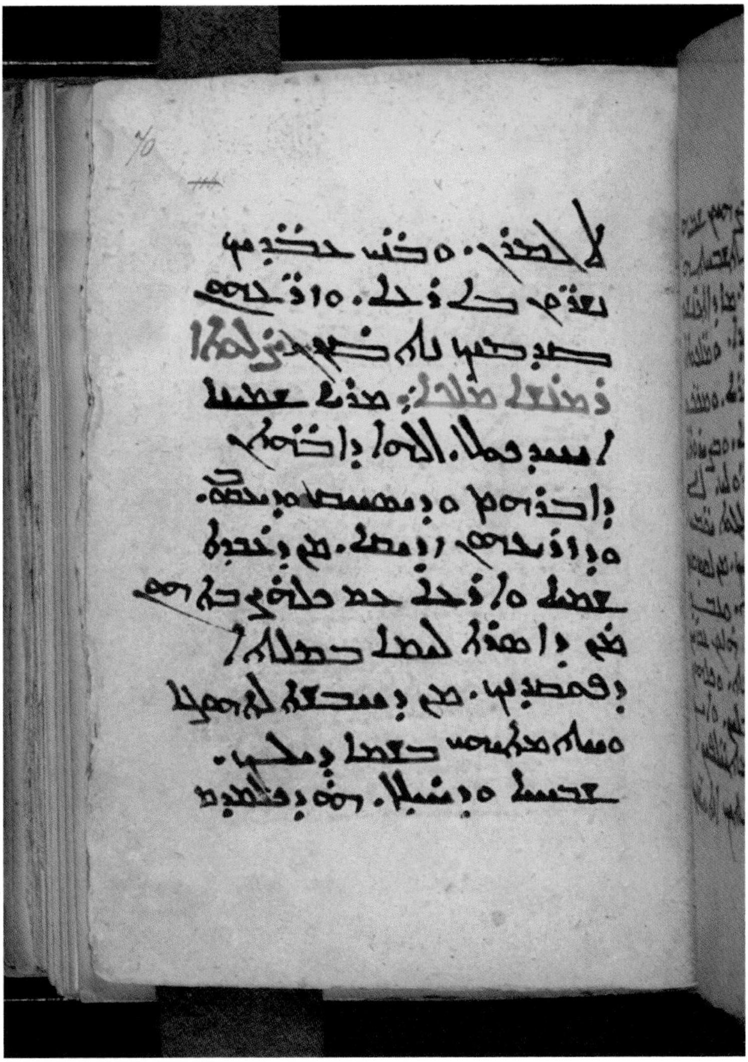

Illustration 9: London, B.M. Add. 14.716 (13H1), fol. 70r

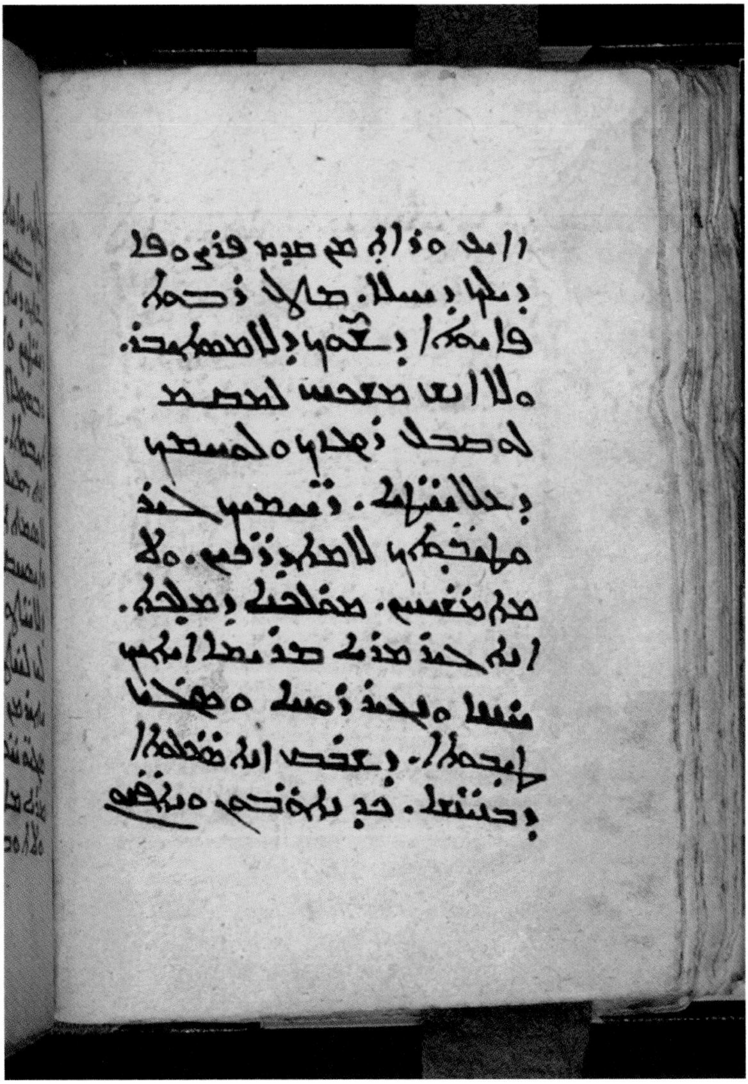

Illustration 10: London, B.M. Add. 14.716 (13H1), fol. 70v

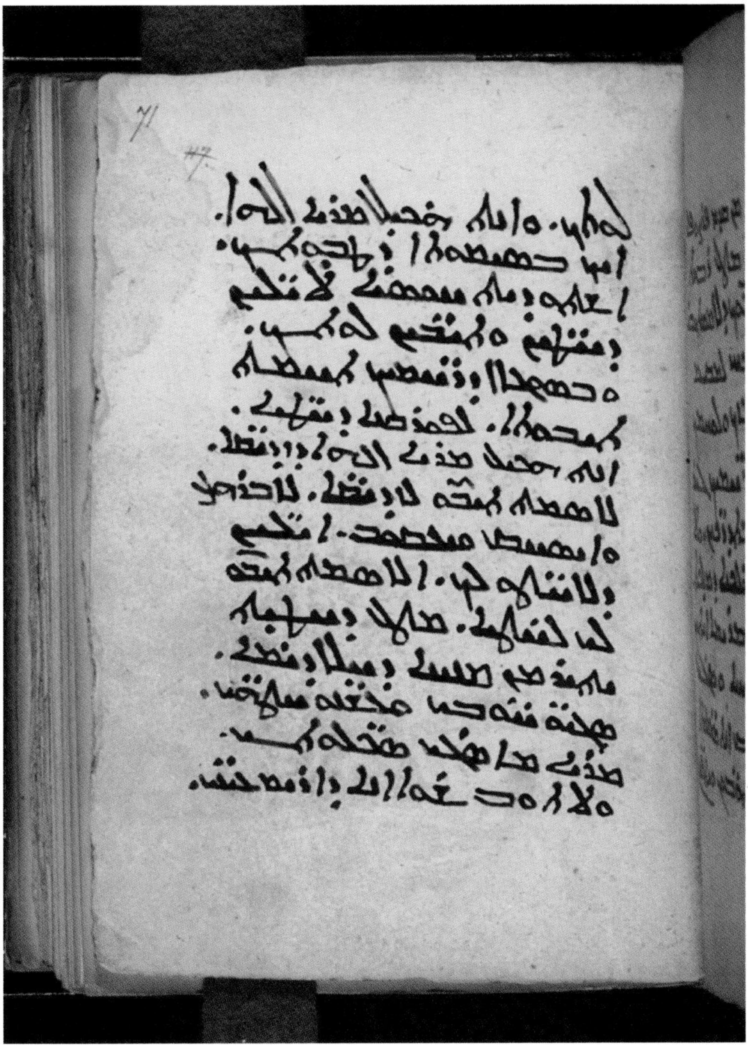

Illustration 11: London, B.M. Add. 14.716 (13H1), fol. 71r

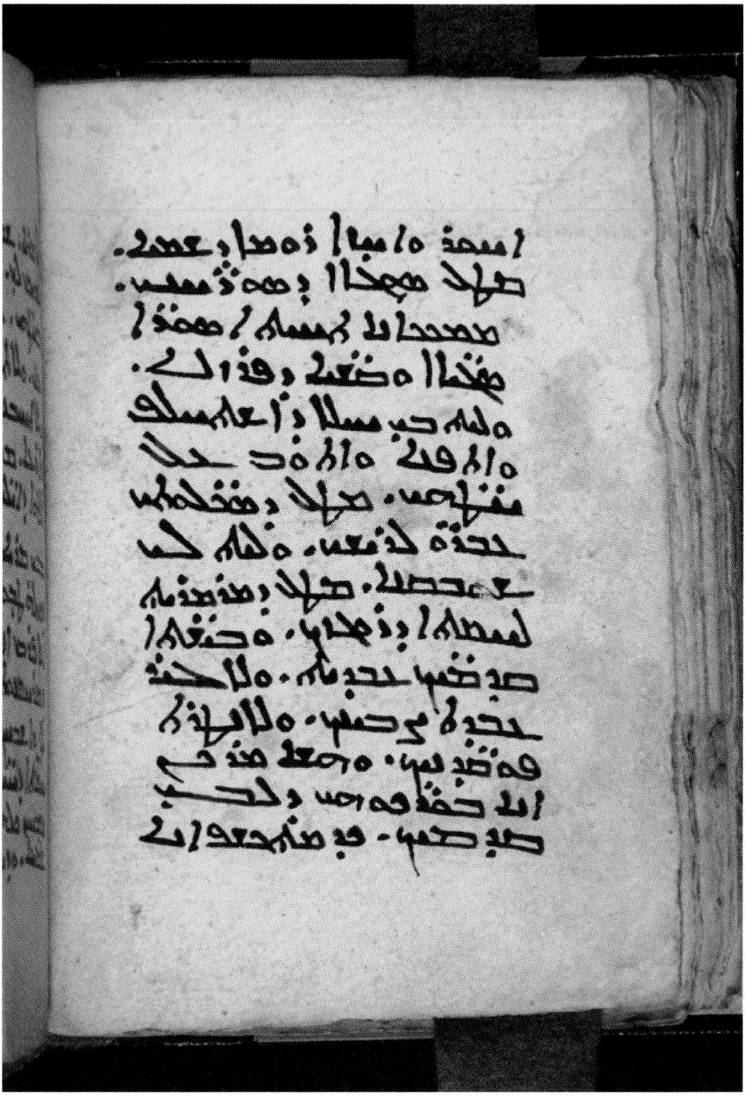

Illustration 12: London, B.M. Add. 14.716 (13H1), fol. 71v

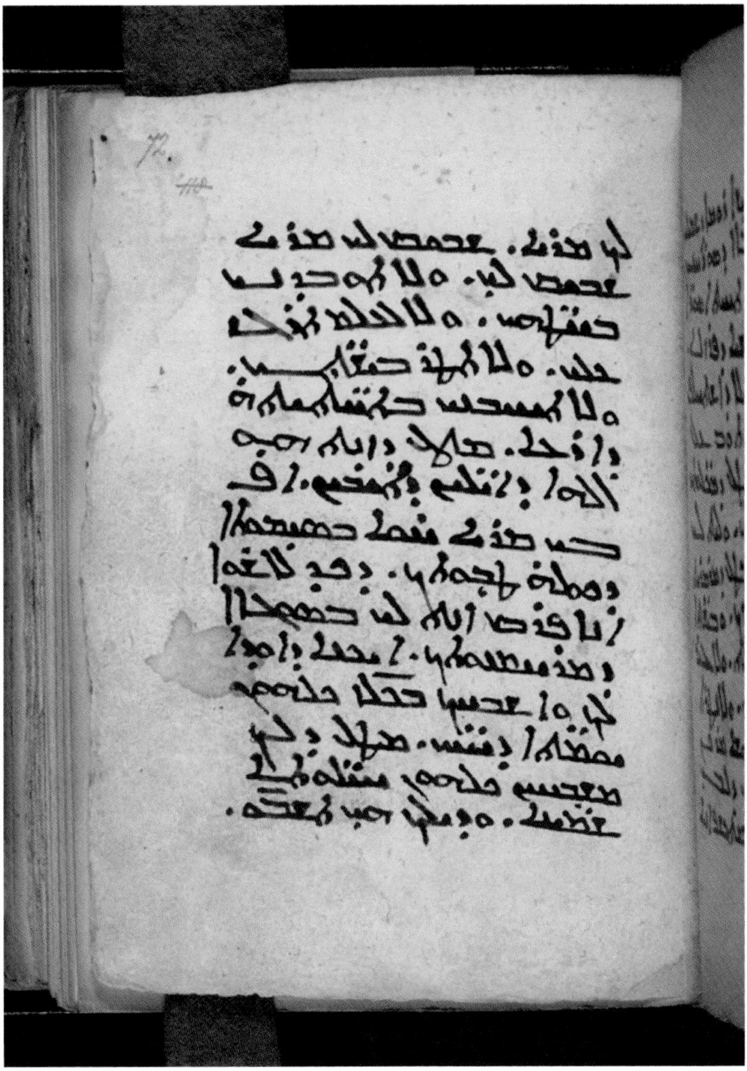

Illustration 13: London, B.M. Add. 14.716 (13H1), fol. 72r

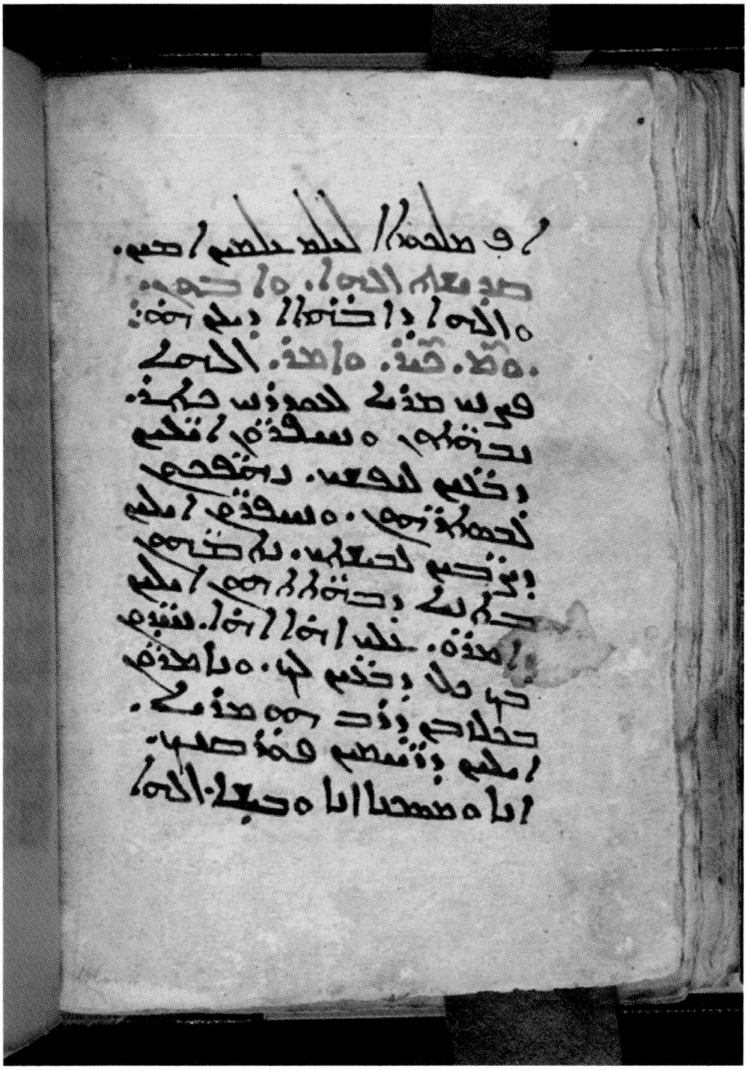

Illustration 14: London, B.M. Add. 14.716 (13H1), fol. 72v

Illustration 15: New York, Public Libr., Spencer Gr. 1, fol. 395v

Illustration 16: Paris, National Libr., Gr. 510, fol. 435v

Illustration 17: Athens, National Libr., Cod. 7, fol. 256v

Illustration 18: Paris, National Libr., Gr. 923, fol. 231v

Illustration 19: London, B.M. Add. 11870, fol. 151r

Illustration 20: Antipas of Pergamum, Monastery of Rousanou, Metéora

Chapter 2

Grammatical Comparison

In this chapter we present a grammatical comparison of the differences and similarities between the two versions of PrMan.[1] Although the two versions are similar in many respects, almost every clause contains various grammatical differences. Thus, our comparison focuses chiefly on the differences between the two versions. Nonetheless, identical clauses are presented as well, when they contribute to the discussion.

The material of this chapter is presented in accordance with our bottom-up linguistic analysis (cf. section 2.2): it starts with a morphological comparison, including orthographical variation (section 2.3), continues with phrase syntax (section 2.4), and ends up by discussing clause syntax (section 2.5). The higher level of clause combining and text hierarchy will be discussed in chapter 4. In the following section, a general introduction to the aims of the comparative analysis is given.

2.1 Introduction to the comparative analysis

The study, interpretation and reconstruction of ancient texts lies at the heart of the domain known as *philology*. Before the invention of the printing press, texts were distributed and transmitted by trained scribes who copied them by hand. More often than not, these copies were not exact duplicates of the original text, since the scribes intro-

[1]We would like to thank Dr Pollet Samvelian (ILPGA, Université Sorbonne Nouvelle) for her useful comments on an earlier version of this chapter.

duced small alterations, sometimes conceived as 'errors' and sometimes as 'corrections'. This made each exemplar of a text (a scroll, a manuscript, a codex) a unique object. The resulting situation should be contrasted with the situation prevailing today, in which multiple copies of the same book can exist without any noticeable difference (not to mention digital copies, which are virtually identical[2]). Thus, contrary to modern literary studies, in which the scholar interprets one 'canonical' text,[3] the philologist is often confronted with the situation in which several different versions of the same text reoccur in different manuscripts, without having an *a priori* knowledge as to which text should be considered 'original' or 'authoritative'. One of the main tasks of the philologist in such cases is to determine, using various techniques, the relationship between the different versions, in order to establish which readings should be considered original and to reconstruct the earliest attainable version of a certain text on the basis of the available manuscripts.

The main activity for establishing the relationship between the various manuscripts, is the **comparison** of the texts. Throughout the years, philologists have developed tools to perform this comparison, such as synopses and concordances, and established rules that account for the different modifications a text can undergo, such as *lectio difficilior potior* and *lectio brevis potior*. These rules represent assumptions about the cognitive mechanisms underlying the process of text-copying, which are converted into assertions regarding the probability (and directionality) of certain textual alterations. Thus the *lectio difficilior* principle presupposes that in general human scribes show the tendency to replace difficult elements in a text such as uncommon words, inconsistencies in a story, or controversial readings, with words or phrases that are more familiar or less controversial.

In an ideal situation these tools and principles help the researcher

---

[2] At the same time, however, the digital medium results in a multiplicity of text forms and versions that to a certain extent resemble the situation of the pre-printing era.

[3] Note, however, the increased attention in literary studies to the growth and development of modern literary works, as reflected, for example, in the author's manuscript and notes preceding the first printed edition or in changes that an author makes in subsequent reprints.

arrange the manuscripts in question in a genealogical chain or a tree, in which each manuscript is a copy of another one. However, the situation is often more complex because the extant material is too scarce or because the relationship between the manuscripts is not solely the result of copying and other diffusion mechanisms are at work as well, such as the translation from a different language, contamination (a copyist consulting more than one manuscript) or oral diffusion.[4] In order to resolve these difficulties, a deeper level of comparison is needed, namely a linguistic comparison.

Philology has always used linguistics as a tool to understand better the texts in question. Indeed, many of the early linguists were philologists, and their linguistic investigations were motivated by their desire to understand better ancient (and sometimes sacred) texts.[5] Since the twentieth century linguistics has adopted as its main goal the uncovering of the cognitive underpinning of language (the so-called 'linguistic competence'[6]), the division between philology and linguists as two separate domains of scholarship, with quite different research questions, is now much more marked. However, as we wish to show in this book, there is still a significant overlap between the two, and mutual enrichment is certainly possible. As mentioned above, a linguistic comparison between two texts (or, in our case, two versions of the same text), can help the philologist to uncover deep affinities or differences between them. For instance, two texts that use similar grammatical constructions with different wordings

[4]By oral diffusion we mean cases in which the copyist does not rely solely on the source version in front of him but, consciously or unconsciously, also on oral traditions he knows, such as recitation of prayers or oral narratives.

[5]This is true not only in the European tradition, but also in non-Western linguistic traditions, even though the domain of philology as such was not an established discipline. The Arabic grammarians, for instance, were interested in knowledge about the linguistic structure of Arabic as a tool to understand better the Quran, and the Sanskrit linguistic tradition probably arose from a concern to codify language and pronunciation in order to ensure a proper performance of the rituals at a time when the number of priests who had a good command of the language was decreasing.

[6]The interest in the cognitive basis of language is of course earlier than the rise of the term 'linguistic competence', and could probably be traced back to Antiquity. In modern times, one can understand the Saussuran notion of *langue* in cognitive terms.

may have more in common (i.e. structural elements) than superficially observed (i.e. in a word-by-word comparison). Conversely, usage of different grammatical constructions to express the same idea may shed light on the period of writing of each text (as grammatical constructions vary through time) or on contact languages (as one construction may be borrowed from a contact language). On the other hand, a thorough comparison of texts (and in particular parallel texts) may contribute to our understanding of the linguistic system in question (see further section 6.1.5).

These considerations have been available to philologists since the advent of the scholarly domain of philology. In biblical studies, for example, sophisticated models and methods for text comparison were developed in the study of the parallel passages in Samuel and Kings on the one hand and Chronicles on the other, in which both historical-literary questions (such as the Chronicler's use of his sources) and linguistic issues (such as the typical features of Late Biblical Hebrew) received due attention. Some of these investigations were extremely exact and elaborate, but others were rather impressionistic. The arrival of the computer age enabled, in principle at least, the creation of a computational platform which would force, so the speak, the scholar into a systematic, consistent and rigorous linguistic and philological analysis of the texts in question, as the computer software requires that every piece of text should be taken into account in one way or another by means of tagging or parsing it, for example. Note that this process is not necessarily done automatically by the computer – in this sense, we speak about 'computer-assisted analysis' rather than 'computational analysis'.[7] Such an approach could yield not only qualitative (and sometimes impressionistic) results, but also quantitative results, as the computer software could easily process numerically the scholar's input. While such an approach was in principle possible also before the invention of computers, in most cases it was impractical.

Such was the aim of the CALAP and Turgama projects, from which this book stems (for a more detailed description of the ap-

[7] We could parallel this distinction with a more common one made in the domain of computational linguistics, namely that between 'unsupervised' and 'supervised' analysis.

proach taken in these frameworks, see section 2.2). Though the methodology and techniques used in the computer-assisted research may differ from the classical philological research, the basic goals and assumptions remain the same: by comparing and analysing our two texts, we wish to arrive at a better understanding of the relationships between them and the linguistic system behind them.

In the previous chapter we presented some of the results of the study of PrMan in traditional scholarship. Although the various versions of PrMan have received much less attention than other parallel texts such as the synoptic Gospels, important progress has been made in the establishment of the relationship between the various versions. The publication of PrMan in the Leiden Peshiṭta edition, with the parallel alignment of the two Syriac versions and a detailed critical apparatus, is an excellent example of how far scholarship in PrMan has advanced. At the same time, however, we have to acknowledge that the most fundamental questions regarding, for example, the linguistic character of the two Syriac versions or their text-historical relationship to the Greek version still remain unanswered. For this reason, a systematic computer-assisted analysis of the two Syriac versions is more than appropriate.

The final results regarding the relationship between the two versions are given in the conclusions in chapter 6. Thus, the reader who is mainly concerned with the textual history of PrMan may content him/herself with reading the introductory chapter and the conclusions. The bulk of the book, however, is dedicated to the interim results of the computer-assisted analysis. In particular, the present chapter is dedicated to a detailed account of the grammatical differences between the two versions from the orthographic word level up to the clause level. This discussion, though it may seem technical (and maybe even tedious) at first sight, is a necessary result of the systematic comparison of the two versions, and is the foundation on which the conclusions are based.

As stated above, the aim of the comparison is two-fold: on the one hand, we wish to expose the differences between the texts in order to draw conclusions regarding the relationship between them and indirectly their relationship to the Greek versions. On the other hand, studying these differences can enhance the discussion on several topics in Syriac grammar, as these variations present grammatical variation coupled often to the same meaning.[8] In order to facilitate the discussion of these subjects, we present at the beginning of each section a short summary of the related Syriac grammar topics. These should not be seen as a comprehensive survey of Syriac grammar, but rather as a reminder of the issues in hand. Note, however, that in some cases we give our own linguistic analysis, since we have not found the existing analysis satisfactory (see especially section 2.5).

Thus, the linguistically-interested reader may benefit from reading throughout this chapter (and the following ones) as it presents various 'case-studies' of different phenomena of Syriac grammar. The non-linguist, on the other hand, may prefer to choose selected topics, either according to the cross-references given in chapter 6, according to the index of verses given at the end of the book, or according to the table of contents.

Before we start presenting our results, we will give a short summary of the method used for our computer-assisted linguistic and comparative analysis.

2.2 METHODOLOGY

For the comparison of the two versions of PrMan we used the model and tools that were developed in the projects CALAP (Computer-Assisted Linguistic Analysis of the Peshiṭta) and its successor, the project 'Turgama: Computer-Assisted Analysis of the Peshiṭta and the Targum: Text, Language and Interpretation'.

CALAP was a joint research project between the Peshiṭta Institute Leiden and the Werkgroep Informatica at the Vrije Universiteit Amsterdam from 1999 to 2005. It concerned the computer-assisted analysis of the Peshiṭta to the books of Kings[9] and Ben Sira.[10] The model of computer-assisted textual analysis and the computer programs required for it were further developed in the Turgama project,

[8] Cf. the section 'Textual Variation and Linguistic Variation' in Van Peursen, 'Language Variation and Textual History', 246–250.

[9] See Dyk–Van Keulen, *Language System, Translation Technique and Textual Tradition.*

[10] See Van Peursen, *Language and Interpretation.*

which started in 2005. In this project they were applied to other parts of the Peshiṭta, namely the books of Judges[11] and Psalms,[12] and to other texts, namely the Targum (also for the book of Judges)[13] and a corpus of original (non-translated) Syriac, namely the *Book of the Laws of the Countries* or the *Dialogue on Fate.*[14] In addition, some smaller pilots were carried out pertaining to the computer-assisted comparison of parallel texts in Hebrew[15] and Syriac.[16]

Since the CALAP/Turgama model has been described in detail elsewhere,[17] we will give here only a short summary of its basic characteristics. In the model the analysis proceeds from a multi-layered linguistic analysis to a comparative textual analysis. This enables a comparison that takes into account not only surface features, but also lexemes, parts of speech, division into phrases and clause parsing. The analysis starts with an independent bottom-up linguistic analysis of the texts to be compared. This involves:

- Word level: Segmentation of words into morphemes. Two auxiliary files – a description of the morphology and a list of lexemes – are used for functional deductions from the morphological analysis and the assignment of lexically determined word functions (e.g. 'collective noun').[18]

---

[11]The research for this project constituent is carried out by Wido van Peursen.

[12]This will be the subject of a PhD dissertation by Jeffrey A. Volkmer, supervised by David K. Taylor and Wido van Peursen and to be defended at the Oriental Institute, Oxford.

[13]The research for this project constituent is carried out by Percy S.F. van Keulen.

[14]This resulted in a PhD dissertation by Dirk Bakker; see Bakker, *Bardaisan's Book of the Laws of the Countries.*

[15]See Van Peursen–Talstra, 'Computer-Assisted Analysis of Parallel Texts in the Bible'.

[16]See Bosker, *A Comparison of Parsers. Delilah, Turgama and Baruch.*

[17]See Talstra–Jenner–Van Peursen, 'How to Transfer the Research Questions into Linguistic Data Types and Analytical Instruments' and other contributions to Van Keulen–Van Peursen, *Corpus Linguistics and Textual History.* and Van Peursen, *Language and Interpretation*, chapters 7–8.

[18] For instance, the active participle ܡܣܝܒܪ *msaybar* 'enduring' is morphologically analysed as `!M!S&JBR[/:d`. The participial prefix ܡ is coded as `!M!`, followed by the root `SBR`. The character `&` indicates that the following `J` is not part of the root. The characters `[` and `/` introduce the verbal and nominal endings, which are ∅

- Phrase level: Combination of words into phrases (e.g. noun + adjective). This entails the morphosyntactic analysis and the systematic adaptations of word classes in certain environments (e.g. participle > adjective; adjective > noun), and the analysis of phrase-internal relations (e.g. attribute, modifier).[19]

- Clause level. Combination of phrases into clauses (e.g. conjunction + verb + determinate Noun Phrase). At this level syntactic functions are assigned (e.g. subject, predicate).[20]

- Text level. Determination of the relationships between clauses. At this level the syntactical functions of the clause within the hierarchy of clauses are assigned (e.g. object clause, attributive clause).

The linguistically analysed texts are the input for the comparative analysis, which consists of the following steps:

- Collation (in the sense of creating a synopsis): interactive parallel alignment of segments that 'belong together', based on the calculation of their correspondences.

- Comparison: comparing the parallel texts with respect to all relevant categories: surface text, lexemes, parts of speech, division into phrases and clause parsing.

---

in this case. The ending `:d` signals that the root is inflected in the 'double' (or 'intensive') stem formation (Paʕʕel); in fact, this is the only coding of the vocalic pattern. From this coding the computer software can deduce that this form is a sg.m. active participle of the root ܣܒܪ in the Paʕʕel stem formation.

[19]For instance, ܒܦܘܩܕܢܐ ܕܡܠܬܗ 'by the commandment of his word' is analysed as `[ B (Prep, n/a) PWQDN> (N, emp) D (Prep, n/a) MLT (N, con) H (PersPN, n/a) ] (PrepP, det)`. This means the expression is interpreted as a Prepositional Phrase which consists of a preposition, a noun in the emphatic state, a second preposition, a noun in the construct state and personal pronoun. Note that only the maximal phrase is marked as such; the internal phrases (constituting the genitive construction) are not delimited.

[20]The clause ܕܐܣܪ ܝܡܐ, for instance, is analysed as `[D-<Re>] [>SR <Pr>] [JM> <Ob>]`: a relativizer followed by a predicate and an object.

2.3 MORPHOLOGY AND ORTHOGRAPHY

In Syriac, as in all Semitic languages, non-concatenative morphology is used extensively: consonantic roots (normally with three consonants) are fused into vocalic patterns to create the language's lexemes.[21] Differences in this domain are discussed in subsection 2.3.1.

Nouns and adjectives are declined for gender (masculine and feminine), number (singular and plural), and state (absolute, construct and emphatic).[22] The state declination is closely related to various syntactic factors, and is discussed in sections 2.4 and 2.5 whenever appropriate. A case of a pure morphological change of gender is discussed below in subsection 2.3.2.

Verbs are conjugated according to the subject, by marking its gender, number, and person indices (1st, 2nd, 3rd), as well as 'tense' (perfect and imperfect), voice and stem formation.[23] Differences in person marking are dealt with in subsection 2.3.3, while stem formation differences are discussed in subsection 2.3.1.

Finally, a short subsection deals with orthographical differences between the two versions (subsection 2.3.4). Although these could not be attributed any morphological significance, it should be noted that the boundary between morphology and orthography is not always clear.[24] For instance, the gender alternation, discussed in sec-

[21] Cf. Muraoka, *Classical Syriac*, 2nd edition, 17, §7. According to Aronoff, *Morphology by Itself*, chapter 5, and specifically pp. 151–154, a combination of a root and a vocalic pattern is a distinct lexeme, though he threats the Paʕʕel and Apʕel patterns as two realizations of the same stem formation (*binyan*). However, in our analytical model every root is treated as a lexeme, and the different stem formations are represented as a combination of prefix morphemes and vocalic pattern morphemes (the `:d` morpheme in footnote 18). This has no real implications for this chapter, but affects the discussion in chapter 3, where vocabulary counts are involved.

[22] Cf. Muraoka, *Classical Syriac*, 2nd edition, 21, §17.

[23] Cf. Muraoka, *Classical Syriac*, 2nd edition, 40, §48.

[24] See Bakker, *Bardaisan's Book of the Laws of the Countries*, 59, 65. This will also be discussed in some other deliverables from the Turgama project (cf. above, section 2.2), including Wido van Peursen's analysis of the Peshiṭta of Judges; see the preliminary remarks in Van Peursen, 'How to Establish a Verbal Paradigm'. This article addresses the distinction between the singular and the plural in the perfect of the third person masculine. The general view that the ending ܘ is a morpheme indicating the plural can be challenged. Another example mentioned in

tion 2.3.2, may be seen as the alternation of different orthographical conventions.

2.3.1 Stem formation

In two cases, the same root appears in the two versions in two different stem formations, without any major shift of meaning: in the verbal domain there is an alternation between the 'heavy' Pa^{ʕʕ}el pattern in version A (ܡܫܒܚܐ 'glorified') and the 'light' P^{ʕ}al pattern in version B (ܫܒܝܚܐ 'glorious') in verse 3. In the nominal domain, there is again an alternation between a 'light' form in version A (ܪ̈ܚܡܝܟ 'your mercy') and a 'heavy' form in version B (ܡܪܚܡܢܘܬܟ, same meaning) in verse 14. In this case the form in B is a newer form, the product of affixal derivation.[25] Nonetheless, both differences could be seen as a choice between alternative lexemes, rather than solely reflecting a morphological difference.

2.3.2 Gender alternation

In one case, in verse 1, there is a formal change of morphological gender, without any change of meaning: In version A, ܐܒ (before suffixes ܐܒܗ) is inflected with a masculine plural suffix, yielding ܐܒ̈ܗܝܢ 'our fathers', while in B a feminine suffix is used, yielding ܐܒ̈ܗܬܢ with the same meaning.[26]

this article is the addition of a Yodh to the perfect 3pl.f., the imperfect 3sg.f. and the perfect 3sg.f., which is an innovation in West Syriac biblical manuscripts. It is a debated issue whether this ending reflects a morpheme that was once pronounced (D. Boyarin) or just an orthographic convention (S. P. Brock).

[25] Thus Professor Alain Desreumaux, personal communication. See also Brock, 'Diachronic Aspects'; According to Brock, the extension of Pa^{ʕʕ}el and Ap^{ʕ}el participles by the suffix *-ānūtā* to produce abstract nouns was 'extremely productive (...) over the period from the fourth to the end of the seventh century' (p. 323).

[26] Cf. Nöldeke, *Syrische Grammatik*, §146; Muraoka, *Classical Syriac*, 2nd edition, 26, §27.1. For masculine nouns taking a plural feminine ending see also Nöldeke, ibid., §82. See also the entry for ܐܒ in Payne Smith, *Compendious Syriac Dictionary*, 1, which gives the two plural forms.

2.3.3 Person inflection

In the first part of the Prayer version B uses consistently the 2nd person (even when this seems less appropriate syntactically), while version A introduces the 2nd person only in verse 4, at the end of the glorifying introduction of the Lord. The differences occur mostly in verbs: (ܬ)ܥܒܕ, (ܬ)ܐܢܗܪ, (ܬ□)ܐܚܕ, (ܬ)ܚܬܡ and in some Noun Phrases: A ܒܦܘܩܕܢܐ ܕܡܠܬܗ / B ܒܡܠܬܐ ܕܦܘܩܕܢܟ (note the transposition) and A ܒܫܡܗ / B ܒܫܡܐ ܕܝܠܟ.

Only in verse 4 is the 2nd person introduced in version A, parallel to its occurrence in version B:

(1) A. ܗܘ ܕܟܠܡܕܡ ܕܚܠ ܘܙܐܥ ܡܢ ܩܕܡ ܚܝܠܟ. (verse 4)
haw d-kol-meddem dāḥel w-zāʾaʿ men
DEM LNK-all.CST-thing fear:AP and-tremble:AP from
qdām ḥayl-āk.
before might-POSS.2

'the one before whose might (2nd person) everything fears and trembles'

B. ܗܘ ܕܟܠ ܡܕܡ ܪܥܠ ܘܡܣܬܪܕ ܡܢ ܩܕܡ ܦܪܨܘܦܐ ܕܚܝܠܬܢܘܬܟ.
haw d-kol-meddem rāʿel
DEM LNK-all.CST-thing quiver:AP
w-mestarrad men qdām parṣopā
and-terrify.INT.REFL:AP from before face
d-ḥayltānut-āk.
LNK-might-POSS.2

'the one in whose face of might (2nd person) everything quivers and is terrified'

This may be explained by the fact that using the 3rd person to refer to the Lord in this verse would cause possibly ambiguity with the 3rd person referring to ܟܠܡܕܡ 'everything'.

Further discussion of the differences in pronouns is given below in section 2.4.1.

2.3.4 Orthography

There are some minor orthographic differences between the two versions (excluding variation in diacritics, which were not treated systematically in the comparison): A ܟܠ ܡܕܡ / B ܟܠܡܕܡ 'everything' (verse 4); A ܬܘܒܕܝܢܝ / B ܬܘܒܕܢܝ '(do not) destroy me' (verse 13b); A ܒ̈ܬܚܬܝܐܬܗ B ܒܬܚܬܝ̈ܬܗ 'in the depths of (earth)' (verse 13b). To these cases we may add also the couple A ܝܐܝܘܬܐ / B ܦܐܝܘܬܐ 'beauty, elegance' (verse 5a), although these words appear as two different lexical entries in the dictionaries.[27]

2.4 Phrase syntax

In our method of computer-assisted analysis, we can encode only one level of phrases, which are serving as 'clause constituents' for the analysis of clauses. For this reason, our phrase encoding is essentially flat, and each phrase is a 'maximal' constituent, be it a Noun Phrase, Prepositional Phrase, Pronominal Phrase etc.[28] Differences in the domain of Pronominal Phrases are treated below in section 2.4.1, and differences between Prepositional Phrases in 2.4.3. In section 2.4.4 we will discuss the way in which ܠܐ is used to negate nominal heads.

In Syriac, as in other Semitic languages, a Noun Phrase can easily be expanded by a genitive construction.[29] The relationship between the head noun and its dependant (normally a noun or a pronoun) can be expressed either morphologically, with the head noun put in the construct state, or syntactically, by means of the particles ܕ or ܕܝܠ.[30] Differences in this domain are treated in section 2.4.2.

On the borderline between phrase syntax and clause syntax stands

[27] For instance, in Payne Smith, *Compendious Syriac Dictionary*, they appear on pp. 184 and 432 with the same denotations: 'beauty, grace, comeliness', though the collocations given are different.

[28] Note, however, that contra some linguistic theories, our Verbal Phrase contains only the verb, and not any complements.

[29] This construction is termed סמיכות *smikut* in Hebrew (cf. Syriac ܣܡܝܟܘܬܐ *smikutā* 'addition, an accessory proposition' [Payne Smith, *Compendious Syriac Dictionary*, 380]) or إضافة *iḍāfa* in Arabic.

[30] Cf. Muraoka, *Classical Syriac*, 2nd edition, 61, §73.

the phenomenon of *apposition*, denoting the relationship between two phrases which fulfil the same syntactic function in the clause. This phenomenon is treated and compared in section 2.4.5.

2.4.1 Pronominal Phrases

In the first part of the Prayer, version A is more consistent in the usage of the 3sg.m. demonstrative pronoun ܗܘ as an apposition or pronominal referent to the vocative head noun ܡܪܝܐ 'the Lord' than version B, which uses also the 2sg.m. personal pronoun ܐܢܬ and the interrogative pronoun ܡܢ.[31] As mentioned in section 2.3.3, the verbal and nominal agreement also differs between the versions. In table 2.1 on page 88 the differences are presented with the relevant pronouns and pronominal suffixes underlined.

The use of the 2nd person starts in version A only at the end of verse 4[32] (possibly to avoid confusion with ܟܠ ܡܕܡ) 'everything'.[33] Grammatically speaking, it seems more logical to use the 3rd person together with the demonstrative pronoun ܗܘ (as in version A) or with the interrogative pronoun ܡܢ (but see also example (2) below). However, the sudden shift of person in verse 4 of version A is also quite odd grammatically, since the 2nd person in the relative clause has as antecedent a 3rd person demonstrative pronoun.

The use of ܡܢ in version B (verse 3) as referring to a unique referent is interesting. This use, unlike its use as an indefinite pronoun, often remains unnoticed in dictionaries and grammars. A similar usage is attested for מי in Rabbinic Hebrew, e.g. Sifre Numbers 78:4 מי שאמר והיה העולם 'the one that spoke and the world was'[34] or in

[31] However, all other Horologion manuscripts (cf. section 1.5.6) use consistently the interrogative pronoun throughout the first three verses instead of ܗܘ and ܐܢܬ (except manuscript 13H2 which simply omits ܐܢܬ). These manuscripts are thus more similar to version A in their consistent structure, though they differ in the choice of the pronoun used. It should be remarked that the term 'interrogative pronoun' does not imply any interrogative function in this context, but is used as a unifying label for ܡܢ in all its pronominal functions.

[32] Charlesworth's comment (Charlesworth, 'Prayer of Manasseh', 365, note m) that 'this is the first occurrence of this pronoun in Syr.' is imprecise, since it applies only to version A.

[33] Cf. also example (1) in section 2.3.3 above.

[34] Cf. Pérez Fernández, *An Introductory Grammar of Rabbinic Hebrew*, 36.

V.	Version A		Version B	
1	O Lord...	...ܡܪܝܐ	O Lord...	...ܡܪܝܐ
2	The one who created (3rd)...	...ܗܘ ܕܒܪܐ	The one who created (2nd)...	...ܗܘ ܕܒܪܬ
3a	The one who bound the sea and placed it	ܗܘ ܕܐܣܪ ܝܡܐ ܘܐܩܝܡܗ	You, who bound it, the sea	ܐܢܬ ܕܐܣܪܬܝܗܝ ܠܝܡܐ
	by the commandment of his word.	ܒܦܘܩܕܢܐ ܕܡܠܬܗ.	by the word of your commandment	ܒܡܠܬܐ ܕܦܘܩܕܢܟ.
3b	The one who held (3rd) the abyss	ܗܘ ܕܐܚܕ ܬܗܘܡܐ	Who held (2nd) the abyss	ܡܢ ܕܐܚܕܬ ܠܬܗܘܡܐ
	and sealed it by his name...	ܘܚܬܡܗ ܒܫܡܗ...	and You sealed it by the name of yours...	ܘܚܬܡܬܝܗܝ ܒܫܡܐ ܕܝܠܟ...
4	The one whom everybody...	...ܗܘ ܕܟܠܡܕܡ	The one whom everybody...	...ܗܘ ܕܟܠ ܡܕܡ
	... before your might.	... ܡܢ ܩܕܡ ܚܝܠܟ.	... in face of your might.	... ܡܢ ܩܕܡ ܦܪܨܘܦܐ ܕܚܝܠܬܢܘܬܟ.
5a	Because... of your honour.	ܡܛܠ ܕ... ܕܬܫܒܘܚܬܟ.	Because ... of your honour.	ܡܛܠ ܕ... ܕܬܫܒܘܚܬܟ.

Table 2.1: Pronouns in verses 1–5

the text from the prayer מי שבירך אבותינו 'the one who blessed our fathers'.[35] In other words, ܡܢ (or Hebrew מי) has the function of being the syntactic head of its relative clause (i.e. it functions as a place holder for an NP), and does not contribute any definite or indefinite value, as that value is derived solely from the semantics of the relative clause.

In another case, version B uses the pronoun ܡܢ, coalesced with the preposition ܐܝܟ to form ܐܟܡܢ, where version A has only the preposition ܐܝܟ:

(2) A. ܐܝܟ ܕܠܐ ܐܪܝܡ ܪܝܫܝ ܠܥܠ. (verse 10a)
ˀa(y)k d-lā ˀarim rēš-(y) l-ˁel.
as LNK-NEG rise.CAUS:IMPF.1 head-POSS.1 to-up
'So I shall not lift my head upwards.'

B. ܐܟܡܢ ܕܠܐ ܡܫܟܚ ܐܢܐ ܕܐܬܗܦܟ ܘܐܪܝܡ ܢܦܫܝ.
ˀak-man d-lā meškaḥ =(ˀ)nā
as-Q LNK-NEG can.CAUS:AP =1
d-ˀethpek w-ˀarim
LNK-turn_around.REFL:IMPF.1 and-rise.CAUS:IMPF.1
napš-(y).
soul-POSS.1
'As one who cannot(1sg.) turn around and lift my soul (or: myself).[36]'

It is noteworthy that in this case, too, version B uses the pronoun ܡܢ with a subsequent 1st, and not 3rd, person. One may be tempted to translate ܐܟܡܢ similarly to version A's ܐܝܟ 'so',[37] but such a translation will miss out the peculiar use of ܡܢ in version B.

The use of different pronouns projects a different kind of hierarchical arrangement of the text, which will be presented in table 4.3 on page 166 and further discussed in section 4.3.

[35] Cf. Wertheimer, משפטים מבוקעים, 23, note 12.

[36] See footnote 138, p. 131.

[37] Such a translation is supported by Payne Smith, *Compendious Syriac Dictionary*, 16, which lists 'as, as if, that' as possible translations of ܐܟܡܢ.

2.4.2 Genitive constructions

In the few cases where the two versions differ regarding genitive constructions, version A has a preference to use a morphological-synthetic construction to mark possession, while version B uses a syntactic-analytic construction:

(3) A. ܒܫܡܗ (verse 3b)
ba-šm-ēh
in-name-POSS.3
'by his name'

B. ܒܫܡܐ ܕܝܠܟ
ba-šmā dil-āk
in-name LNK-POSS.2
'by the name of yours'

(4) A. ܪܘܓܙܟ ܘܚܡܬܟ (verse 5b)
rugz-āk w-ḥemt-āk
rage-POSS.2 and-fury-POSS.2
'your rage and your fury'

B. ܚܡܬܐ ܘܪܘܓܙܐ ܕܝܠܟ
ḥemtā w-rugzā dil-āk
before fury and-rage LNK-POSS.2
'the fury and rage of yours'

In example (3) and (4) A attaches the possessive pronoun directly to the nominal base (which is consequently in the construct state), while B has an analytic construction: the noun (in emphatic state) is followed by the possessive particle ܕܝܠ + possessive suffix.[38] It is hard to discern a functional difference between the two constructions, but according to T. Muraoka, the construction with ܕܝܠ is often used 'with some emphasis on the possessive pronoun'.[39] In example (4)

[38] It is possible to analyse ܕܝܠ as being in apposition to the head noun, in which case this can be seen as a specific case of the preference of version B for apposition (see section 2.4.5); cf. Goldenberg, 'Attribution in Semitic Languages', 4.

[39] Muraoka, *Classical Syriac for Hebraists*, §87; see also Nöldeke, *Syrische Grammatik*, §225A; Joosten, *Syriac Language*, 57–58.

also the lexeme order changes, though this is probably unrelated.

In some cases one of the versions prefers the 'double' genitive in which the genitive is marked both syntactically by means of the linking particle ܕ, and morphologically on the head noun by means of a suffixed possessive pronoun agreeing with the genitive noun. For instance, A uses this construction in example (5) and B uses it in (6) (embedded in a bigger genitive construction) and (7).

(5) A. ܒܝܫܬܗܘܢ ܕܒܢܝܢܫܐ (verse 7a)
bišāt-hon da-bnay-nāšā.
evil.F.PL-POSS.3PL LNK-son.CST.PL-man
'the evil deeds (of them) of humans'

B. ܒܝܫܬܐ ܕܒܢܝܢܫܐ
bišātā da-bnay-nāšā.
evil.F.PL LNK-son.CST.PL-man
'the evil deeds of humans'

(6) A. ܚܠܐ ܕܝܡܐ (verse 9a)
ḥālā d-yammā
sand LNK-sea
'the sand of the sea'

B. ܡܢܝܢܐ ܕܚܠܗ ܕܝܡܐ.
menyānā d-ḥāl-ēh d-yammā.
number LNK-sand-POSS.3 LNK-sea
'the amount of the sand of the sea'

(7) A. ܪܘܡܐ ܗܘ ܕܫܡܝܐ. (verse 10a)
rawmā haw da-šmayyā.
height DEM LNK-heaven
'the height, that of heaven'

B. ܪܘܡܗ ܕܫܡܝܐ. (verse 9a)
rāwmā-h da-šmayyā.
height-POSS.3F LNK-heaven
'the height (of it) of heaven'

Example (7) is especially interesting.[40] Version B uses a double genitive construction, but version A uses a highly elaborate analytic construction: the head noun ܪܘܒܐ stands in apposition to the demonstrative pronoun ܗܘ, which in turn is the head of the genitive construction.[41]

As with the object construction with pronominal agreement (see example (26) on page 114) there seems to be at least a certain degree of functional equivalence (because no functional difference can be observed) as well as distributional equivalence (the constructions alternate in variant readings in the textual witnesses).[42]

In this context we can also mention example (37), quoted on page 122, in which A ܠܟ is parallel to B ܕܠܟ; but this example is less convincing since the two phrases appear in quite distinct syntagms.

It should be noted that in most cases the two versions agree as to the way of expressing the genitive construction, be it morphological or syntactical, such as in the following examples:

(8) A. ܝܐܝܘܬܐ ܕܬܫܒܘܚܬܟ (verse 5a)
yāyutā d-tešboḥt-āk
beauty LNK-honour-POSS.2
'the beauty of your honour'

B. ܦܐܝܘܬܐ ܕܬܫܒܘܚܬܟ
pāyutā d-tešboḥt-āk.
elegance LNK-honour-POSS.2
'the elegance of your honour'

[40] For the alignment of verses 9 and 10, see table 4.9.

[41] This is, in fact, a concrete example of the syntactic analysis given in Goldenberg, 'Attribution in Semitic Languages', for genitive constructions. In Goldenberg's analysis ܕ has a pronominal nature and stands in apposition to the head noun. In the example above, it has been expanded with a real demonstrative pronoun. While this example supports the syntactic logic of Goldenberg's view, it shows as well that from the point of view of the language user, ܕ has no pronominal power, as it can follow a pronoun. If ܕ were a 'real' pronoun, there would be no need, semantically speaking, to expand it by another pronoun. Indeed, synchronically, it is more correct to analyse it as a linking particle.

[42] For cases of similar variant readings in the additional manuscripts, see the tables in chapter 5.

(9) A. ܡܪܝܐ ܐܠܗܐ ܕܙܕܝܩܐ (verse 8)
mārya ʔalāhā d-zaddiqē
Lord God LNK-righteous.PL
'O Lord, God of the righteous'
B. ܡܪܝܐ ܐܠܗܐ ܕܙܕܝܩܐ
O Lord, God of the righteous

(10) A. ܒܬܐܚܬܝܬܗ ܕܐܪܥܐ (verse 13b)
b-ta(?)ḥtāyāt-āh d-ʔarʕā.
in-lower_part.PL-POSS.3F LNK-earth
'in the depths of earth'
B. ܒܬܚܬܝܬܗ ܕܐܪܥܐ
in the depths of earth

2.4.3 Prepositional Phrases

In several cases the two versions use different prepositions. In two cases, this does not lead to a major change of meaning:

(11) A. ܣܡܬ ܬܝܒܘܬܐ ܠܝ ܕܝܠܝ ܚܛܝܐ. (verse 8)
sāmt tyābutā l-i dil-(y) ḥaṭṭāyā.
put:PRF.2 repentance to-POSS.1 LNK-POSS.1 sinner
'You have put repentance for me, I who am a sinner.'
B. ܣܡܬ ܬܝܒܘܬܐ ܥܠܝ ܕܝܠܝ ܚܛܝܐ.
sāmt tyābutā ʕl-ay dil-(y) ḥaṭṭāyā.
put:PRF.2 repentance on-POSS.1 LNK-POSS.1 sinner
'You have put repentance on me, I who am a sinner.'

(12) A. ܦܪܩ ܐܢܬ ܠܝ ܐܝܟ ܣܘܓܐܐ ܕܪ̈ܚܡܝܟ (verse 14)
pāreq =ʔa(n)t l-i ʔa(y)k sog(?)ā
redeem:AP =2 to-POSS.1 as multitude
d-raḥmay-k.
LNK-mercy.PL-POSS.2
'You will redeem me, according to the greatness of your mercies.'

B. ܡܫܘܙܒ ܐܢܬ ܠܝ ܒܣܘܓܐܐ ܕܡܪܚܡܢܘܬܟ.
mšawzeb =ˀa(n)t l-i
deliver.INT:AP=2 to-POSS.1 in-multitude
b-sog(ˀ)ā da-mraḥmānut-āk.
LNK-mercy-POSS.2
'You will deliver me with the greatness of your mercy.'

In another case, though, the change of preposition may be interpreted as leading to a different meaning:

(13) A. ܘܠܐ ܬܘܒܕܝܢܝ ܥܡ ܣܟܠܘ̈ܬܝ. (verse 13b)
w-lā tawbd-ayn(y) ˁam
and-NEG perish.CAUS:IMPF.2-OBJ.1 with
saklwāt-(y).
transgression.PL-POSS.1
'Do not destroy me with my transgressions.'
B. ܘܠܐ ܬܘܒܕܢܝ ܒܚܛ̈ܗܝ.
w-lā tawbd-an(y) b-ḥṭāh-ay.
and-NEG perish.CAUS:IMPF.2-OBJ.1 in-sin.PL-POSS.1
'Do not destroy me with/because of my sins.'

These two phrases may be interpreted as expressing the same meaning ('with my transgressions/sins') or as expressing different meanings ('with my transgressions' versus 'because of my sins'). For the parallelism between the two prepositional complements compare verse 10a ܣܟܠܘ̈ܬܝ ܘܚܛ̈ܗܝ 'my transgressions and my sins', but note that this occurs only in B.[43] In A verse 13 is the only occurrence of ܣܟܠܘܬܐ.

[43] In other Horologion manuscripts (related to version B) ܣܟܠܘܬܐ appears also as a variant reading of ܒܝ̈ܫܬܐ ('evil deeds') in verse 7, or of ܥܘ̈ܠܝ ܘܚܘ̈ܒܝ ('iniquities and debt') in verse 9, thus strengthening this interpretation. Compare Psalm 51:3[5], where the Peshitta has ܡܛܠ ܕܣܟܠܘ̈ܬܝ ܝܕܥ ܐܢܐ 'because I know my transgressions', corresponding to Hebrew כי פשעי אני אדע.

2.4.4 Phrase negation

The negator ܠܐ can negate nominal heads, as reflected in example (14):[44]

(14) A. ܕܠܐ ܣܟܐ ܕܝܢ ܘܕܠܐ ܟܝܠܐ (verse 6)
d-lā sākā dēn wa-d-lā kaylā
LNK-NEG limit however and-LNK-NEG measure
'without limit, however, and without measure'

B. ܠܐ ܡܬܡܫܚܢܐ ܗܘ ܟܝܬ ܘܠܐ ܡܬܥܩܒܢܐ.
lā metmašḥānā =(h)u kit w-lā metˁaqbānā
NEG finite =3 indeed and-NEG scrutable
'infinite, indeed, and inscrutable'

On top of the lexical difference between these two phrases (see section 3.2), we see that the two versions use different means to negate the nominal heads of the phrases: in version A ܕܠܐ 'without' is used, while in version B ܠܐ is used as a nominal negator, similar to English 'un-' or 'in-'.[45]

Note also the expression ܠܐ ܣܟ serving as an emphatic negation 'not at all', presented in example (21).

2.4.5 Appositions

In our linguistic model, we view two successive phrases as standing in apposition to each other if they fill the same syntactic slot, have the same referent and are not connected syndetically.[46] We adopt here the view that also adjectives should be treated as appositions, since

---

[44] On ܠܐ as a clause negator see below, section 2.5.3.

[45] Both these uses are listed under the entry ܠܐ in Payne Smith, *Compendious Syriac Dictionary*, 233. The expressions ܠܐ ܡܬܡܫܚܢܐ and ܠܐ ܡܬܥܩܒܢܐ are listed under their nominal heads in Payne Smith, *Compendious Syriac Dictionary*, 319, 320.

[46] In some cases, the two phrases may portray the referent in quite different ways, thus obscuring the co-referentiality. See for instance (18) where 'all times' and 'all days of my life' may seem to refer to two different time stretches, but in the context of the prayer can also be analysed as co-referential. On the complexities related to the definition of 'apposition', see Acuňa-Farina, 'On Apposition'.

they fulfil the above conditions.[47]

In this analysis, we see that version B uses more appositions than version A, which prefers to use the conjunction ܘ (examples (17), (18)) or omit the second constituent altogether (examples (15), (16)).[48] Note, however, that the structure of example (16) in both versions is quite similar: ܡܪܝܐ 'the Lord' together with an appositive qualification (either A: ܐܠܗܐ ܕܐܒܗܝܢ 'God of our fathers' or B: ܫܡܝܢܐ ܐܚܝܕ ܟܠ 'celestial, almighty'), followed by a *pāsoqā* and a second apposition (A: ܐܠܗܗ ܕܐܒܪܗܡ 'God of Abraham', B: ܐܠܗܐ ܕܐܒܗܬܢ 'God of our fathers', parallel to this expression in version A). Version B continues with ...ܕܐܒܪܗܡ 'of Abraham (etc.)' (which is parallel to the NP in version A) as a further apposition to ܕܐܒܗܬܢ 'of our fathers' in the second NP.

Example (16) is also marked by the addition of ܟܠܗ 'all of it' in version B. The 3rd person genitive pronoun can be analysed as quasi-appositive to the noun ܙܪܥܗܘܢ 'their seed', but it is better seen as part of the ܟܠ construction.[49]

(15) A. ܨܠܘܬܐ ܕܡܢܫܐ. (superscription)
ṣlotā da-mnašše
prayer LNK-Manasseh
'Prayer of Manasseh'[50]

---

[47]In this view, an adjective is essentially a qualifying nominal phrase, which is co-referential to its head noun. See Goldenberg, 'Attribution in Semitic Languages', 8–11.

[48]For variation among textual witnesses regarding the presence or absence of an apposition cf. Van Peursen, *Language and Interpretation*, 214 (but that discussion deals with differences between the Syriac, Hebrew and Greek witnesses, rather than with inner-Syriac variation). See also footnote 50.

[49] The adjective ܙܕܝ̈ܩܐ 'righteous (pl.)' suggests that ܙܪܥܗܘܢ is a plural noun, although it is not marked as such by a , or *seyame* mark. On the other hand, the genitive pronoun of ܟܠܗ is singular. Thus, it seems that either there is an error in the agreement, or this construction has become partly fossilized, though other examples in the text do show a 'correct' accord, such as ܟܠܗܘܢ ܚܝ̈ܠܘܬܐ ܕܫܡܝܐ 'all the heavenly powers' (verse 15, both versions). Notice that all the Horologion manuscripts, except 13H5, omit ܟܠܗ. 13H5, on the other hand, adds a *seyame* mark on ܙܪܥܗܘܢ. Of the A family, manuscript 14/8a1 adds ܟܠܗ but has no *seyame* on ܙܪܥܗܘܢ.

[50] Other textual witnesses to version A add the apposition ܡܠܟܐ ܕܝܗܘܕܐ 'the king

B. ܨܠܘܬܐ ܕܡܢܫܐ ܡܠܟܐ ܕܒܢܝ̈ ܐܝܣܪܝܠ

ṣlotā da-mnašše, malkā da-bnay ˀisrāˀyel
prayer LNK-Manasseh king LNK-son.CST.PL Israel
'Prayer of Manasseh, King of Israel'

(16) A. ܡܪܝܐ ܐܠܗܐ ܕܐܒܗ̈ܝܢ. ܐܠܗܗ ܕܐܒܪܗܡ ܘܕܐܝܣܚܩ ܘܕܝܥܩܘܒ ܘܕܙܪܥܗܘܢ ܙܕܝܩܐ. (verse 1)

mārуā ˀalāhā d-ˀabāhay-n. ˀalāh-ēh
Lord God LNK-father.PL-POSS.1PL God-POSS.3
d-ˀabrāhām wa-d-ˀisḥāq wa-d-yaˁqob
LNK-Abraham and-LNK-Isaac and-LNK-Jacob
wa-d-zarˁ-hon zaddiqā.
and-LNK-seed-POSS.3PL righteous.SG

'O Lord, God of our fathers, God of Abraham, of Isaac and of Jacob and of their righteous seed'

B. ܡܪܝܐ ܫܡܝܢܐ ܐܚܝܕ ܟܠ. ܐܠܗܐ ܕܐܒܗ̈ܬܢ ܕܐܒܪܗܡ ܘܕܐܝܣܚܩ ܘܕܝܥܩܘܒ ܘܕܟܠܗ ܙܪܥܗܘܢ ܙܕܝܩ̈ܐ

māryā šmayānā ˀāḥid kol. ˀalāhā
Lord heavenly hold:AP all.ABS God
d-ˀabāhāt-an. d-ˀabrāhām wa-d-ˀisḥāq
LNK-father.PL-POSS.1PL LNK-Abraham and-LNK-Isaac
wa-d-yaʿqob wa-d-koll-ēh zarʿ-hon
and-LNK-Jacob and-LNK-all-POSS.3 seed-POSS.3PL
zaddiqē.
righteous.PL

'O celestial Lord, almighty, God of our fathers, of Abraham, of Isaac and of Jacob and of all their righteous seed'

of Judah' (17a8) or ܡܠܟܐ ܕܐܝܣܪܝܠ 'the king of Israel' (16g7) or even two appositions: ܡܠܟܐ ܕܝܗܘܕܐ ܒܪ ܚܙܩܝܐ ܡܠܟܐ 'king of Judah, the son of king Hezekiah' (14/8a1).

(17) A. ܡܪܝܐ ܢܓܝܪ ܪܘܚܐ. ܘܡܪܚܡܢܐ ܘܣܓܝ ܚܢܢܐ. (verse 7a)

mārya ngir ruḥā wa-mraḥmānā w-saggi
Lord long.CST spirit and-merciful and-great
ḥnānā.
compassion
'the Lord, long-suffering and merciful and of great compassion' [51]

B. ܡܪܝܐ ܡܪܝܡܐ. ܚܢܢܐ ܢܓܝܪ ܪܘܚܐ. ܘܣܓܝ ܛܝܒܘܬܐ

mārya mrimā. ḥannānā ngir ruḥā.
Lord high compassionate long.CST spirit
w-saggi ṭaybutā
and-great.CST grace
'the Lord, Most High, compassionate, long-suffering and of great grace'

(18) A. ܒܟܠܙܒܢ. ܘܒܟܠܗܘܢ ܝܘܡܬܐ ܕܚܝܝ. (verse 15)

b-kol-zban, wa-b-kol-hon yawmātā
in-all.CST-time and-in-all-POSS.3PL day.PL
d-ḥayy-ay.
LNK-life.PL-POSS.1
'at all times and at all days of my life'

B. ܒܟܠܙܒܢ. ܒܟܠܗܘܢ ܝܘܡܬܐ ܕܚܝܝ.

b-kol-zban. b-kol-hon yawmātā
in-all.CST-time in-all-POSS.3PL day.PL
d-ḥayy-ay.
LNK-life.PL-POSS.1
'at all times, at all days of my life'

It is fascinating to see how the differences in grammatical structure between the two versions go side by side with differences in the interpunction used in the Syriac manuscripts. The two appositive constituents are sometimes separated by a *pāsoqā* (ܦܣܘܩܐ.)[52], which

[51] See also example (59) on page 150 for the lexical correspondences.

[52] In this paragraph we attach the punctuation mark under discussion to the end of its Syriac name for the benefit of the reader.

is never present in the case of a conjunction. Instead, the second element of the conjunction follows a *taḥtāyā* (. ܬܚܬܝܐ), as in example (18), or an *ʿeṣyānā* (· ܥܨܝܢܐ)[53], as in example (17). Such is also the case in example (29) on page 116, where the adjunct is separated by a *šwayyā* (: ܫܘܝܐ)[54] and the apposition by a *pāsoqā*. In this respect, the usage of the *pāsoqā* is quite different from the modern usage of the full stop in many Western scripts, but also from its established usage in the Syriac tradition, in which it has more or less the same function as the full stop in English.[55] It should be noted, however, that 10t1, the basic text of version B, has a less developed system of interpunction, in which only the single dot is used.

2.5 CLAUSE SYNTAX

2.5.1 Introductory remarks

The clause structure in Syriac has drawn a fair amount of research, but yet many issues are still controversial or unresolved. As the aim of this section is introductory, we will only present the different issues, some much debated, and some yet to be researched, without presenting a detailed analysis. Nonetheless, in some cases we have ventured to propose our own proper analysis, as we have found it more adequate for explaining the data in question. Such is for instance the case for our proposal of the Focus Phrase as a constituent of the Syriac clause (see below, section 2.5.1). It should be borne in mind, however, that we do not intend to discuss all issues related to Syriac clause syntax, but rather those that relate to the instances presented in the rest of this chapter.

---

[53] According to the East Syriac tradition this would be a *mziʿna* (ܡܙܝܥܢܐ), on which Segal, *The Diacritical Point and the Accents in Syriac*, 82, writes that it comes 'before a co-ordinate clause, usually introduced by the conjunction ܘ'.

[54] This could also be a *taḵsa* to indicate an interrogative tone. See Segal, *The Diacritical Point and the Accents in Syriac*, 127.

[55] See Muraoka, *Classical Syriac*, 2nd edition, 10, §5e. Segal, *The Diacritical Point and the Accents in Syriac*, 133, notes that the *pāsoqā* 'marked the conclusion of a definite clause, whether in the middle or at the end of a verse', though in the latter case it was renamed *šḇima* (ܫܒܝܡܐ). See also Weiss, *Zur Ostsyrischen Laut- und Akzentlehre*, 46; Stanley Jones, 'Early Syriac Pointing', 439–440.

A core distinction within Syriac clause syntax is made between nominal clauses (NCs) and verbal clauses (VCs). Verbal clauses are those that contain a finite verb (i.e. a verb in the perfect, imperfect or imperative forms), while the remaining clauses are labelled nominal clauses.[56] The predicate of a nominal clause is usually a Noun Phrase, but it can also be an Adjectival Phrase, a Prepositional Phrase or even an Adverbial Phrase.[57] For this reason they are also called non-verbal clauses.[58] The following two sections treat each of these clause types.

Nominal clauses and Focus Phrases

Apart from their non-verbal predicate, nominal clauses are marked by the fact that their predicate is quite often followed by an enclitic personal pronoun (e.p.p.). There has been much debate regarding the status of this e.p.p.; T. Muraoka sees it as a third element added to the basic structures P-S or S-P, serving as a focus marker.[59] Alternatively, G. Goldenberg sees the e.p.p. together with the predicate as forming a nuclear nominal clause of the form P-s (Predicate-[lesser] subject), and any other NP denoting the subject as an extraposed element, not forming part of this internal clause. The NP denoting the subject may be in front extraposition, i.e. S || P-s, or in rear extraposition, i.e. P-s || S.[60] Both views agree that functionally the e.p.p. marks the most salient information in the clause, be it the 'focus', 'rheme' or 'comment'.

It will be argued below (section 2.5.6) that the enclitic pronoun is better analysed as a second-position clitic embedded inside the domain of the predicate, or the focus.[61] In such a view, the predicate

56 Cf. Muraoka, *Classical Syriac*, 2nd edition, 82, §101.

57 Cf. Goldenberg, 'On Syriac Sentence Structure', 99.

58 Thus Joosten, *Syriac Language*, 77, distinguishes between nominal clauses, in which the Predicate is a noun, and other non-verbal clauses such as adverbial clauses. See also Baasten, *Non-Verbal Clause in Qumran Hebrew*.

59 Muraoka, *Classical Syriac*, 2nd edition, 83, §104.

60 Cf. Goldenberg, 'On Syriac Sentence Structure'. It should be noted that such a P-s construction is indeed sufficient to create an independent clause.

61 For the idea of a clitic attaching to a certain phrase or domain, see for instance Klavans, 'Cliticization', §1.3. In this article Klavans gives a general framework for clitic positioning, and in particular second-position clitics. For a general treatment of such clitics, see Anderson, *Aspects of the Theory of Clitics*.

together with the e.p.p. may be termed a 'Focus Phrase' (FocP), analogous to the verb in the Verbal Phrase. Just like the Verbal Phrase, the Focus Phrase can constitute a clause by itself, or it can be accompanied by other elements.[62] This view endorses the tight relationship between the predicate and the e.p.p. as proposed by Goldenberg, while taking into account Muraoka's objections for considering them as forming together a clause within a larger (matrix) clause.[63] In this respect it is a synthesis of the two approaches.

This analysis clarifies cases in which another argument besides the subject is fronted or extraposed,[64] either before the subject in Goldenberg's S || P-s pattern (see example (37)) or following the subject in the P-s || S pattern (see example (39)). In Goldenberg's analysis one has to assume that in such a case two elements are extraposed.[65] This is unnecessary if the internal 'clause' is analysed as

---

[62]One may be tempted to call this type of phrase a 'Predicative Phrase', since the relationship between the e.p.p. and the head element of the phrase is that of a nexus. For instance, M. Azar, in his study of Modern Hebrew (Azar, *The Emphatic Sentence in Modern Hebrew*, 212) uses the notion PredP as containing both the predicate NP and the pronominal copula. However, as argued in Van Peursen, 'Response to the Responses', 201–202, in some cases the e.p.p. joins the subject of the clause forming an S–e.p.p.–P pattern. In this case, the function of the phrase is solely focal and not predicative. Goldenberg analyses such cases as P-s || S patterns since he gives preference to the information-structure definition of subject (=topic) and predicate (=comment) over their grammatical definitions in terms of agreement and definiteness. In our view, these two notions should be kept apart, although many times they coincide. Indeed, other languages with focus particles allow subject focus as well. See for instance Tosco, *Information Packaging in Somali Texts*.

[63]Semantically, though, it is possible to speak of two propositions. Thus Caron, 'Assertion et préconstruit', 7, characterizes the notion Focus in the following way: 'Focus consists in the imbrication of two propositions within a single speech unit: a predicative relation and the identification of one term of this predicative relation, the focused term. What is asserted is the identification of the focused term, while the predicative relation is given the status of a preconstruct.' See also Lambrecht, *Information Structure and Sentence Form*, 213, who defines 'Focus' in terms of difference between the 'presupposition' and the 'assertion'.

[64]For the distinction between fronting and extraposition see the following section.

[65]Cf. Van Peursen, *Language and Interpretation*, 332: '[Goldenberg's] argument would be weakened if we were to find examples where the tripartite clause is preceded by another extraposed element, because an analysis with two elements in extraposition such as X || Su || Pr-s is odd.'

a Focus Phrase, in which case the subject NP is not extraposed (see table 2.3).

Our proposal may also help resolve the dispute around the structure that Goldenberg has referred to as 'imperfectly-transformed cleft sentence', such as ܐܢܬ ܗܘ ܐܡܪܬ 'it is you who said'.[66] These sentences may contain both a finite verb and an e.p.p., in which case Goldenberg regards the element followed by the e.p.p. (in this example: ܐܢܬ) as the predicate and the finite verb (in this example: ܐܡܪܬ) as the 'virtually nominalized' topic of the clause.[67] Others, including Muraoka, do not accept this analysis, but analyse these sentences as verbal clauses and the e.p.p. as a 'focusing' particle.[68] Indeed, if we acknowledge the existence of a Focus Phrase, we may see this structure as a Verbal Clause containing a Focus Phrase (in this example: ܐܢܬ ܗܘ), without the latter being the grammatical predicate of the clause.

Some seemingly nominal predicates, such as verbal participles and most adjectives, show several characteristics of verbal predicates, such as the lack of a 3rd person e.p.p. following them.[69] Moreover, verbal participles take complements just as their finite verbal counterparts, and thus may be seen just as another 'tense' of the verb.[70] These participials can be analysed as predicative NPs, not forming part of a Focus Phrase (analysing them as part of a Focus Phrase would require the postulation of a ∅-realized e.p.p. of the 3rd person).[71] In this respect, our proposal makes a sharp distinction at

---

[66] Cf. Goldenberg, 'Imperfectly-Transformed Cleft Sentences'; see also Van Peursen, *Language and Interpretation*, chapter 24.

[67] In other words, he takes the verb as part of a subject relative clause, introduced by a ∅ relativizer.

[68] Muraoka, 'Response to Van Peursen', 194–196; cf. Muraoka, *Classical Syriac*, 2nd edition, 87, §110.

[69] These predicates have been termed *participials* by G. Goldenberg; See Van Peursen, *Language and Interpretation*, chapter 20.

[70] Cf. Muraoka, *Classical Syriac*, 2nd edition, 40, §48: 'Syriac knows three "tenses", traditionally termed perfect, imperfect and participle, the last of which is often nominalised.' In Eastern Neo-Aramaic, the participle has entirely entered into the verbal domain and replaced the former finite forms.

[71] This is somewhat similar to Pat-El's view, who calls them *inherent predicates* (See Pat-El, 'Syntactical Aspects of Negation in Syriac'). Non-3rd person e.p.p.'s can either by analysed as focus markers or as subject pronouns. See the discussion

the syntactic level between these clauses and the 'tripartite' nominal clauses: the former have an NP as their predicate (albeit a restricted group of nouns can occupy this category), and the latter have a FocP as predicate.

Clauses of existence form a special class of nominal clauses, as their predicate is normally taken to be the existential particle ܐܝܬ.[72] Intriguingly, as will be seen below in example (36), this particle can sometimes replace the e.p.p., thus serving as a kind of copula.

Verbal clauses and word order

In general linguistic tradition it is common to see the verb as the predicate of the clause, forming together with its complements a VP, to which a subject is added as a specifier. However, another common view in Semitic linguistics sees the verb not as the predicate but rather as a complex morphological form encapsulating both the subject (=the pronominal agreement), the predicate (=the verbal lexeme) and the nexus (=the predicative relation between the two). In this view, the verb itself forms a nuclear clause to which an external subject NP may stand in extraposition.[73]

While we agree with the view that the verb is an independent unit that contains a predication (and thus our VP is the verb alone without any complements),[74] we do not analyse an explicit subject as being necessarily in extraposition. The problem with saying that the explicit subject always stands in extraposition is similar to the problem we noticed with the analysis of the tripartite nominal clause as an extraposition construction: sometimes the subject takes a slot that denies such an analysis. It may intervene, for example, between

---

of examples (39) and (40).

[72] For a different view, which takes these clauses as 'subject-only' clauses and ܐܝܬ as a predication marker (rather than the predicate) see Van Peursen, *Language and Interpretation*, 339, with further references.

[73] This view is especially advocated by Goldenberg, for example in Goldenberg, 'On Verbal Structure and the Hebrew Verb', though he attributes it to former linguistic traditions.

[74] See Van Peursen, *Language and Interpretation*, 280, with reference to Hoftijzer, 'A Preliminary Remark on the Study of the Verbal System in Classical Hebrew', 647, note 8.

a complement and the verb.

For this reason we prefer to analyse an explicit subject NP, just as any other argument or modifier of the verb, as a satellite element expanding the nucleus of the phrase being the verbal complex. The subject argument has the peculiarity that it is obligatorily expressed by means of pronominal agreement in the verbal complex, but it is not the only such argument: many times an object argument is expressed pronominally as well in the verb.

When an explicit object NP follows the verb with such an object pronoun, this is often called 'prolepsis' or 'anticipatory pronominal agreement',[75] and when it precedes the verb, it is called 'extraposition'. However, the two phenomena reflect the same 'tendency to put small pronominal elements close to the verb or, in other words, to complete the valency of the verb before the agents and patients are specified'.[76] This tendency is also reflected in verbal complements consisting of preposition + suffix pronoun, which often take a position immediately after the verb, whether or not being resumed elsewhere in the clause.[77]

Since the subject is always expressed in the verbal complex, it may come as no surprise that the subject NP can appear before or after the verb, though a slight skewing towards a VS order does appear.[78]

[75] Cf. Khan, *Studies in Semitic Syntax*.

[76] Van Peursen, *Language and Interpretation*, 326. As Van Peursen notes there, this happens also in Bantu languages. Another example could be Somali, mentioned already in footnote 62 above for marking its focus. Tosco, *Information Packaging in Somali Texts*, 28, writes: 'the order of constituents is syntactically free, and all grammatical information is found within the "Verbal Complex", which contains in rigid order object pronouns, adpositions, and adverbials and is ended by the verbal form'.

[77] Cf. Van Peursen, *Language and Interpretation*, 326. Because of the impact of verbal government on the structure of the clause, the question of whether or not an element forms part of the verbal valency (i.e. whether or not it is an obligatory or semi-obligatory argument) is a core distinction in our encoding system. This, together with its form (NP or PP) determines the labels we attach to it (see table 2.2 in section 2.5.4).

[78] In data gathered by D. Bakker from the *Book of the Laws of the Countries*, 49 out of 80 (61%) verbal clauses with an explicit subject NP have a VS order, showing a preference for this order (if the word order is free, the probability for getting as strong a skewing by chance is $\alpha = \frac{1}{2^{80}} \Sigma_{i=49}^{80} \binom{80}{i} \approx 0.03$ using the cumulative distribution function of the binomial distribution). See Bakker, *Bardaisan's Book of*

As for the object, a distinction should be made between the notions of 'extraposition' and 'fronting'. By 'extraposition' we mean cases in which the object is positioned before the main clause, and is referred to later by a resumptive pronoun in the main clause (either on the verb or in a PP), as in ܟܠܒܐ ܘܩܛܠܬܗ. When no resumptive pronoun is used, we speak about 'fronting', such as ܠܟܠܒܐ ܘܩܛܠܬ.[79] However, the latter phenomenon is quite uncommon: whenever the (direct) object is not encoded pronominally, it has a very strong tendency to occur after the verb, yielding a VO order.[80]

These observations fit well with T. Nöldeke's views regarding word order in Syriac, summarized neatly by R. Kuty:

> Nöldeke [p. 248] claims that the word order is 'very free' in Syriac. His notes suggest that the subject sometimes precedes, sometimes follows, sometimes even interrupts the predicate; he adds that in narrative clauses the verb is preferably placed before the subject, but that this is by no means an absolute rule. P_1-placement appears to be used for the marking of Topic and Focus constituents (ibid.). As for the object, it occurs most frequently after the verb, but also often before it. [p. 250].[81]

---

the Laws of the Countries, 180 for detailed data.

[79]Cases of fronted/extraposed PPs, such as in the clause ܠܟܠܒܐ ܘܩܛܠܬܗ, are less straight-forward. They can be analysed either as the result of a fronting operation on a pronominal agreement construction (ܘܩܛܠܬܗ ܠܟܠܒܐ), or as cases of extraposition with retention of the case marking of the object. The latter analysis would go againt Khan, *Studies in Semitic Syntax*, xxvi, who requires the object to be unmarked. In the text of PrMan there are no such cases. The only case that might be interpreted as an extraposed verbal complement introduced by Lamadh occurs in example (39)B (page 124), but in that case the object is not resumed in the main clause and the reason for analysing it as a case of extraposition is different (namely, the possibility that the element following the complement should be analysed as extraposed as well).

[80]In the *Book of the Laws of the Countries* 110 out of 126 (87.3%) verbal clauses without pronominal object marking had a VO order, showing a strong preference for this order ($\alpha \approx 0$). However, whenever pronominal object marking was used, the object appeared always in a front-extraposition. Similar data were also found for indirect objects. As for adjuncts, temporal adverbs showed no skewing, while locatives showed a preference to appear after the verb: 14 out of 41 cases (34%, $\alpha \approx 0.03$).

[81]Kuty, *Studies in the Syntax of Targum Jonathan to Samuel*, 299, citing Nöldeke,

Thus the notion of 'free' word order should be understood as applying mostly to the subject placement, rather than to the object placement.[82]

Combining the tendency to VS order together with the VO order may seem to yield the conclusion that Syriac has a typical VSO order. Thus Edwald writes:

> Die ruhige Folge der Worte ist: Verbum, Subject, Object, oder wenn das Verbum das Subject in sich enthält, Verbum, Object; mehr gesondert ist das Subject oder Object von vorn, zumal wenn es an sich schon eine längere Beschreibung enthält, wodurch oft ein grosser Halt der Stimme entsteht.[83]

Indeed, some research seems to support this claim. For instance, in his study on the Peshiṭta to Psalms 90–150, I. Carbajosa has demonstrated that on the one hand there are many cases where the Peshiṭta follows the free word order of the Hebrew text, whereas on the other hand the order is often modified towards the 'normal' order of VSO.[84]

However, other data show that the VSO order is not as common as usually thought. Such is the case with the data collected by D. Bakker from the *Book of the Laws of the Countries*.[85] Thus, it seems

---

Syrische Grammatik, 248–250.

[82]Brockelmann is less clear regarding this point, as he writes about free word order: 'Die Wortstellung ist sehr frei. Wenn auch die altsemit. Regel, daß in Verbalsätzen das Prädikat, in Nominalsätzen das Subjekt voran steht, noch oft beobachtet wird, so sind doch Abweichungen davon ebenso häufig.' ('The word order is very free. Even though the Old Semitic rule that in verbal clauses the predicate comes first, and in nominal clauses the subject, is still often observed, deviations from it are equally frequent.') (Brockelmann, *Syrische Grammatik*, 118).

[83]'The smoothly flowing word order is: verb, subject, object, or, if the verb includes the subject: verb, object. The subject or the object is more separated at the beginning, especially when it includes a longer description in itself, by which often a greater pause in the voice is created.' (Ewald, 'Über das syrische Punctationssystem', 106).

[84]Or, more precisely: verb + subject + direct object + indirect object + adverbial modifier; Carbajosa, *The Character of the Syriac Version of Psalms*, 21–22. In his study on Biblical Aramaic, R. Buth assumes a 'unique VSO pattern' in Biblical Aramaic; see Buth, *Word order in Aramaic from the Perspectives of Functional Grammar and Discourse Analysis*.

[85]In Bakker's data, in a sample of 25 clauses with explicit subject and object

to us that a more prudent and restricted conclusion would be that Syriac is a VO language, certainly in the strict sense, and possibly also in the typological sense suggested by W. Lehmann,[86] i.e. a head-initial language. Such a generalization fits well, for instance, with the fact that Syriac exclusively uses prepositions, and that in general the adjectives follow their nouns.

2.5.2 Mood

We shall now move on to a survey of the differences between the two versions in the domain of clause syntax. We start with variation regarding the simple clause (verbal and then nominal) and finish with variation regarding complex clauses.

In one example, version A uses the imperative mood whereas version B uses the indicative mood as expressed by the participle followed by a pronominal subject:

(19) A. ܐܦ ܗܟܝܠ ܚܘܐ ܡܪܝ ܛܝܒܘܬܟ (verse 14)
ˀāp hākēl ḥawwā mār-(y)
even therefore show.INT:IMPT Lord-POSS.1
ṭaybut-āk.
grace-POSS.2
'Truly, thus, show, my Lord, your goodness.'

NPs, only 5 (20%) have a VSO order. See Bakker, *Bardaisan's Book of the Laws of the Countries*, 180.

[86] See Lehmann, 'A Structural Principle of Language'. Note also his comment regarding subject position: 'As we may note from consistent OV languages like Japanese and from consistent VO languages like Hebrew, subjects are by no means primary elements in sentences. Including them among the primary elements, as in the attempt to classify SVO and VSO languages as major types in the same way as VO and OV languages, has been a source of trouble for typologists as well as for linguistic theorists in general.' (ibid., p. 51). See also the discussion in Comrie, *Language Universals and Linguistic Typology*, 94–102.

B. ܘܒܝ ܡܚܘܐ ܐܢܬ ܟܠܗ ܛܝܒܘܬܟ

w-b-i mḥawwē =ˀa(n)t koll-āh
and-in-POSS.1 show.INT:AP =2 all-POSS.3F
ṭaybut-āk.
grace-POSS.2
'And in me You show all your goodness.'

Note the parallelism between the 2sg.m. subject in B ܐܢܬ and the vocative ܡܪܝ 'my Lord' in A, and the added locative expression ܒܝ 'in me' in version B.

In another case, both versions use the imperative:[87]

(20) A. ܫܒܘܩ ܠܝ ܡܪܝܐ ܘܠܐ ܬܘܒܕܝܢܝ ܥܡ ܣܟܠܘܬܝ (verse 13b)

šboq l-i māryā w-lā
forgive:IMPT.SG to-POSS.1 Lord and-NEG
tawbd-ayn(y) ʕam saklwāt-(y).
perish.CAUS:IMPF.2-OBJ.1 with folly.PL-POSS.1
'Forgive me, Lord, and do not destroy me with my follies.'

B. ܫܒܘܩ ܠܝ ܡܪܝܐ ܫܒܘܩ ܠܝ ܘܠܐ ܬܘܒܕܢܝ ܒܚܛܗܝ

šboq l-i māryā šboq
forgive:IMPT.SG to-POSS.1 Lord forgive:IMPT.SG
l-i w-lā tawbd-an(y)
to-POSS.1 and-NEG perish.CAUS:IMPF.2-OBJ.1
b-ḥṭāh-ay.
in-sin.PL-POSS.1
'Forgive me, Lord, forgive me, and do not destroy me with my sins.'

Apart from the repetition of the imperative in version B,[88] the two versions use the same construction. Note also the typical usage of a negated imperfect to form a negative imperative.[89]

[87] For the difference of prepositions, see discussion of example (13).
[88] Cf. section 6.1.3.
[89] For the difference in orthography, see section 2.3.4.

2.5.3 Clause negation

The most common means of negation in the text is the negator ܠܐ. It is used in many parallel places in the two versions, as several examples throughout the text show (such as examples (20), (34), (35), (40)).

In one case, in verse 9, version B uses the emphatic negator ܠܐ ܣܟ 'not at all, by no means'.[90] According to the discussion in section 4.6 this negation is paralleled by the negation ܐܦܠܐ 'not even, nor' in version A, verse 10 (see table 4.9).

(21) A. ܐܦܠܐ ܓܝܪ ܫܘܐ ܐܢܐ (verse 10a)
ʾāp-lā gēr šāwē =(ʾ)nā
even-NEG indeed be_worth:AP =1
'Nor, indeed, am I worthy'

B. ܘܠܐ ܣܟ ܫܘܐ ܐܢܐ (verse 9a)
w-lā sāk šāwē =(ʾ)na
and-NEG limit.ABS be_worth:AP =1
'and I am not worthy at all.'

Negation scope

(22) A. ܘܠܐ ܠܥܠܡ ܬܪܓܙ ܥܠܝ. ܘܠܐ ܬܛܪ ܠܝ ܒܝܫܬܝ.. (verse 13b)
w-lā l-ʿālam tergaz ʿl-ay,
and-NEG to-eternity.ABS be_angry:IMPF.2 on-POSS.1
w-lā teṭṭar l-i bišāt-(y).
and-NEG keep:IMPF.2 to-POSS.1 evil.F.PL-POSS.1
'And do not be angry at me forever, and do not keep for me my evils.'

B. ܘܠܐ ܠܥܠܡ ܬܪܓܙ ܥܠܝ ܘܬܛܪ ܒܝܫܬܝ.
w-lā l-ʿālam tergaz ʿl-ay
and-NEG to-eternity.ABS be_angry:IMPF.2 on-POSS.1
w-teṭṭar bišāt-(y).
and-keep:IMPF.2 evil.F.PL-POSS.1
'And do not be angry at me forever nor keep my evils.'

[90] See under ܣܟ in Payne Smith, *Compendious Syriac Dictionary*, 376.

(23) A. ܘܠܐ ܬܚܝܒܢܝ ܘܬܐܫܕܢܝ ܒܬܐܚܬܝܬܗ ܕܐܪܥܐ. (verse 13b)
w-lā ṯḥayyb-an(y)
and-NEG owe.INT:IMPF.2-OBJ.1
w-tē(ˀ)šd-an(y) b-ta(ˀ)ḥtāyāt-āh
and-pour_out:IMPF.2-OBJ.1 in-lower_part.PL-POSS.3F
d-ˀarˁā.
LNK-earth
'And do not condemn me and banish me to the depths of earth.'

B. ܘܠܐ ܬܚܝܒܢܝ ܒܬܚܬܝܬܗ ܕܐܪܥܐ.
w-lā ṯḥayyb-an(y)
and-NEG owe.INT:IMPF.2-OBJ.1
b-taḥtāyāt-āh d-ˀarˁā.
in-lower_part.PL-POSS.3F LNK-earth
'And do not condemn me to the depths of earth.'

These two examples, following each other in verse 13, show the same syntactic phenomenon in different places. In example (22), the negator in version B has scope over two clauses, whereas in version A it is repeated in the second clause.[91] In example (23) it is version A which uses one negator for two clauses, the second clause, ܬܐܫܕܢܝ 'banish me', being a plus vis-à-vis version B.

These examples show that the usage of the negator ܠܐ in PrMan is more diverse than that attested in the Peshiṭta of Kings, according to the study of J. W. Dyk and P. S. F. van Keulen. In their study they observed that the range of government of the negative particle is more restricted in the Peshiṭta than in the Masoretic Text. There are a number of cases that show that '[i]n the Masoretic text it is possible for the negative to occur once and yet apparently to affect a number of items listed thereafter', whereas '[i]n the Peshitta, the negative is repeated with each of the items affected'.[92] In PrMan this

[91] See also the discussion about the complement in these examples, given under example (32). Note that in the English translation of verse B we use the conjunction 'nor' for clarity. In Syriac both versions use the neutral conjunction ܘ 'and'. However, in version A the two clauses are separated by a *taḥtaya* punctuation mark (.). See also footnote 53, p. 99.

[92] Quotation from semi-final draft of Dyk–Van Keulen, *Language System, Trans-*

observation does not hold, as both negation strategies are used in both versions.

lā (h)wā construction

(24) A. ܠܐ ܗܘܐ ܠܙܕܝܩܐ <u>ܣܡܬ ܬܝܒܘܬܐ:</u> (verse 8)

lā =(h)wā l-zaddiqē sāmt tyābutā
NEG =be:PRF.3 to-righteous.PL put:PRF.2 repentance
'It is not for the righteous that You have put repentance.'

B. ܠܐ ܣܡܬ ܬܝܒܘܬܐ ܠܙܕܝܩܐ.

lā sāmt tyābutā l-zaddiqē.
NEG put:PRF.2 repentance to-rigtheous.PL
'You did not put repentance for the righteous.'

In example (24) version A uses a construction with the negation ܠܐ ܗܘܐ *lā (h)wā* whereas B has an ordinary negated verbal clause with the negator ܠܐ *lā*. The effect of the construction in A is to put contrastive focus on the element following ܠܐ ܗܘܐ, i.e. ܠܙܕܝܩܐ 'the righteous',[93] which is evident from the continuation of the verse ܐܠܐ ܣܡܬ ܬܝܒܘܬܐ ܠܝ 'but You have put repentance for me', common to both versions but for the preposition.[94]

In G. Goldenberg's analysis, such a construction implies a negative cleft construction in which ܠܙܕܝܩܐ is the comment and the rest of the clause (the underlined part) is the 'virtually nominalized' subject (=topic).[95] In other words, this is the negation of the positive cleft sentence ܠܙܕܝܩܐ ܗܘ ܣܡܬ ܬܝܒܘܬܐ 'it is for the righteous that You

---

lation Technique and Textual Tradition; see also Carbajosa, *The Character of the Syriac Version of Psalms*, 29.

[93]Cf. Nöldeke, *Syrische Grammatik*, §328B.

[94]See example (11). For the difference in final punctuation see section 2.4.5 (end).

[95]Cf. Goldenberg, 'Bible Translations and Syriac Idiom', 27: 'The rest of the sentence is thus implicitly nominalized to become the "glose" of a cleft sentence'; ibid. 32–33: 'The new grammatical predicate of the lā-w X or the lā (h)wā X nuclear construction is obviously the X; its subject is the virtually nominalized rest of the sentence'; see also Van Peursen, *Language and Interpretation*, 359.

have put repentance'.[96] However, in accordance with our claims regarding the e.p.p. (see sections 2.5.1 and 2.5.6), one may claim that ܠܐ ܗܘܐ forms a negated Focus Phrase together with the following element, without altering the basic structure of the clause.[97]

2.5.4 Verbal complements

The distinction between 'direct object', 'indirect object' and 'adjunct' is a debated issue. Our analytical model uses a two-fold distinction: functionally, we distinguish between 'objects', which take part in the verbal valency (i.e. they are obligatory or semi-obligatory), and 'adjuncts', which do not. Subsequently, we distinguish between 'direct objects' and 'indirect objects' solely on formal grounds: direct objects are not introduced by a preposition, while indirect objects are.[98] Thus, the traditional 'direct object introduced by Lamadh'[99] is classified by us as an indirect object (cf. examples (26) and (27)). A similar formal distinction is done also in the realm of non-obligatory arguments: we label adverbs or NPs serving as adverbs as 'modifiers', while PPs are labelled simply 'adjuncts'.[100] To distinguish some semantically privileged kinds of adjuncts/modifiers, we use also the terms 'time expressions' and 'locatives'.

In our bottom-up linguistic analysis (cf. section 2.2), it is our aim to build the analysis at each linguistic level upon the informa-

---

[96] Cf. Pat-El, 'Syntactical Aspects of Negation in Syriac', 339: 'We may, therefore, rightly call ^{h}*wā* the negative counterpart, syntactically speaking, of the clitic ^{h}*w*'. According to this view ܗܘܐ is necessarily a fossilized non-conjugating particle.

[97] Note that unlike an affirmative cleft sentence, the focused element itself does not contain new information, but rather the negation itself is the new information. In modern colloquial Hebrew, it is possible to put only the negation in the vedette position of the cleft sentence: ...זה לא ש 'it is not that...', marking this phenomenon syntactically.

[98] Cf. Rodrigue-Scharzwald–Sokoloff, *A Hebrew Dictionary of Linguistics and Philology*, 105.

[99] Cf. Muraoka, *Classical Syriac*, 2nd edition, 77, §96a.

[100] Since it is sometimes difficult to distinguish between indirect objects and adjuncts, we register both in our analysis of verb valency. The list of valency patterns that is generated in the computer-assisted analysis gives the verb and all elements outside the verb and includes subjects, direct and indirect objects and adjuncts; cf. Dyk, '1 Kings 2:1–9: Some Results of a Structured Hierarchical Approach', 292–293.

tion from the lower levels. Thus, at clause level analysis we use the formal properties of the phrase as analysed in the phrase level analysis (in this case: whether it is a PP or not) which we combine with a further functional and semantic analysis. The resulting terminology is summarized in table 2.2.

	[+ valency]	[- valency]
[+ preposition]	indirect object	adjunct (time expression / locative)
[- preposition]	direct object	modifier (time expression / locative)

Table 2.2: Verbal complements terminology

As shall be seen below, version B uses an indirect object several times, each time introduced by a Lamadh, whereas A has a direct object or an adjunct (all underlined).

Pronominal agreement

(25) A. ܕܐܣܪ ܝܡܐ (verse 3a)
haw d-ˀesar yammā
DEM LNK-bind:PRF.3 sea
'Who bound the sea.'
B. ܕܐܣܪܬܝܗܝ ܠܝܡܐ
ˀa(n)t d-ˀesart-āy(hy) l-yammā
2 LNK-bind:PRF.2-OBJ.3 to-sea
'(You) who bound it, the sea.'

In example (25) version B uses the 'specifier' or 'pronominal agreement'[101] construction, whereas A has a regular verbal clause; the direct object of A (ܝܡܐ 'sea') is an indirect object in B, which specifies a pronominal cataphoric direct object preceding it (ܝܗܝ–). Although some rules or tendencies determining the distribution of these two object constructions have been identified in the scholarly literature,

[101] Muraoka, *Classical Syriac*, 2nd edition, 88, §112 refers to such a construction as 'direct object prolepsis'.

no fixed rules can be given.[102] There seems to be at least a certain degree of functional equivalence (because no functional difference can be observed) as well as distributional equivalence (the constructions alternate in variant readings in textual witnesses).

Direct/indirect alternation and object fronting

(26) A. ܕܐܚܝܕ ܬܗܘܡܐ (verse 3b)
d-ˀeḥad thomā
LNK-hold:PRF.3 Abyss
'who held the abyss'

B. ܕܐܚܝܕܬ ܠܬܗܘܡܐ
d-ˀeḥadt la-thomā
LNK-hold:PRF.3 to-Abyss
'(You) who held the abyss'

(27) A. ܘܡܛܠ ܕܝܕܥ ܐܢܐ ܚܛܗܝ (verse 12)
w-meṭṭol d-yādaˁ =(ˀ)nā ḥtāh-ay
and-because LNK-know:AP =1 sin.PL-POSS.1
'Because I know my sins.'

B. ܘܠܥܘܠܝ ܐܢܐ ܝܕܥ ܐܢܐ
wa-l-ˁawl-ay ˀenā yādaˁ =(ˀ)nā
and-to-iniquity.PL-POSS.1 1 know:AP =1
'And my iniquities I know.'

Example (26) shows variation between a direct and an indirect object, which does not imply any functional/semantic difference.[103] This is also the case in example (27), though in this example the marking of the object by a Lamadh is motivated by its fronted position.[104] Traditionally these examples would be described in terms

[102] Cf. Van Peursen, *Language and Interpretation*, 325; and further Williams, *Peshitta of 1 Kings*, 325; Khan, 'Object Markers and Agreement Pronouns', 473; Joosten, *Syriac Language*, 40–41.

[103] The difference of person in the verb (3rd person vs. 2nd person) is probably not related.

[104] Thus, the Lamadh identifies it unequivocally as an object, notwithstanding its thematic (fronted) position. This is somewhat similar to phenomena of Differential

of 'simple object' versus 'object introduced by Lamadh'.[105] Indeed, these examples strengthen the view that the Lamadh is merely used in such cases as an accusative marker, without adding any semantic content. Example (27) is dealt with also in section 2.5.6 where two different analyses of it are given (see table 2.3). The clause just preceding this example is given below as example (31).

Object/adjunct alternation

(28) A. ܘܒܣܘܓܐ ܕܪ̈ܚܡܝܟ ܣܡܬ ܬܝܒܘܬܐ ܐܝܟ ܕܠܚ̈ܝܝܗܘܢ ܕܚ̈ܛܝܐ (verse 7b)

wa-b-sog(ˀ)ā d-raḥmay-k
and-in-multitude LNK-compassion.PL-POSS.2
sāmt tyābutā ˀa(y)k da-l-ḥayyay-hon
put:PRF.2 repentance as LNK-to-life.PL-POSS.3PL
d-ḥaṭṭāyē.
LNK-sinner.PL

'And in the greatness of your compassion, You have put repentance, as for the life of the sinners.'

B. ܘܒܣܘܓܐ ܕܪ̈ܚܡܝܟ ܬܚܡܬ ܬܝܒܘܬܐ ܠܦܘܪܩܢܐ ܕܚ̈ܛܝܐ

wa-b-sog(ˀ)ā d-raḥmay-k
and-in-multitude LNK-compassion.PL-POSS.2
tḥamt tyābutā l-purqānā d-ḥaṭṭāyē.
fix:PRF.2 repentance to-redemption LNK-sinner.PL

'And in the greatness of your compassion, You have fixed repentance for the redemption of sinners.'

Object Marking exhibited by some languages: objects that are prone to be identified as themes or agents are explicitly marked as objects (typically by an accusative case). Here it is not the nature of the object that requires this marking, but rather its position in the clause.

[105] For our labelling see table 2.2.

(29) A. ܠܙܕܝܩܐ (...): ܐܝܟ ܕܠܐܒܪܗܡ ܘܠܐܝܣܚܩ ܘܠܝܥܩܘܒ ܗܢܘܢ (verse 8)

l-zaddiqē ... ʔa(y)k da-l-ʔabrāhām
to-righteous.PL ... as LNK-to-Abraham
wa-l-ʔisḥāq wa-l-yaʕqob hānnon
and-to-Isaac and-to-Jacob DEM.PL
'for the righteous ..., as for Abraham, for Isaac for Jacob, those ...'

B. ܠܙܕܝܩܐ. ܠܐܒܪܗܡ ܘܠܐܝܣܚܩ ܘܠܝܥܩܘܒ ܗܢܘܢ

l-zaddiqē. l-ʔabrāhām wa-l-ʔisḥāq
to-rigtheous.PL to-Abraham and-to-Isaac
wa-l-yaʕqob hennon
and-to-Jacob 3.PL
'for the righteous, for Abraham, for Isaac, and for Jacob, those ...'

In example (28) version A uses an adjunct ܐܝܟ ܕܠܚܝܝܗܘܢ ܕܚܛܝܐ 'as for the life of the sinners' while version B has an indirect object ܠܦܘܪܩܢܐ ܕܚܛܝܐ 'for the redemption of sinners', though the latter may be analysed as a purpose adjunct, if it not seen as part of verbal valence. Example (29) is similar: A has an adjunct where B has an apposition to a verbal complement (note that both versions continue with the demonstrative ܗܢܘܢ as apposition to ܐܒܪܗܡ ܘܐܝܣܚܩ ܘܝܥܩܘܒ 'Abraham, Isaac and Jacob', i.e. the complement of the ܠ headed Prepositional Phrase).[106] This explains also the difference in punctuation: the adjunct is preceded by a colon while the apposition is preceded by a full stop (see section 2.4.5 on appositions).[107]

[106] In A the diacritic is that of the demonstrative pronoun (ܗܢܘܢ), in B that of the personal pronoun (ܗܢܘܢ).

[107] On this example see further the discussion of the *la (h)wa* construction on page 111, example (24)).

Objects/adjuncts as pluses

(30) A. ܘܗܫܐ ܗܐ ܟܐܦ ܐܢܐ ܒܘܪܟܘܗܝ ܕܠܒܝ ܩܕܡܝܟ. (verse 11)

w-hāšā hā kāʔep =(ʔ)nā burkaw-(hy)
and-now behold bend:AP =1 knee.PL-POSS.3
d-leb-(y) qdāmay-k,
LNK-heart-POSS.1 before-POSS.2

'And now, behold, I am bending the knees of my heart before You.'

B. ܘܗܫܐ ܡܪܟܢ ܐܢܐ ܒܘܪܟܘܗܝ ܕܠܒܝ.

w-hāšā marken =(ʔ)nā burkaw(hy)
and-now incline:AP =1 knee.CST.PL
d-leb-(y).
LNK-heart-POSS.1

'And now I am inclining the knees of my heart.'

(31) A. ܚܛܝܬ ܡܪܝܐ ܚܛܝܬ. (verse 12)

ḥṭēt māryā ḥṭēt.
sin:PRF.1 Lord sin:PRF.1

'I have sinned, O Lord, I have sinned.'

B. ܚܛܝܬ ܠܟ ܡܪܝܐ ܚܛܝܬ.

ḥṭēt l-āk māryā ḥṭēt,
sin:PRF.1 to-POSS.2 Lord sin:PRF.1

'I have sinned before You, O Lord, I have sinned.'

(32) A. ܘܠܐ ܠܥܠܡ ܬܪܓܙ ܥܠܝ. ܘܠܐ ܬܛܪ ܠܝ ܒܝܫܬܝ. (verse 13b)

w-lā l-ʕālam tergaz ʕl-ay,
and-NEG to-eternity.ABS be_angry:IMPF.2 on-POSS.1
w-lā teṭṭar l-i bišāt-(y).
and-NEG keep:IMPF.2 to-POSS.1 evil.F.PL-POSS.1

'And do not be angry at me forever, and do not keep for me my evils.'

B. ܘܠܐ ܠܥܠܡ ܬܪܓܙ ܥܠܝ ܘܬܛܪ ܒܝܫܬܝ.
w-lā l-ʿālam tergaz ʿl-ay
and-NEG to-eternity.ABS be_angry:IMPF.2 on-POSS.1
w-teṭṭar bišāt-(y).
and-keep:IMPF.2 evil.F.PL-POSS.1
'And do not be angry at me forever nor keep my evils.'

(33) A. ܐܦ ܗܟܝܠ ܚܘܐ ܡܪܝ ܛܝܒܘܬܟ (verse 14)
ʾāp hākēl ḥawwā mār-(y)
even therefore show.INT:IMPT Lord-POSS.1
ṭaybut-āk.
grace-POSS.2
'Truly, thus, show, my Lord, your goodness.'

B. ܘܒܝ ܡܚܘܐ ܐܢܬ ܟܠܗ ܛܝܒܘܬܟ
w-b-i mḥawwē =ʾa(n)t koll-āh
and-in-POSS.1 show.INT:AP =2 all-POSS.3F
ṭaybut-āk.
grace-POSS.2
'And in me You show all your goodness.'

In example (30) version A has two pluses as compared to version B: the adjunct ܩܕܡܝܟ 'before You' and the presentative particle ܗܐ 'behold!'.[108] In fact, ܗܐ appears only in version A and only one more time, in verse 9: ܕܗܐ ܐܣܝܪ ܐܢܐ 'behold, I am a prisoner'.[109] Semantically, these two pluses yield a more content-full (and marked) structure in version A.

In example (31), which appears in the text just before example (27), version B has an additional indirect object (serving as a kind of malfactive) where version A has no object or complement. Semantically, this yields a more elaborated clause.

---

[108]The latter is normally analysed as an interjection, but in accordance with table 2.2 it may be analysed as a modifier. Semantically, it reinforces the assertive power of utterance, thus operating on the nexus, just as a negative participle denies the nexus.

[109]Other manuscripts of the A family add a further ܗܐ in the same verse: ܗܐ ܡܬܐܠܨ ܐܢܐ 'behold, I am afflicted' (all except 17a6–9, 16D2) or ܗܐ ܡܬܛܪܦ ܐܢܐ 'behold, I am harassed' (16g7, 13D1).

In example (32), the first clause is identical in both versions, but the second clause has an additional 1sg. indirect object ܠܝ (again, a malfactive) as well as an additional negator ܠܐ in version A.[110] Both these pluses can be explained syntactically: in version A two independent clauses are conjuncted, and thus the indirect object as well as the negation are repeated in each clause. In version B the conjunction is done at the VP level, and thus neither the negation nor the indirect object are repeated.[111] This is also apparent in the fact that version A has a *pāsoqā* lacking in version B.

Example (33) has an extra adjunct ܒܝ 'in me' in version B. The preposition ܒ can be analysed here either as a locative preposition (albeit in a figurative sense) 'in me', or as an instrumental preposition 'by me'. The addition of this adjunct compensates for the usage of the weaker conjunction in version B (see example (56) on page 137). It can less easily be linked to the difference of mood (see example (19) on page 107).

2.5.5 Impersonal clauses

In version B, we see two impersonal clauses (i.e. clauses which have no overt subject; the subject is understood to be generic), in places where version A has a grammatical subject (underlined).

(34) A. ܠܐ ܡܣܬܝܒܪܐ ܪܒܘܬ ܝܐܝܘܬܐ ܕܬܫܒܘܚܬܟ (verse 5a)

lā	mestaybrā	rabbut	yāyutā
NEG	endure.INT.REFL:AP.3.EMPH	greatness.CST	beauty

d-tešboḥt-āk
LNK-honour-POSS.2

'The greatness of the beauty of your honour cannot be endured.'

[110] See also the discussion of the negation under example (22).

[111] The two different prepositional phrases ܥܠܝ 'at me' and ܠܝ 'to me' of version A are subsumed under one prepositional phrase ܥܠܝ in version B. This is possible because syntactically both prepositions function as indirect object markers.

B. ܠܐ ܡܣܝܒܪ ܠܪܒܘܬ ܦܐܝܘܬܐ ܕܬܫܒܘܚܬܟ
lā msaybar l-rabbut pāyutā
NEG endure.INT:AP.3 to-greatness.CST elegance
d-tešboḥt-āk.
LNK-honour-POSS.2
'One does not endure the greatness of the elegance of your honour.'

(35) A. (...) ܘܠܐ ܐܢܫ ܡܫܟܚ (verse 5b)
w-lā (?)nāš meškaḥ ...
and-NEG man.ABS can.CAUS:AP ...
'No man can ...'

B. (...) ܘܠܐ ܡܫܟܚ
w-lā meškaḥ ...
and-NEG can.CAUS:AP ...
'It is not possible ...'

In the first example, the complement of B (which can arguably be seen as the theme of the clause) is rendered in A as the grammatical subject; as an alternative to the impersonal subject of B (denoting a generic agent) A uses a middle verbal form (ܡܣܬܝܒܪܐ) thus yielding approximately the same meaning.[112] In the second example, A has an overt generic subject (ܐܢܫ) whereas B has a covert generic subject, yielding an impersonal clause. The two constructions in A and B are also functionally equivalent, though syntactically different.[113]

---

[112] It is worth noting that only three other manuscripts (14/8a1, 16g7 and 13H5) have the impersonal construction, though the two former do not mark ܪܒܘܬ as an object with a Lamadh (probably since they are related to the A version). On the other hand, all manuscripts that use the middle form omit the Lamadh. Peculiary, some B-related manuscripts (13H1–3.6) use the masculine middle form ܡܣܬܝܒܪ, maybe due to analogy to B's ܡܣܝܒܪ. In these cases, the subjecthood of the NP ܪܒܘܬ ܦܐܝܘܬܐ ܕܬܫܒܘܚܬܟ (f.) is less clear. For a general discussion of the impersonal construction as part of the middle voice semantic category see Kemmer, *The Middle Voice*, 148; for an application of this study to Syriac and other forms of Aramaic see Farina, *An Outline of Middle Voice in Syriac*.

[113] Cf. Lambert, 'L'impersonnel', 297.

2.5.6 Clauses with an enclitic personal pronoun

The enclitic personal pronoun (e.p.p.) can be used as the third element in a tripartite nominal clause or as the rhematizer in clauses that G. Goldenberg has coined 'imperfectly-transformed cleft sentences'.[114] The e.p.p. in tripartite nominal clauses can either be analysed as a copula or as a subject of a nuclear clause (see below, discussion of example (39)). The e.p.p. tends to be attached directly to the predicate, but as the examples below show, it may be better analysed as a second-position clitic situated inside the Focus Phrase (see above, section 2.5.1, and especially note 61).

Nominal clauses

B has a tendency to use tripartite nominal clauses with the e.p.p. (underlined) where A avoids them:

(36) A. ܕܠܐ ܣܟܐ ܕܝܢ ܘܕܠܐ ܟܝܠܐ ܐܝܬܝܗܘܢ ܪ̈ܚܡܐ ܕܡܘܠܟ̈ܢܝܟ. (verse 6)

d-lā sākā dēn wa-d-lā kaylā
LNK-NEG limit however and-LNK-NEG measure
ʔitay-hon raḥmē d-mulkānay-k.
EXP-POSS.3PL mercy.PL LNK-promise.PL-POSS.2
'Without limit, however, and without measure is the tenderness of your promises.'

B. ܠܐ ܡܬܡܫܚܢܐ ܗܘ ܟܝܬ ܘܠܐ ܡܬܥܩܒܢܐ ܛܘܝܒܐ ܕܫܘܕ̈ܝܟ.

lā metmašḥāna =(h)u kit w-lā metʕaqbānā
NEG finite =3 indeed and-NEG scrutable
ṭuyābā d-šu(w)day-k.
readiness LNK-promise.PL-POSS.2
'Infinite, indeed, and inscrutable is the readiness of your declarations.'

[114] See Goldenberg, 'Imperfectly-Transformed Cleft Sentences'; Goldenberg, 'Bible Translations and Syriac Idiom', 26–28 (section on 'Rhematization'); Goldenberg, 'On Some Niceties of Syriac Syntax', 338–340 ('Focalization/Rhematization'). Muraoka, 'Response to Goldenberg', 43, uses the term 'rhematizer'.

(37) A. ܘܠܟ ܡܙܡܪܝܢ ܠܥܠܡ ܘܠܥܠܡ ܥܠܡܝܢ܀ (verse 15)

w-l-āk mzammrin l-ˁālam
and-to-POSS.2 sing.INT:AP.PL to-eternity.ABS
wa-l-ˁālam ˁālmin.
and-to-eternity.CST eternity.PL.ABS
'And (they) sing for You forever and ever.'

B. ܘܕܝܠܟ ܗ̱ܝ ܬܫ̈ܒܘܚܬܐ ܘܩܘܠܣܐ ܘܪܘܡܪܡܐ ܠܥܠܡ ܘܠܥܠܡ ܥܠܡܝܢ

w-dil-āk =(h)i tešbo[ḥtā] w-qulāsā
and-LNK-POSS.2 =3F hymn and-praise
w-rumrāmā l-ˁālam wa-l-ˁālam
and-exaltation to-eternity.ABS and-to-eternity.CST
ˁālmin
eternity.PL.ABS
'And Yours are the hymns and praise and exaltation forever and ever.'

In example (36) B has a tripartite nominal clause with the e.p.p. ܗܘ, whereas A uses the existential particle ܐܝܬ.[115] The same kind of variation can be observed by comparing verse 7 of both versions to the variant reading in the Horologion manuscripts:[116]

(38) A. ܐܝܬ ܗ̱ܘ ܡܪܝܐ ܢܓܝܪ ܪܘܚܐ. (verse 7a)

ˀa(n)t =(h)u māryā ngir ruḥā
2 =3 Lord long.CST spirit
'You are the Lord, long suffering'

---

[115] All the other Horologion manuscripts use active participles as predicates in this verse and thus do not use the e.p.p.: ܪ̈ܚܡܝܟ ܓܝܪ ܘܛܝܒܘܬܟ ܠܐ ܡܬܕܪܟܝܢ ܘܠܐ ܡܬܚܫܒܝܢ. ܡܘܠܟܢܐ ܕܡܠܟܬ. 'Your mercy, indeed, and your kindness are not comprehended and infinite (as is) the promise which You ordained.'

[116] The subject focus in versions A and B (ܐܝܬ being part of the Focus Phrase) can be explained as sentence focus, portraying all the clause as new information. See Lambrecht, *Information Structure and Sentence Form*, 233–235. For an illustration of Lambrecht's framework, see Tosco, *Information Packaging in Somali Texts*, 30–31, which applies it to Somali.

B. ܐܢܬ ܗܘ ܓܝܪ ܡܪܝܐ ܡܪܝܡܐ.
ˀa(n)t =(h)u gēr māryā mrimā.
2 =3 indeed Lord high
'You are indeed the Lord, Most High.'

H. ܐܢܬ ܓܝܪ ܡܪܝܐ ܡܪܝܡܐ ܐܝܬܝܟ
ˀa(n)t gēr māryā mrimā ʾit-ēk
2 indeed Lord high EXP-POSS.2
'You are indeed the Lord, Most High.'

A similar distributional equivalence of the e.p.p. and copulaic ܐܝܬ is attested, for example, in parallel passages in the synoptic Gospels.[117] Whether this shows that the two constructions are also functionally equivalent is more difficult to decide. The e.p.p. in B comes immediately after the first minimal unit of the predicate, which is continued by a parallel element following the e.p.p. and the second-position conjunction ܓܝܪ, while the existential particle in A is in the penultimate position, that is to say, after the parallel element. Thus, it seems correct to analyse the e.p.p. as embedded inside the Focus Phrase, as a second-position clitic, while the existential particle stands outside the predication,[118] and is normally adjacent to the subject NP.[119] Except for that, the two clauses exhibit a parallel syntax, though the lexemes used are different.

Example (37) shows a more extreme difference: the clauses can be claimed to be parallel only because of their position in the text (specifically, their parallel conjunction to the previous clause, which is rendered below as example (41)). Syntactically and lexically they are very different. Here we can observe that in A there is a plain verbal (participial) clause, while B has a nominal clause with an e.p.p. Note

[117]Cf. Matt 21:25 // Mark 11:30 and see further Van Peursen, 'Three Approaches to the Tripartite Nominal Clause in Syriac', 159.

[118]Cf. Van Peursen, *Language and Interpretation*, 339, with reference to Joosten, *Syriac Language*, 97–98; compare also footnote 72 on page 103.

[119]For the position of the e.p.p. after the first minimal unit of the clause see Van Peursen, *Language and Interpretation*, 250–251, 269 and further Van Peursen–Falla, 'The Particles ܓܝܪ and ܕܝܢ in Classical Syriac', 72–74. As for the adjacency of the existential particle and the subject NP, see Muraoka, *Classical Syriac*, 2nd edition, 86, §109.

again the second position of the e.p.p., and its agreement as a feminine singular pronoun with the first noun of the subject (ܬܫܒܘܚܬܐ given in a abbreviated form).[120] The adjunct that follows the subject NP in version B (ܠܥܠܡ ܘܠܥܠܡ ܥܠܡܝܢ 'forever and ever'), identical to the one in version A, casts doubt on the analysis of the subject NP as an extraposed subject (see above, section 2.5.1 and footnote 65).

In both these examples, the predicate together with the e.p.p. (i.e. the Focus Phrase) appears at the beginning of the clause, while the subject NP appears at the end. Whether this is a marked order or not remains to be investigated. In example (41) below we shall see a clear example where the fronting of the predicate is used for focusing.

Clauses with an an e.p.p. and an active participle

As explained in section 2.5.1, the participles, and particularly the active participle, can be seen as intermediate forms between verbal predicates and nominal predicates.[121] Whenever the subject is a 3rd person, the e.p.p. is not needed.[122] However, for the other persons the e.p.p. is used, as the following example shows.

(39) A. ܘܡܛܠ ܕܝܕܥ ܐܢܐ ܚܛܗܝ (verse 12)
w-meṭṭol d-yādaʿ =(ʔ)nā ḥṭāh-ay
and-because LNK-know:AP =1 sin.PL-POSS.1
' And because I know my sins.'

B. ܘܠܥܘܠܝ ܐܢܐ ܝܕܥ ܐܢܐ.
wa-l-ʿawl-ay ʔenā yādaʿ =(ʔ)nā
and-to-iniquity.PL-POSS.1 1 know:AP =1
'And my iniquities I know.'

[120] Cf. Nöldeke, *Syrische Grammatik*, §322, and further Costaz, *Grammaire syriaque*, 175, §628, who writes: 'Quand il y a plusieurs sujets, le verbe peut s'accorder avec le plus rapproché'. It seems that the e.p.p. follows the same rule here. It should be noted that version A does not use the feminine pronoun ܗܝ at all.

[121] Goldenberg, 'On Syriac Sentence Structure', 113, following Cohen, 'Phrase nominale et verbalisation', considers the participles to be in the 'third [=maximal] degree of verbalization'. See also Cohen, *La phrase nominale et l'évolution du système verbal*.

[122] See page 102; for an example see above, footnote 115.

In this example each version uses another construction: Version A has a VSO clause, while B has an OSV(s) clause.[123] Moreover, in A the object is a direct object, while in B it is an indirect object. The clause-internal differences can be explained by the different environments in which the clauses appear: in A it is an adjunct clause, connected syntactically to the following clause (ܡܬܟܫܦ ܐܢܐ ܩܕܡܝܟ 'I pray humbly before You'), whereas the clause in B is an independent clause (terminated by a *pāsoqā* sign).[124] Topicalization of the object within an adjunct clause would result in a cumbersome construction (*ܘܡܛܠ ܠܫܬܩܗ, ܢܕܒ ܐܢܐ) and thus is avoided in version A.

It should be noted that there are two possible ways to analyse the e.p.p. ܐܢܐ of version B (as every e.p.p., in fact). Either it is seen as the subject of an internal clause ܢܕܒ ܐܢܐ, parallel to the clause of version A, or it is analysed as a focus marker,[125] a third element added to the nuclear clause ܐܢܐ ܢܕܒ, which has an inverse (possibly marked) order relative to version A. An elaboration of the latter idea, which we adopt here, is to integrate the focus-marker together with the participle into a Focus Phrase, which in turn serves as the predicate of the clause.[126] The two analyses are summarized in table 2.3.[127]

---

[123]The lower case 's' is used for 'lesser subject'; cf. section 2.5.1 and Van Peursen, 'Three Approaches to the Tripartite Nominal Clause in Syriac', 158.

[124]In version A, a *pāsoqā* appears just before the clause, showing that the backward connection, marked by the coordinating conjunction ܘ, is not as strong as in version B, where the same conjunction ܘ is preceded by a *ʕeṣyana*.

[125]Another option would be to analyse the e.p.p. as a copula, i.e. a marker of predication without any added semantic value at the level of information structure. However, in such a case the position of the e.p.p. after the predicate would be largely arbitrary, which is certainly not the case. A more reasonable alternative would be to see the e.p.p. following a participle as an agreement morpheme, similar to the agreement exhibited by other verbal forms.

[126]This analysis provides a synthesis of Goldenberg's approach (doing justice to the tight relationship between the e.p.p. and the preceding element) and Muraoka's approach (avoiding the problems connected with the extraposition-analysis). See discussion on page 100 (section 2.5.1), as well as the discussion of example (41) below.

[127] In this table and in table 2.4 $[_x\ ]_y$ denotes phrase/clause boundaries, with *x* denoting the phrase (or clause) type and *y* its function in the surrounding clause. We use the following abbreviations: CL=Internal Clause, FOC=Focus Phrase, PRED=Predicate, ex.=extraposed, fr.=fronted.

	ܐܢܐ	ܝܕܥ	ܐܢܐ	ܠܥܘܠܝ
	=(ˀ)nā	yādaˁ	ˀenā	l-ˁawl-ay
[CL	subject	predicate]	ex. subject (focus)	ex. object (topic)
[FOC	focus-marker	particple]PRED	subject	fr. object (topic)

Table 2.3: Two analyses of example (39)

The first analysis poses an analytical problem in regard to the status of the object: since no resumptive pronoun refers to it in the internal clause, we are inclined to see it as a fronted object (i.e. in the first position within the predication structure) rather than an extraposed object (i.e. outside the predication structure). However, since in this analysis it is followed by an extraposed subject, we are obliged to see it as standing outside the internal clause and hence necessarily in extraposition.[128] From the semantic point of view both analyses imply a marked structure: the first analysis has an extraposed subject in a focus position (since it follows the extraposed object in the topic position) yielding the interpretation 'As for my sins, *I*, I know them', while the second analysis has the marked SV order with a Focus Phrase emphasizing the predication ('as for my sins, I *know* them'). Unlike in version B, in version A no emphasis is given, as the unmarked VSO order is used. Moreover, the emphasis in B is further marked by the independent status of the clause (as opposed to the subordinated status in A), and the fact that the preceding clause (example (31)) is more elaborated, and thus more content-full semantically. The second analysis provides a synthesis of Goldenberg's approach (doing justice to the tight relationship between the e.p.p. and the preceding element) and Muraoka's approach (avoiding the problems connected to the extraposition-analysis).[129]

In other cases, however, both versions use a bipartite construction, in which the subject is solely expressed by means of a (possibly enclitic) pronoun following the participle. This is, for instance the

[128] Cf. above, section 2.5.1 and footnote 65.

[129] See discussion on page 100.

case in example (40) below:

(40) A. ܘܟܕ ܠܐ ܫܘܐ ܐܢܐ ܦܪܩ ܐܢܬ ܠܝ (verse 14)
w-kad lā šāwē =(ˀ)nā pāreq =ˀa(n)t
and-when NEG worth:AP =1 redeem:AP =2
l-i
to-POSS.1
'And although I am not worthy, You will redeem me.'

B. ܘܟܕ ܠܐ ܫܘܐ ܐܢܐ ܡܫܘܙܒ ܐܢܬ ܠܝ
w-kad lā šāwē =(ˀ)nā mšawzeb
and-when NEG be_worth:AP =1 deliver.INT:AP=2
=ˀa(n)t l-i
to-POSS.1
'And although I am not worthy, You will deliver me.'

'Imperfectly-transformed cleft sentences'

As indicated in section 2.5.1, the 'imperfectly-transformed cleft sentences' constitute a much-debated category of Syriac syntax. In addition to the *la (h)wa* construction in example (24), p. 111, which in Goldenberg's approach constitutes a negative cleft construction, PrMan contains one other example of this category:

(41) A. ܡܛܠ ܕܠܟ ܡܫܒܚܝܢ ܟܠܗܘܢ ܚܝܠܘܬܐ ܕܫܡܝܐ. (verse 15)
meṭṭol d-l-āk mšabbḥin kol-hon
because LNK-to-POSS.2 praise.INT:AP.PL all-POSS.3PL
ḥaylwātā da-šmayyā.
power.PL LNK-heaven
'Because all the heavenly powers praise You.'

B. ܡܛܠ ܕܠܟ ܗܘ ܡܫܒܚܝܢ ܟܠܗܘܢ ܚܝܠܘܬܐ ܕܫܡܝܐ
meṭṭol d-l-āk =(h)u mšabbḥin
because LNK-to-POSS.2 =3 praise.INT:AP.PL
kol-hon ḥaylwātā da-šmayyā
all-POSS.3PL power.PL LNK-heaven
'Because it is You that the heavenly powers praise.'

Example (41) is a case of an additional e.p.p. in version B (note again the second position in the clause). Here, too, we are dealing with two constructions that are distributionally equivalent, as appears from many cases in which Syriac manuscripts of the same text show variation regarding the presence or absence of the e.p.p.[130] Functionally, both versions put emphasis on the indirect object ܠܟ, as is evident from its fronted position.[131] However, version B further focalizes the object by attaching the e.p.p. to it. The 3sg.m. e.p.p. ܗܘ clearly does not agree in gender and number with the pl.f. subject ܫ̈ܠܝܛܘܬܐ (contrast example (37)B in which ܗܝ appears). This is not exceptional and can be explained in several ways: according to G. Goldenberg's analysis, the e.p.p. agrees (by 3sg.m. agreement) with the 'virtually nominalised' clause ܡܫ̈ܒܚܝܢ ܠܗܘܢ ܫ̈ܠܝܛܘܬܐ ܕܥܝܪ̈ܐ, which serves thus as an appositive subject.[132] In such a case, the sentence is understood as an 'imperfectly-transformed cleft sentence', as the translation above suggests. In this view, the information-structure and the grammatical structure of the clause are equated, and the grammatical parallelism with version A is lost. Another method, which keeps the information structure and grammatical structure apart, is to analyse the e.p.p. ܗܘ as a focus-marker, while the other sentence constituents keep their grammatical functions in the sentence. This is, essentially, the view advocated by T. Muraoka. In this view, the e.p.p. serves as a pure focus-marker devoid of any subject marking; as such it is a fossilized element.[133]

As we explain in the introductory section 2.5.1, we propose a third analysis, which forms a synthesis of the two former analyses. In our view, the e.p.p. is indeed a focus marker, but it is not a direct constituent of the clause but rather forms together with the focused element (in this case, the indirect object) a Focus Phrase ܠܟ ܗܘ par-

[130] Cf. Joosten, 'Comments', 185–186; for a similar variation regarding the e.p.p. in tripartite nominal clauses see Van Peursen, 'Response to the Responses', 199–200.

[131] Cf. footnote 80 on page 105 for the infrequency of such an order.

[132] See footnote 67 on page 102.

[133] See Van Peursen, 'Three Approaches to the Tripartite Nominal Clause in Syriac', 161–162 and 167 note 40, for a discussion of the fossilization of the e.p.p. in NCs. Another possibility would be to argue tentatively that the position of the e.p.p. before the predicate and subject precludes it from agreement (similarly to the lack of number agreement in an initial verb in classical Arabic).

allel to the non-focused PP ܠܟ in version A.[134]. We note that the FP 'inherits' the valency role of the focused element, and acts as the object of the participial predicate (just as the parallel PP in version A).[135] This eliminates the need for postulating a constituent which is not governed by the predicate's valency, as is the case in Muraoka's original analysis. Moreover, this analysis establishes a perfect symmetry between the two versions at the clause-level analysis: both sentences have the same number of immediate constituents with the same grammatical functions. In this respect, this analysis is preferable both to Muraoka's and Goldenberg's analyses. As a general principle, we believe that whenever two constructions present an affinity both at the level of form (*signifiant*) and semantics (*signifié*), it is preferable to analyse them as syntactically similar as well, if possible. In this respect, the tight parallelism and distributional equivalence between the two versions at this point seem to justify our analysis. The three analyses are given below in table 2.4.[136]

ܟܠܗܘܢ...	ܡܫܒܚܝܢ	ܗܘ	ܠܟ
...kol-hon	mšabbḥin	=(h)u	l-āk
$[_{\text{CL}}$ subject	predicate $]_{\text{SUBJ}}$	(lesser) subject	predicate
subject	predicate	focus-marker	fr. object
subject	predicate	$[_{\text{FOC}}$ focus-marker	object $]_{\text{OBJ}}$

Table 2.4: Three analyses of example (41)

2.5.7 Embedded clauses

The use of embedded clauses varies between the two versions. In some cases A has an embedded clause where B has not and in some cases *vice versa*. In the following examples the differing embedded

[134]Cf. Van Peursen, *Language and Interpretation*, 374–376, §24.3.

[135]It should be emphasized that the designation FP is a phrase-level analysis, and it can receive different grammatical functions in the clause level, as can a PP or an NP.

[136]We follow the notational conventions explained in footnote 127, with the following additions: SUBJ=Subject, OBJ=Object.

clauses, and their non-embedded counterparts are underlined.[137]

Embedded clauses replacing objects

(42) A. ܘܠܐ ܐܢܫ ܡܫܟܚ ܡܣܝܒܪ ܕܢܩܘܡ ܩܕܡ ܪܘܓܙܟ ܘܚܡܬܟ (verse 5b)

w-lā (ʔ)nāš meškaḥ msaybar
and-NEG man.ABS can.CAUS:AP endure.INT:AP
da-nqum qdām rugz-āk w-ḥemt-āk
LNK-stand:IMPF.3 before rage-POSS.2 and-fury-POSS.2
'And no man can endure standing in front of your rage and fury.'

B. ܘܠܐ ܡܫܟܚ ܠܡܩܡ ܩܕܡ ܚܡܬܐ ܘܪܘܓܙܐ ܕܝܠܟ

w-lā meškaḥ la-mqām qdām ḥemtā
and-NEG can.CAUS:AP to-stand:INF before fury
w-rugzā dil-āk
and-rage LNK-POSS.2
'It is not possible to stand in front of the fury and rage of yours.'

(43) A. ܘܬܐܒ ܐܢܬ ܥܠ ܒܝܫܬܗܘܢ ܕܒܢܝ̈ܢܫܐ (verse 7a)

w-tāʔeb =ʔa(n)t ʕal bišāt-hon
and-repent:AP =2 on evil.F.PL-POSS.3PL
da-bnay-nāšā.
LNK-son.CST.PL-man
'And You repent on the evils of humans.'

[137] In this section we will not repeat the discussion about debated cases of embedding treated elsewhere in this chapter. For example, if one considers the part of the sentence following the e.p.p. in the 'imperfectly-transformed cleft sentence' discussed above to be 'implicitly subordinate' (cf. Goldenberg, 'Comments', 179), such a case displays embedding as well.

B. ܘܩܘܫܬܐ ܡܬܬܘܝܢܐ ܕܥܠ ܒܝܫܬܐ ܕܒܢܝܢܫܐ

w-quštā mettawyānā d-ʕal bišātā
and-true feeling_sorry.EMPH LNK-on evil.F.PL
da-bnay-nāšā.
LNK-son.CST.PL-man
'And rightly You are repentant on evils of humans.'

(44) A. ܐܝܟ ܕܠܐ ܐܪܝܡ ܪܝܫܝ ܠܥܠ. (verse 10a)

ʔ(y)k d-lā ʔarim rēš-(y) l-ʕel.
as LNK-NEG rise.CAUS:IMPF.1 head-POSS.1 to-up
'So I shall not lift my head upwards.'

B. ܐܟܡܢ ܕܠܐ ܡܫܟܚ ܐܢܐ ܕܐܬܗܦܟ ܘܐܪܝܡ ܢܦܫܝ.

ʔak-man d-lā meškaḥ =(ʔ)nā
as-Q LNK-NEG can.CAUS:AP =1
d-ʔethappak
LNK-turn_around.INTREFL:IMPF.1
w-ʔarim napš-(y).
and-rise.CAUS:IMPF.1 soul-POSS.1
'As one who cannot(1sg.) turn around and lift my soul (or: myself).[138]'

In example (42) version A uses a relative clause whereas B has an infinitival clause. Note also that A adds an extra auxiliary verb ܡܣܝܒܪ. Semantically, this seems superfluous, but stylistically it agrees with the verb ܡܣܬܝܒܪܐ at the beginning of the verse (see example (34)).[139]

[138] The noun ܢܦܫ may also be understood as an analytic reflexive pronoun (in contrast to a morphologically marked reflexive verb); cf. Farina, *An Outline of Middle Voice in Syriac*, 3, esp. note 7. However, in this case it is not clear whether it is used grammatically (indicating reflexivity) or with full semantic content (meaning 'soul'). The parallelism with ܪܝܫ 'head' in version A does not help, since this noun can also be interpreted either in a concrete or in a figurative way.

[139] Cf. Charlesworth, 'Prayer of Manasseh', 635, note p: 'In Syr.—but not in Gk.—5a and 5b are linked by different forms of the same verb (sbr, "to endure"; in Ethpaial in 5a, Paiel in 5b). The Syr. of this verse is superior to the Gk.'; note that Charlesworth's comment applies only to version A. Compare also verse 11 where ܟܐܦ '(I) am bending (my knees)' in A occurs parallel to ܡܪܟܢ in B; the reading in A establishes a lexical connection with ܟܦܝܦ '(I) am bent (by a multitude of iron chains)', in verse 10.

The verb ܡܫܟܚ 'can' itself is added as an auxiliary verb in version B of example (44), transforming the clause ܕܐܬܗܦܟ ܘܐܙܩܦ ܪܫܝ to an object clause in version B (note that the verb ܐܬܗܦܟ 'turn around' is a plus of version B as well[140]). See also example (2) on p. 89 for a discussion regarding the pronoun ܗܝ.

Example (43) presents two phenomena: A uses the participle ܬܐܒ 'repent' as a verbal predicate of an independent conjunct clause while B expresses the same meaning with the participle ܡܬܬܘܝܐ 'feel sorry', which forms part of a series of adjectives. Apart from the lexical difference,[141] a syntactical difference emerges: the indirect object of version A ܥܠ ܒܝܫܬܗܘܢ 'on the evils (of them)' directly governed by the predicate, which acts a verb, while in B the parallel expression ܥܠ ܒܝܫܬܐ 'on evils' is preceded by the subordinating conjunction ܕ, since it is seen as a complement of a Noun Phrase (the participle ܡܬܬܘܝܐ serving as a predicative NP).[142]

Embedded clauses replacing non-predicative particles

(45) A. ܐܢܬ ܗܘ ܓܝܪ ܐܠܗܐ ܕܬܝܒܐ. (verse 13b)
ˀa(n)t =(h)u gēr ˀalāhā d-tayyābē.
2 =3 indeed God LNK-repenter.PL
'You are, indeed, the God of the repenters.'

B. ܡܛܠ ܕܐܢܬ ܗܘ ܐܠܗܐ ܕܐܝܠܝܢ ܕܬܝܒܝܢ.
meṭṭol d-ˀa(n)t =(h)u ˀalāhā d-ˀāylēn
because LNK-2 =3 God LNK-Q.PL
d-tāybin.
LNK-repent:AP.PL
'Because You are the God of those who repent.'

---

[140] This verb could also be interpreted as an auxiliary indicating repetition: 'as one who cannot lift *again* his head', a usage that is well-known for the Pᶜal of ܗܦܟ.

[141] See below, section 3.1.

[142] The use of ܕ before a Prepositional Phrase modifying a Noun Phrase is idiomatic in Syriac (see Van Peursen, *Language and Interpretation*, 224). However, as manuscript 14/8a1 shows, it is not strictly necessary: in this manuscript the subject ܐܢܬ is omitted, thus reinforcing the nominal nature of the participle ܬܐܒ by making it part of a series of adjectives, but the subsequent Prepositional Phrase is not introduced by ܕ.

In example (45) two phenomena are present: first, the clause in B is connected with a conjunction to the preceding clause, making it an adjunct clause, while the clause in A is connected via the conjunction (or rather 'connective adverb'[143]) ܕܝܢ 'indeed'. Secondly, the (synthetic) noun ܬܝܒܐ 'repenters' in A corresponds to the analytic expression ܐܝܠܝܢ ܕܬܝܒܝܢ 'those who repent' in B. The part-of-speech difference between the two versions is signalled by the usage of two different vocalic patterns, one nominal and non-participial, as well as a difference of state (emphatic vs. absolute state).[144] Syntactically, the result is that the former is a noun, without any predicative power, while the latter is a verbal counterpart of it, enabling it to be the predicate of the embedded clause.

Differences in disposition

(46) A. ܐܫܬܘܕܝܬ ܫܘܒܩܢܐ ܠܐܝܠܝܢ ܕܬܝܒܝܢ ܡܢ ܚܛܗܝܗܘܢ (verse 7b)

ʔeštawdit šubqānā l-ʔaylēn
promise.REFL:PRF.2 forgiveness to-Q.PL
d-tāybin men ḥṭāhay-hon.
LNK-repent:AP.PL from sin.PL-POSS.3PL

'You promised forgiveness for those who repent of their sins.'

B. ܐܫܬܘܕܝܬ ܬܝܒܘܬܐ ܕܫܘܒܩܢܐ ܠܐܝܠܝܢ ܕܚܛܘ ܠܟ

ʔeštawdit tyābutā d-šubqānā
promise.REFL:PRF.2 repentance LNK-forgiveness
l-ʔaylēn d-ḥṭaw l-āk.
to-Q.PL LNK-sin:PRF.3PL to-POSS.2

'You promised repentance of forgiveness for those who sinned before You.'

In (46) the same content is partitioned differently between a main clause and a subordinate clause. Version A introduces the idea of

[143] See below, section 2.5.8 (end).

[144] Admittedly, as the original text is not vocalized, we can only infer the vocalic difference by the context. An alternative reading of ܬܝܒܐ as *tāybē* (=repent:AP.PL.EMPH) is possible, but less idiomatic.

repentance in the participle serving as the predicate of the subordinated clause (ܬܝܒܝܢ 'repent'; see also above, example (45)), while in B it appears as a noun in the main clause (ܬܝܒܘܬܐ) 'repentance', taking part in a somewhat cumbersome genitive Noun Phrase ܬܝܒܘܬܐ ܕܫܘܒܩܢܐ 'repentance of forgiveness',[145] where version A has only ܫܘܒܩܢܐ 'forgiveness'. Consequently, the 'sins' expressed nominally in A (ܚ̈ܛܗܝܗܘܢ 'their sins') reappear as the verb ܚܛܘ 'they sinned' in the subordinate clause of B.

2.5.8 Conjunctions and clause connectors

Throughout the two texts there are several cases where different conjunctions are used. Moreover, the versions differ sometimes in that one version uses a subordinating conjunction and the other a coordinating conjunction.[146] The varying conjunctions are underlined:

(47) A. ܕܠܐ ܣܟܐ ܕܝܢ ܘܕܠܐ ܟܝܠܐ ܐܝܬܝܗܘܢ ܪ̈ܚܡܐ ܕܡܘܠܟܢܝ̈ܟ (verse 6)

d-lā sākā dēn wa-d-lā kaylā
LNK-NEG limit however and-LNK-NEG measure
ˀitay-hon raḥmē d-mulkānay-k.
EXP-POSS.3PL mercy.PL LNK-promise.PL-POSS.2
'Without limit, however, and without measure is the tenderness of your promises.'

[145] Cf. section 1.9.4 for parallels to this phrase. Note that the meaning of the root ܬܘܒ is slightly different in the two versions. In version A the 'repentance' is portrayed as a human action, while in version B it is a gift given by God. See section 3.1 for a further discussion of the latter interpretation.

[146] Similar types of variation are attested in the two versions of the Epistle of Baruch (cf. above, section 2.2); see Bosker, *A Comparison of Parsers. Delilah, Turgama and Baruch*, 24–27.

B. ܠܐ ܡܬܡܫܚܢܐ ܗܘ ܟܝܬ ܘܠܐ ܡܬܥܩܒܢܐ ܛܘܝܒܐ ܕܫܘ̈ܕܝܟ

lā metmašḥāna =(h)u kit w-lā metʕaqbānā
NEG finite =3 indeed and-NEG scrutable.ABS
ṭuyābā d-šu(w)day-k.
readiness LNK-promise.PL-POSS.2
'Infinite, indeed, and inscrutable is the readiness of your declarations.'

(48) A. ܡܛܠ ܕܐܢܬ ܗܘ ܡܪܝܐ ܢܓܝܪ ܪܘܚܐ. (verse 7a)

metṭol d-ˀa(n)t =(h)u māryā ngir ruḥā
because LNK-2 =3 Lord long.CST spirit
'Because You are the Lord, long-suffering.'

B. ܐܢܬ ܗܘ ܓܝܪ ܡܪܝܐ ܡܪܝܡܐ.

ˀa(n)t =(h)u gēr māryā mrimā.
2 =3 indeed Lord high
'You are, indeed, the Lord, Most High.'

(49) A. ܐܢܬ ܡܪܝܐ (verse 7b)

ˀa(n)t māryā
2 Lord
'You, O Lord'

B. ܐܢܬ ܗܟܝܠ ܡܪܝܐ

ˀa(n)t hākē(y)l māryā
2 therefore Lord
'You, therefore, o Lord '

(50) A. ܕܐܦܠܐ ܚܛܘ ܠܟ. (verse 8)

d-ˀāp-lā ḥṭaw l-āk.
LNK-even-NEG sin:PRF.3PL to-POSS.2
'Who truly did not sin against You.'

B. ܕܠܐ ܚܛܘ ܠܟ.

d-lā ḥṭaw l-āk.
LNK-NEG sin:PRF.3PL to-POSS.2
'Who did not sin against You.'

(51) A. ܘܠܝܬ ܠܝ ܢܦܝܫܐ (verse 9a)

w-la-(ˀ)yt l-i npēšā
and-NEG-EXP to-POSS.1 rest
'And I do not have a rest.'[147]

B. ܘܠܝܬ ܠܝ ܡܟܝܠ ܐܣܝܘܬܐ. (verse 10a)

w-la-(ˀ)yt l-i mekkēl ˀāsyutā.
and-NEG-EXP to-POSS.1 therefore cure
'And I do not have, therefore, a cure.'

(52) A. ܐܦܠܐ ܓܝܪ ܫܘܐ ܐܢܐ (verse 10a)

āp-lā gēr šāwē =(ˀ)nā
even-NEG indeed be_worth:AP =1
'Nor, indeed, am I worthy.'

B. ܘܠܐ ܣܟ ܫܘܐ ܐܢܐ (verse 9a)

w-lā sāk šāwē =(ˀ)nā
and-NEG limit.ABS be_worth:AP =1
'And I am not at all worthy.'

(53) A. ܘܐܩܝܡܬ ܦܬܟܪܐ ܘܐܣܓܝܬ ܛܢܦܘܬܐ. (verse 10b)

w-ˀaqimet ptakrē
and-stand.CAUS:PRF.1 idol.PL
w-ˀasgit ṭanputā.
and-multiply.CAUS:PRF.1 abomination
'And I set up idols, and multiplied abominations.'[148]

B. ܠܐ ܓܝܪ ܥܒܕܬ ܨܒܝܢܟ ܘܠܐ ܢܛܪܬ ܦܘܩܕܢܝܟ.

lā gēr ˁebdet ṣebyān-āk w-lā neṭret
NEG indeed do:PRF.1 will-POSS.2 and-NEG keep:PRF.1
puqdānay-k.
commandment.PL-POSS.2
'Indeed, I did not do your will, and I did not keep your commandments.'

---

[147] The alignment between verses 9 and 10 is based on the transpositional analysis presented in table 4.9 of section 4.6.

[148] See section 3.2.2 for a further discussion of this example.

(54) A. ܘܒܥܐ ܐܢܐ ܡܢ ܒܣܝܡܘܬܟ (verse 11)
w-bāʕē =(ʔ)nā men bassimut-āk.
and-beseech:AP =1 from sweetness-POSS.2
'And I am beseeching your sweetness.'

B. ܟܕ ܒܥܐ ܐܢܐ ܡܢ ܒܣܝܡܘܬܟ
kad bāʕē =(ʔ)nā men bassimut-āk.
when beseech:AP =1 from sweetness-POSS.2
'While I am beseeching your sweetness.'

(55) A. ܐܢܬ ܗܘ ܓܝܪ ܐܠܗܐ ܕܬܝ̈ܒܐ (verse 13b)
ʔa(n)t =(h)u gēr ʔalāhā d-tāybē.
2 =3 indeed God LNK-repenter.PL
'You are, indeed, the God of the repenters.'

B. ܡܛܠ ܕܐܢܬ ܗܘ ܐܠܗܐ ܕܐܝܠܝܢ ܕܬܝ̈ܒܝܢ
meṭṭol d-ʔa(n)t =(h)u ʔalāhā d-ʔāylēn
because LNK-2 =3 God LNK-Q.PL
d-tāybin.
LNK-repent:AP.PL
'Because You are the God of those who repent.'

(56) A. ܐܦ ܗܟܝܠ ܚܘܐ ܡܪܝ ܛܝܒܘܬܟ (verse 14)
ʔāp hākēl ḥawwā mār-(y)
even therefore show.INT:IMPT Lord-POSS.1
ṭaybut-āk.
grace-POSS.2
'Truly, thus show, my Lord, your goodness.'

B. ܘܒܝ ܡܚܘܐ ܐܢܬ ܟܠܗ ܛܝܒܘܬܟ
w-b-i mḥawwē =ʔa(n)t koll-āh
and-in-POSS.1 show.INT:AP =2 all-POSS.3F
ṭaybut-āk.
grace-POSS.2
'And in me You show all your goodness.'

(57) A. ܡܛܠܗܕܐ ܐܫܒܚܟ (verse 15)
mettol-hādē ˀeššabbḥ-āk
because-DEM.F praise.INT:IMPF-OBJ.1
'Because of this, I shall praise You'

B. ܘܐܫܒܚܟ
w-ˀeššabbḥ-āk
and-praise.INT:IMPF.1-obj.2
'And I shall praise You'

In some cases version A uses a 'light' conjunction (either semantically or syntactically speaking) while version B uses a 'heavy' conjunction: This is the case in example (54), where version A uses the neutral and symmetric coordinator ܘ 'and', while B uses the content-full 'asymmetric coordinator' or 'subordinator' ܟܕ 'when, after; although, even if; because; while'.[149] A similar trend is seen in example (55): version B uses the asymmetric subordinator ܡܛܠ ܕ 'because of, by reason of, on account of, in order that', while version A uses the weaker coordinator ܓܝܪ 'for, but, indeed, however'. Other examples are (53), where B has the conjunction ܓܝܪ 'indeed' and A ܘ 'and', or examples (49) and (51), where version B has as pluses the conjunctions ܗܟܝܠ and ܡܟܝܠ respectively (both translated 'therefore').

In other cases, the opposite is true. In example (56), for instance, it is version A that uses the 'heavy' coordinator ܐܦ 'also, and truly, even, nevertheless', while version B uses the 'light' coordinator ܘ 'and'. Moreover, version A uses here an extra conjunction/modifier ܗܟܝܠ 'therefore'.[150] In examples (50) and (52), A uses the conjunction ܐܦ 'even', coalesced with the negator ܠܐ, while in version B we have a ∅ (no parallel conjunction) or ܘ 'and' respectively (and note also the added ܓܝܪ 'indeed' in (52)A[151]). The same is true as well as for example (57): Version A uses a meaningful phrase ܡܛܠܗܕܐ 'because of this' while B has only the coordinator ܘ 'and'.

[149] The English equivalents in this section are taken from Payne Smith, *Compendious Syriac Dictionary*.

[150] Compare with example (49).

[151] Version B, however, uses an emphatic negator ܠܐ ܡܕܡ 'not at all'; see the discussion in section 2.4.4.

The distinction in example (47) between ܕܝܢ 'but, however, for, then' as against ܟܝܬ 'scilicet, that is to say, indeed', seems to be mostly lexical. The distinction in examples (48) and (55) – a subordinating ܡܛܠ ܕ 'because of' versus a connective adverb ܓܝܪ 'indeed' (see below) – creates a difference in the text hierarchy (see respectively sections 4.4 and 4.7). The differences are summarized in the table 2.5 (the 'heavier' conjunctions are underlined).

Example	Verse	A	B
(47)	6	ܕܝܢ	ܟܝܬ
(48)	7a	ܡܛܠ ܕ	ܓܝܪ
(49)	7b	Ø	<u>ܗܟܝܠ</u>
(50)	8	<u>ܕܐܦܠܐ</u>	ܕܠܐ
(51)	9a/10a	Ø	<u>ܡܟܝܠ</u>
(52)	10a/9a	<u>ܕܐܦܠܐ ܓܝܪ</u>	ܘܠܐ
(53)	10b	ܘ	<u>ܓܝܪ</u>
(54)	11	ܘ	<u>ܟܕ</u>
(55)	13b	ܓܝܪ	ܡܛܠ ܕ
(56)	14	<u>ܐܦ ܗܟܝܠ</u>	ܘ
(57)	15	<u>ܡܛܠܗܕܐ</u>	ܘ

Table 2.5: Clause connectors

Elsewhere we have argued that ܓܝܪ and ܕܝܢ should be called 'connective adverbs' rather than 'conjunctions', because of the syntactical and functional differences between these particles and 'real' conjunctions such as ܘ or ܡܛܠ ܕ. Thus whereas a conjunction serves to indicate a connection between clauses, but is not part of one of them, the syntactic rules that determine the position of ܓܝܪ and ܕܝܢ within the clause make them capable of being a constituent of the clause (*satzgliedfähig*). Moreover, the presence of a clause-initial conjunction does not rule out the presence of ܓܝܪ or ܕܝܢ later on in the clause.[152] A similar argument can be made for ܟܝܬ, and perhaps also for ܗܟܝܠ. It is interesting to note, however, that in two cases (examples (48) and (55)) ܓܝܪ in one version corresponds to the conjunction

[152] Van Peursen–Falla, 'The Particles ܓܝܪ and ܕܝܢ in Classical Syriac', 66–67. See e.g. verse 10 in version A: ܐܦܠܐ ܓܝܪ ܫܘܐ ܐܢܐ 'nor, indeed, am I worthy'.

ܡܛܠ ܕ in the other version. This suggests that there is at least some semantic overlap between the two.

Chapter 3

Lexical Analysis

In this chapter we investigate the vocabulary of the two versions using several approaches. In section 3.2 we present a qualitative survey of lexical correspondences between the two versions. This is not intended to be exhaustive, but rather covers the cases which have not already been addressed in chapter 2. In section 3.3 we take a quantitative and non-linear approach to obtain a tentative numerical measure of difference or 'distance' between the two versions. This will be preceded by a case study of the *metanoia* terminology in PrMan in section 3.1. In this section we will examine S. von Stemm's argument regarding the importance of the 'penitence' notion in the Prayer, in order to show the importance of a rigorous, rather than impressionistic, approach when dealing with vocabulary. We will also argue that we should be hesitant to speak of '*the* vocabulary of the Syriac version of PrMan' or even, more generally, '*the* vocabulary of PrMan', because of the considerable variation that the different versions show with regard to their vocabulary.

3.1 Case Study: *Metanoia* Terminology

3.1.1 Word frequencies

Since it is generally acknowledged that PrMan is a prayer of penitence, it seems appropriate to devote a small case study to words for penitence in the Greek and Syriac versions. According to Sönke von Stemm, the *metanoia* terminology (i.e. the words μετανοεῖν 'to repent' and μετάνοια 'repentance') is dominant in PrMan.[1] At first sight this claim agrees with the general character of PrMan, but the question arises as to whether such a claim is justified.

If such a claim about the dominance of a certain terminology is based on our impression as to what motif or theme plays an important role in the Prayer, regardless of word frequencies, one could equally consider, for example, ܫܘܐ 'to be worthy of, to deserve' to preponderate, because it marks an important contrast between the deserved punishment and the undeserved salvation (version A vv. 9, 10, 14; version B vv. 9, 14).

If, however, we want claims regarding the question as to what terminology is dominant to be based on word frequencies, we should take into account, for example, that both in the Greek and in the Syriac versions the words for sin (even if we restrict ourselves to words of the root ἁμαρτ- / ܚܛ and ignore other words belonging to the same semantic field, such as ܒܝܫܬܐ 'evil', ܥܘܠܐ 'iniquity', ܚܘܒܐ 'debt', ܦܬܟܪܐ 'idol', ܛܢܦܘܬܐ 'abomination' and ܒܐܝܫܘ 'harm, wickedness'[2]) outnumber the words for *metanoia*, as appears from tables 3.1 and 3.2.[3]

Lexeme	Version A	Version B	Lexeme	LXX
ܬܘܒ (verb)	3	1	μετανοεῖν	2
ܬܝܒܘ (noun)	3	5	μετάνοια	2
Total	6	4		2

Table 3.1: 'Metanoia-terminology' in the Greek and Syriac versions of PrMan

From these tables it appears that the word frequency numbers do not unequivocally support the claim that the *metanoia* terminology is dominant in PrMan. No-one will object to calling PrMan a penitential prayer, but this does not necessarily mean that the terminology of penitence/repentance is predominant. The interaction

[1]Cf. Von Stemm, *Der betende Sünder vor Gott*, 121–134.

[2]For the various Syriac words belonging to this semantic field see Greenberg, 'Sin, Iniquity, Wickedness and Rebellion in the Peshitta to Isaiah and Jeremiah'.

[3]The numbers given for the Septuagint (LXX) are based on the Greek text in Rahlfs, *Psalmi cum Odis*.

Lexeme	Version A	Version B	Lexeme	LXX
ܚܛܐ (verb)	5	3	ἁμαρτάνω	4
ܚܛܗ (noun)	3	3	ἁμαρτία	1
ܚܛܝ (adjective)	3	3	ἁμαρτωλός	2
Total	11	9		7

Table 3.2: Words for 'sin' in the Greek and Syriac versions of PrMan

between genre, theme, and word frequencies is more complicated.

3.1.2 Distribution and use

Leaving aside the question of how dominant the *metanoia* terminology is in PrMan, we will now have a look at its distribution and use. It appears that the distribution of the μετάνοια / ܬܘܒ terminology differs between the Greek and Syriac versions as well as between the Syriac versions A and B.[4] In the Syriac versions, words of the root ܬܘܒ occur, just like the *metanoia* terminology in the Greek version, referring to (a) God's feeling sorry over people's sin; (b) repentance as a gift of God to the people[5]; and (c) those who repent.

With regard to the first usage, there is a difference between A and B in verse 7a (see above, example (43) on page 130) in that A has ܘܬܐܒ ܐܢܬ 'And You repent (of the evils of humans)' where B has ܘܒܫܪܪܐ ܡܬܬܘܝܢܐ 'and truly You are repentant (of evils of humans)'. According to J.H. Charlesworth, ܡܬܬܘܝܢܐ indicates more

[4] Cf. Ehrmann, *Klagephänome im zwischentestamentlicher Literatur*, 131, on the equivalence of Hebrew שׁוב and Greek μετανοεῖν. In the Septuagint שׁוב is often translated with ἐπιστρέφειν.

[5] According to Ryle, 'The Prayer of Manasses', 616, 'the statement that "repentance" is appointed by God for certain persons, and not for others', is 'characteristic of Jewish religious thought', and according to Dancy, *The Shorter Books of the Apocrypha*, 246–247, 'it is a common Jewish idea that repentance is granted or withheld by God'. This idea is indeed also expressed in Wisdom of Solomon 11:23; 12:10, 19. Since, however, it occurs also in Acts 11:18 ('This means that God has granted life-giving repentance to the Gentiles also'; Dancy, ibid.), the idea was not foreign to the early Christian community, and hence it does not argue against a Christian authorship of PrMan. (References to Wisdom taken from Jervell, *Die Apostelgeschichte*, 316); cf. above, section 1.9.4

clearly 'feel sorry over', rather than 'repent'.[6] Elsewhere in the Bible we find that God 'repents' or 'turns away' from his anger (cf. Joel 2:13; Jonah 3:9), but that understanding of ܬܐܒ does not fit the present context. In A (but not in B) we further have ܘܬܐܒ ܐܢܬ ܥܠ ܒܝܫܬܗܘܢ ܕܒܢܝܢܫܐ (...) ܠܐܝܠܝܢ ܕܬܝܒܝܢ ܡܢ ܚܛܗܝܗܘܢ 'and You repent of the evils of humans (...) those who repent of their sins'. In the same verse B has ܐܫܬܘܕܝܬ ܬܝܒܘܬܐ ܕܫܘܒܩܢܐ 'You promised repentance of forgiveness'[7] as against ܐܫܬܘܕܝܬ ܫܘܒܩܢܐ 'You promised forgiveness' in A. In verse 13b we find ܐܠܗܐ ܕܬܝܒܐ (A) / ܐܠܗܐ ܕܐܝܠܝܢ ܕܬܝܒܝܢ (B) 'the God of the repenters / those who repent'.

There are more occurrences of ܬܘܒ in variant readings to version B. Thus in verse 7a ܒܝܫܬܐ ܕܒܢܝܢܫܐ '(You feel sorry over) the evils of humans' is followed in all manuscripts (except for the main text, 10t1) by ܟܕ ܬܝܒܝܢ ܘܦܢܝܢ ܠܘܬܟ 'when they repent and turn to You' and for ܕܚܛܘ ܠܟ 'who sinned before You' they have ܕܚܛܝܢ ܘܬܝܒܝܢ ܠܘܬܟ 'who sin and repent/return to You' (cf. version A). In verse 10a they have a variant that expresses the inability of the sinner to repent, and hence agrees with the view that repentance is a gift from God: ܘܠܝܬ ܒܝ ܚܝܠܐ ܕܐܬܚܠܡ ܘܐܬܦܢܐ ܘܐܬܘܒ ܥܠ ܚܛܗܝ 'And I do not have strength that I should recover and turn and repent of my sins'.

Since Von Stamm's discussion of the *metanoia* terminology in PrMan does not take into account the Syriac text,[8] he misses the ܬܝܒܝܢ in verse 7b and does not mention the variation attested in the Syriac versions in those places where the Greek text has μετανοεῖν or μετάνοια.[9] For details see table 3.3.

---

[6]Cf. Charlesworth, 'Prayer of Manasseh', 636, note v. Note that version B also has ܐܬܬܘܝ 'he felt sorry' in its introduction, referring to Manasseh (cf. section 1.7).

[7]Cf. Luke 3:3 ܬܝܒܘܬܐ ܠܫܘܒܩܢܐ ܕܚܛܗܐ 'repentance (leading) to the forgiveness of sins' (Dancy, *The Shorter Books of the Apocrypha*, 246). cf. section 1.9.4; see also the discussion of example (46) on page 133.

[8]Although he admits on p. 107 that this is 'die älteste erreichbare Version des Gebetes'.

[9]The same can be said of the discussion in Ehrmann, *Klagephänome im zwischentestamentlicher Literatur*, 164–165.

Table 3.3: Distribution of the μετάνοια / ܬܘܒ terminology

V.	Version A	Version B	LXX
7a	ܘܬܐܒ ܐܢܬ ܥܠ ܒܝܫܬܗܘܢ ܕܒܢܝܢܫܐ. And You repent of the evils of humans.	ܘܫܪܝܪܐ ܡܬܬܘܝܢܐ ܕܥܠ ܒܝܫܬܐ ܕܒܢܝܢܫܐ. ... and truly You feel sorry over the evils of humans. Variant + (*omnes*): ܟܕ ܬܝܒܝܢ ܘܡܬܦܢܝܢ ܠܘܬܟ when they repent and turn to You	καὶ μετανοῶν ἐπὶ κακίαις ἀνθρώπων And repenting of the evils of humans.
7b	ܐܫܬܘܕܝܬ ܫܘܒܩܢܐ ܠܐܝܠܝܢ ܕܬܝܒܝܢ ܡܢ ܚܛܗܝܗܘܢ. You promised forgiveness for those who repent of their sins. Variant (14/8a1): ܐܫܬܘܕܝܬ ܬܝܒܘܬܐ ܠܐܝܠܝܢ ... You promised forgiveness for those...	ܐܫܬܘܕܝܬ ܬܝܒܘܬܐ ܕܫܘܒܩܢܐ ܠܐܝܠܝܢ ܕܚܛܘ ܠܟ. You promised repentance of forgiveness for those who sinned before You. Variant (*omnes*-13H5): ܕܚܛܝܢ ܘܬܝܒܝܢ ܠܘܬܟ. who sin and repent/return to You.	
7b	ܣܡܬ ܬܝܒܘܬܐ ܐܝܟ ܕܠܚܝܝܗܘܢ ܕܚܛܝܐ. You have put repentance, as for the life of sinners.	ܐܣܡܬ ܬܝܒܘܬܐ ܠܦܘܪܩܢܐ ܕܚܛܝܐ. You have fixed repentance for the redemption[10] of sinners.	

[10] Cf. Dancy, *The Shorter Books of the Apocrypha*, 247: (on 'repentance... as the way to salvation'): 'This sounds at first like a Christian phrase, but in fact a parallel to it is found in a Jewish work of about 100 B.C.', after which Dancy refers to The

Table 3.3: Distribution of the μετάνοια / ܬܘܒ terminology (contd.)

V.	Version A	Version B	LXX
8	ܠܐ ܗܘܐ ܠܙܕܝܩܐ ܣܡܬ ܬܝܒܘܬܐ: It is not for the righteous that You have put repentance.[11]	ܠܐ ܣܡܬ ܬܝܒܘܬܐ ܠܙܕܝܩܐ. You have not put repentance for the righteous.	οὐκ ἔθου μετάνοιαν δικαίοις You have not put repentance for the righteous.
8	ܐܠܐ ܣܡܬ ܬܝܒܘܬܐ ܠܝ ܕܝܠܝ ܚܛܝܐ. But You have put repentance for me, the sinner.	ܐܠܐ ܣܡܬ ܬܝܒܘܬܐ ܥܠܝ ܕܝܠܝ ܚܛܝܐ. But You have put repentance for me, the sinner.	ἀλλ᾽ ἔθου μετάνοιαν ἐμοὶ τῷ ἁμαρτωλῷ But You have put repentance for me, the sinner.
10a		Variant (*omnes*): ܘܠܝܬ ܒܝ ܚܝܠܐ ܕܐܬܚܠܦ ܘܐܬܦܢܐ ܘܐܬܘܒ ܥܠ ܚܛܗ̈ܝ.	

Testament of Gad 5:7. Note, however, that the attribution of the Testaments of the Twelve Patriarchs to a Jewish author can be seriously challenged (see section 1.9.2) For other parallels, including a New Testament passage such as 2 Corinthians 7:9–10, see Hollander, 'The Testaments of the Twelve Patriarchs', 330. For the reading in version A with ܠܚܝܝܗܘܢ 'for their life', cf. above, footnote 5, on Acts 11:18, which is translated in the Peshiṭta by ܟܒܪ ܐܦ ܠܥܡܡܐ ܐܠܗܐ ܝܗܒ ܬܝܒܘܬܐ ܠܚܝܐ 'apparently, God has given repentance for live to the Gentiles also'.

[11]For the idea that the righteous do not need repentance, Dancy, *The Shorter Books of the Apocrypha*, 247 refers to Luke 5:32 and 15:7; vice versa, in their comment on Luke 15:7, Strack and Billerbeck, *Kommentar zum Neuen Testament aus Talmud und Midrasch*, 210, refer to PrMan 8, as well as many places in later Rabbinic literature, where a contrast is created between the 'man of repentance' (בעל תשובה), and the 'completely righteous one' (צדיק גמור). Contrast Ben Sira 8:5 (Genizah manuscript A) אל תכלים איש שב מפשע זכר כי כלנו חייבים 'do not put to shame a man who returns from his transgression; remember that we are all guilty', for which the Peshiṭta has: ܠܐ ܬܒܣܪ ܠܒܪܢܫܐ ܕܬܐܒ ܡܢ ܚܛܗ̈ܘܗܝ، ܐܬܕܟܪ ܕܟܠܢ ܚܛ̈ܝܢ. Note also that it has been argued that in Luke 15:7 'who need no repentance' is meant ironically, i.e. 'who think they do not need repentance'; cf. Reiling–Swellengiebel, *A Translator's Handbook on the Gospel of Luke*, 543–544.

Table 3.3: Distribution of the μετάνοια / ܬܘܒ terminology (contd.)

V.	Version A	Version B	LXX
		And I do not have strength that I should recover and turn and repent of my sins	
13b	ܐܢܬ ܗܘ ܓܝܪ ܐܠܗܐ ܕܬܝܒ̈ܐ. You are, indeed, the God of the repenters.	ܡܛܠ ܕܐܢܬ ܗܘ ܐܠܗܐ ܕܐܝܠܝܢ ܕܬܝܒ̈ܝܢ. Because You are the God of those who repent.	ὁ θεὸς τῶν μετανοούντων the God of the repenters.[12]

3.2 LEXICAL CORRESPONDENCES

This section summarizes the lexical correspondences that are not part of a wider syntactic or morphological difference (treated earlier in chapter 2). By 'correspondences' we refer to words that occur in the same place and with the same syntactic function in the two versions, but are not necessarily semantically equivalent.[13] Most of the correspondences in the two versions are between two words with identical or similar meaning. We will call these pairs 'synonymous', indicating that the two words have a similar meaning, without entering the linguistic debate as to what precisely makes two words synonymous and whether 'words with identical meaning' exist at all.[14] In other cases,

[12]For the argument that 'God of the repenters' is a Rabbinic idiom and suggests a late date for PrMan, see footnote 158 on page 42.

[13]Compare P.G. Borbone's definition of 'corresponding word' in Borbone, 'Correspondances lexicales entre Peshitta et TM du Pentateuque', 2. See further Borbone, Jenner *et al.*, *Concordance*, xii, and Dyk, 'Lexical Correspondence and Translation Equivalents', 311, note 1; for the way in which correspondences can be established in the computer-assisted comparative analysis of parallel texts see Dyk, 'A Synopsis-Based Translation Concordance'.

[14]For a discussion of this question in relation to Syriac lexicography see Falla, 'A Conceptual Framework for a New Comprehensive Syriac-English Lexicon', 47–48. An interesting computational treatment of the notion of 'near-synonymy' is given

one version uses a more specific term than the other, or a different term altogether.

3.2.1 Synonymous and non-synonymous correspondences

Although we are aware of the problems related to the definition of 'synonyms' and the identification of similar meaning, we will facilitate our discussion of lexical correspondences by making a tentative distinction between 'synonymous' and 'non-synonymous' correspondences. A summary of the synonymous correspondences together with translations (adapted from Payne Smith, *Compendious Syriac Dictionary*) is given in table 3.4 while the non-synonymous correspondences are given in table 3.5. Note that the correspondences for verses 9–10 are established according to their transpositional analysis, as given in table 4.9.[15] The words are given as they appear in the text with any affixes or clitics.

Table 3.4: 'Synonymous' lexical correspondences between versions A and B

V.	Version A		Version B	
4	to fear, dread	ܕܚܠ	to be made to quake, be terrified	ܡܬܪܬܪ
4	to be moved, shaken to and fro	ܙܐܥ	to oscillate; to be swayed, shaken	ܢܕܠ
4	might, power, force	ܚܝܠܟ	might, ability	ܫܠܝܛܘܬܟ
6	endless	ܕܠܐ ܣܟܐ	immeasurable	ܠܐ ܡܬܡܫܚܐ
6	promise, declaration	ܫܘܠܚܝܟ	promise, declaration	ܫܘܘܕܝܟ

in Edmonds–Hirst, 'Near-Synonymy and Lexical Choice', who characterize near-synonyms as having the same 'essential' meaning, but differing at a granular level (ibid., 12–13).

[15] In such cases we give first the verse number of version A and then the verse number of version B, whenever they differ.

Table 3.4: 'Synonymous' lexical correspondences between versions A and B (contd.)

V.	Version A		Version B	
7a	merciful	ܡܪܚܡܢܐ	compassionate	ܚܢܢܐ
7a	compassion	ܚܢܢܐ	goodness, favour	ܛܝܒܘܬܐ
7b	to put, set	ܣܡܬ	a) to limit; b) to settle, fix	ܬܚܡܬ
10a/9a	to look, behold, gaze	ܐܚܘܪ	to fix the eye, gaze intently	ܐܕܝܩ
10a/9a	harm, iniquity	ܡܒܐܫܘܬܐ	iniquity, injustice	ܥܘܠ
11	to bend, curve, bow	ܟܐܦ	to turn, bend downwards	ܟܪܡ
12	sin; a sin, fault	ܚܛܗܝ	iniquity, injustice	ܥܘܠ
13a	to pray in a low voice, supplicate	ܬܬܟܫܦ	to ask, entreat	ܫܐܠ
13b	transgressions[16]	ܣܟܠܘܬܝ	sins	ܚܛܗܝ
14	to redeem, save	ܦܪܩ	deliver, redeem	ܡܦܨܐ

The synonymous lexical correspondences of verse 4 are established under the assumption of a transposition:

(58) A. ܗܘ ܕܟܠܡܕܡ ܕܚܠ ܘܙܐܥ ܡܢ ܩܕܡ ܚܝܠܟ. (verse 4)
haw d-kol-meddem dāḥel w-zāʔaʕ men
DEM LNK-all.CST-thing fear:AP and-tremble:AP from
qdām ḥayl-āk.
before might-POSS.2
'The one before whose might everything fears and trembles.'

[16] See discussion of example (13) on page 94.

B. ܗܘ ܕܟܠ ܡܕܡ ܪܥܠ ܘܡܣܬܪܕ ܡܢ ܩܕܡ ܦܪܨܘܦܐ ܕܚܝܠܬܢܘܬܟ.
haw d-kol-meddem rāʕel
DEM LNK-all.CST-thing quiver:AP
w-mestarrad men qdām parṣopā
and-terrify.INT.REFL:AP from before face
d-ḥayltānut-āk.
LNK-might-POSS.2
'The one before whose face of might everything quivers and is terrified.'

In the above example ܕܚܠ *dāḥel* corresponds to ܡܣܬܪܕ *mestarrad* while ܙܐܥ *zāʔaʕ* corresponds to ܪܥܠ *rāʕel*. In addition, the lexeme ܦܪܨܘܦܐ *parṣopā* 'face' is added in version B, and ܚܝܠܬܢܘܬܟ *ḥayltānut-āk* 'Your might' corresponds to ܚܝܠܟ *ḥayl-āk*.

A similar case arises in verse 7a (treated also as example (17) on page 98):

(59) A. ܡܛܠ ܕܐܢܬ ܗܘ ܡܪܝܐ ܢܓܝܪ ܪܘܚܐ ܘܡܪܚܡܢܐ ܘܣܓܝ ܚܢܢܐ. (verse 7a)
mettol d-ʔa(n)t =(h)u māryā ngir ruḥā
because LNK-2 =3 Lord long.CST spirit
wa-mraḥmānā w-saggi ḥnānā.
and-merciful and-great.CST compassion
'Because You are the Lord, long-suffering and merciful and of great compassion.'

B. ܐܢܬ ܗܘ ܓܝܪ ܡܪܝܐ ܡܪܝܡܐ. ܚܢܢܐ ܢܓܝܪ ܪܘܚܐ. ܘܣܓܝ ܛܝܒܘܬܐ
ʔa(n)t =(h)u gēr māryā mrimā. ḥannānā
2 =3 indeed Lord high compassionate
ngir ruḥā. w-saggi ṭaybutā
long.CST spirit and-great.CST grace
'You are indeed the Lord, Most High, compassionate, long-suffering and of great grace.'

However, in this case the correspondences are less straightforward. One assumption could be that ܢܓܝܪ ܪܘܚܐ *ngir ruḥā* is parallel in both versions even though occurring in different locations. We should note that this cannot be said of the form ܚܢܢܐ since in version A it is the noun ܚܢܳܢܳܐ *ḥnānā* 'compassion' while in version B it corresponds to the adjective ܚܰܢܳܢܳܐ *ḥannānā* 'compassionate', as is shown also by the *rwaḥa* above the ܢ. Instead, on semantic grounds we relate B's ܚܢܢܐ *ḥannānā* to A's ܡܪܚܡܢܐ *mraḥmānā* 'merciful' (underlined). In this analysis B's ܡܪܝܡܐ *mrimā* 'high' remains as a plus, though interestingly the pair of adjectives ܡܪܝܡܐ. ܚܢܢܐ *mrimā ḥannānā* in B alliterates with ܡܪܚܡܢܐ *mraḥmānā* in A. Under this assumption ܚܢܢܐ *ḥnānā* 'compassion' in version A corresponds to ܛܝܒܘܬܐ *ṭaybutā* 'goodness, favour' in version B.[17]

Other lexical correspondences are not synonymous. They are given in table 3.5.

V.	Version A		Version B	
6	without measure	ܕܠܐ ܟܝܠܐ	inscrutable	ܠܐ ܡܬܥܩܒܢܐ
6	tenderness, mercy	ܪܘܚܡܐ	preparation, readiness	ܛܘܝܒܐ
9a/10a	breathing; rest, refreshment	ܢܝܚܐ	the healing art, a remedy, cure	ܐܣܝܘܬܐ
10a	head[18]	ܪܫܝ	self, soul[19]	ܢܦܫܝ

Table 3.5: 'Non-synonymous' lexical correspondences between versions A and B

The lexical correspondences of verse 6 which are not synony-

[17] Von Stemm's observation (in a discussion on the references to Exod 34:6–7) that 'im Gebet Manasses werden abweichend von allen übrigen Exodus-Zitaten nur drei Adjektive zur Charakerisierung des gnädigen Gottes genannt' (Von Stemm, *Der betende Sünder vor Gott*, 121) does not apply to version B. On the function of the partial citation of Exod 34:6–7 in PrMan see also Newman, 'The Form and Settings of the Prayer of Manasseh', 110–111.

[18] According to our linear analysis, presented in table 4.8, ܥܝܢܝ 'my eyes' would come here. However, the linear alignment presented by Baars–Schneider, 'Prayer of Manasseh', 5, agrees with the above given correspondence.

[19] See footnote 138, p. 131, for the interpretation of ܢܦܫ.

mous (marked below with double underline), are nonetheless from the same semantic field. They occur together with other lexical correspondences which are synonymous (marked with single underline):

(60) A. ܕܠܐ ܣܟܐ ܕܝܢ ܘܕܠܐ ܟܝܠܐ ܐܝܬܝܗܘܢ ܪ̈ܚܡܐ ܕܡܘܠܟܢܝܟ (verse 6)

d-lā sākā dēn wa-d-lā kaylā
LNK-NEG limit however and-LNK-NEG measure
ʔitay-hon raḥmē d-mulkānay-k.
EXP-POSS.3PL mercy.PL LNK-promise.PL-POSS.2
'Without limit, however, and without measure is the tenderness of your promises.'

B. ܠܐ ܡܬܡܫܚܢܐ ܗܘ ܟܝܬ ܘܠܐ ܡܬܥܩܒܢܐ ܛܘܝܒܐ ܕܫܘܕ̈ܝܟ

lā metmašḥāna =(h)u kit w-lā metʕaqbānā
NEG finite =3 indeed and-NEG scrutable.abs
ṭuyābā d-šu(w)day-k.
readiness LNK-promise.PL-POSS.2
'Infinite, indeed, and inscrutable is the readiness of your declarations.'

The correspondence between ܢܦܝܫܐ *npēšā* 'rest' in verse 9a of version A and ܐܣܝܘܬܐ *ʔāsyutā* 'cure' in verse 10a of version B is based upon the correspondence between these two clauses:

(61) A. ܘܠܝܬ ܠܝ ܢܦܝܫܐ (verse 9a)

w-la-(ʔ)yt l-i npēšā
and-NEG-EXP to-POSS.1 rest
'and I do not have a rest'

B. ܘܠܝܬ ܠܝ ܡܟܝܠ ܐܣܝܘܬܐ. (verse 10a)

w-la-(ʔ)yt l-i mekkēl ʔāsyutā.
and-NEG-EXP to-POSS.1 therefore cure
'and I do not have, therefore, a cure'

This correspondence rests chiefly on the similar construction of the two clauses; however, the lexical content and the surrounding context are quite distinct.[20]

We can conclude, thus, that almost all of the lexical correspondences are drawn from the same semantic field, whether they are synonymous or not

3.2.2 Antonymous correspondences

In one section of the Prayer, at the end of verse 10b, the same idea, of upsetting God, is expressed in opposite ways in each version:

(62) A. ܘܐܩܝܡܬ ܦܬܟܪܐ ܘܐܣܓܝܬ ܛܢܦܘܬܐ. (verse 10b)
w-ʔaqimet ptakrē
and-stand.CAUS:PRF.1 idol.PL
w-ʔasgit ṭanputā.
and-multiply.CAUS:PRF.1 abomination
'and I set up idols, and multiplied abominations.'

B. ܠܐ ܓܝܪ ܥܒܕܬ ܨܒܝܢܟ ܘܠܐ ܢܛܪܬ ܦܘܩܕܢܝܟ.
lā gēr ʕebdet ṣebyān-āk w-lā neṭret
NEG indeed do:PRF.1 will-POSS.2 and-NEG keep:PRF.1
puqdānay-k.
commandment.PL-POSS.2
'Indeed, I did not do your will, and I did not keep your commandments.'

In version A the evil deeds are spelled out in an affirmative manner, while in version B they are expressed in a negative manner, as non-obedience of God. The lexemes used cannot be considered generally as antonyms, but in the context in which they are given they provide us with opposite notions. Thus A ܦܬܟܪܐ *ptakrē* 'idols' ≠ B ܨܒܝܢܟ *ṣebyān-āk* 'your will'; A ܛܢܦܘܬܐ *ṭanputā* 'abominations' ≠ B ܦܘܩܕܢܝܟ *puqdānay-k* 'your commandments'. Incidentally, the Greek version agrees here with version A.

[20] See discussion in section 4.6.

3.3 VOCABULARY COUNTS

Our discussion of lexical correspondences in the preceding section was synopsis-based: First it was established which phrases and clauses are parallel, and then the correspondences at word level within the corresponding phrases and clauses were established. In this approach a text is primarily taken as a sequence of elements, and the difference between the two texts concerns the different elements in corresponding positions. Another way to analyse the difference between two texts is to compare the lexemes they contain, without taking into account the sequence in which they occur. In such an approach it is not the syntagmatic order that plays a role, but rather an over-all lexical comparison is made.

This 'bag of words' approach can be carried out in two distinct ways: either we count the lexemes of the texts as they would appear in a glossary; i.e. each lexeme is counted only once, and repetitions of it or inflectional variations are ignored. This we shall label 'lexeme count'. Another possible approach is to count the occurrences of the lexemes (or 'tokens') as they appear in the text (with or without taking into account inflectional variation). In this approach it is not only the appearance of a lexeme in a text that counts, but also its relative frequency. If in one text a lexeme appears more times than in the other, the additional occurrences are seen as version-specific. This approach we shall call 'token count'. Both methods are useful to establish a numeric measure of 'distance' between two texts.[21] The lexeme count is useful if we want to compare the vocabularies of two texts.[22]

The token count can be used as a complementary method of a syntagmatic (linear) comparison, since it levels out the effects of transpositions: two transposed sections are not caught as parallels in a linear comparison, since they appear in different places. However,

[21] Cf. Van Peursen, 'Plagiaatbestrijding en analyse van oude bijbelvertalingen'. This approach is not restricted only to lexemes. We may apply it to the inventories of syntactical constructions or morphological patterns as well. However, the lexical comparison is the easiest since it does not require any thorough analysis of the text.

[22] What we call here 'lexeme-count' and 'token count' is sometimes referred to as the more general type-token distinction; cf. McEnery–Wilson, *Corpus Linguistics*, 66–71.

the token count would give us a small measure of 'distance' between the texts, since the tokens used are in fact the same.[23]

In the following discussions we regard nouns as single lexemes, disregarding their morphological inflection and possessive suffixes.[24] Verbal forms are treated as a single lexeme whenever they share the same root, including participles.[25] We start with a lexeme count, but these assumptions are also true for the following token count.

Under these assumptions, we can establish that the two versions have a shared vocabulary of 115 lexemes. As for the version-specific vocabulary, we can distinguish between lexemes that have a correspondence in the other version (parallel lexemes), and those that are essentially pluses.[26] Version A has 25 lexemes that do not appear in version B (18% of all its lexemes). These are presented in table 3.6. Version B, on the other hand, has 49 (30%) lexemes, which are presented in table 3.7.[27]

[23]This is, of course, most useful for long texts, where the transpositions cannot always be easily identified or treated. For a short text such as PrMan it is possible to treat the transpositions on a case-by-case basis. This is done, for example, in section 4.6 regarding verses 9–10 of the Prayer.

[24]The possessive suffixes are in fact treated as pronominal lexemes in their own right; cf. Sikkel, 'Lexeme Status of Pronominal Suffixes'.

[25]Another possibility is to see the combination of a root with a stem formation as a lexeme, in accordance with Aronoff, *Morphology by Itself*, chapter 5. See also note 21, p. 83.

[26]The correspondence is not necessarily on word level, but may also be at phrase level or clause level (as part of a parallel construction).

[27]For our way of listing Third-Weak verbs, e.g. ܗܘܝ rather than ܗܘܐ, see Bakker, 'Lemma and Lexeme: The Case of Third-Alaph and Third-Yodh Verbs'.

Parallels		Pluses	
also, even	ܐܦ	eye	ܥܝܢ
these	ܗܢܘܢ	pour out	ܐܫܕ
beauty	ܝܐܘ	be tormented	ܐܠܝ (ܡܬܐܠܝ)
pray in a low voice	ܒܨܦ (ܡܬܒܨܦ)	behold	ܗܐ
without measure	ܟܝܠ (ܕܠܐ ܟܝܠ)	this	ܗܕܐ
		be	ܗܘܝ
harm, wickedness	ܡܒܐܫܘ	rightly, justly	ܒܟܐܢܐܝܬ
		the Lord	ܡܪܐ
merciful	ܡܪܚܡ	be shaken	ܛܪܦ (ܡܬܛܪܦ)
promise	ܡܘܠܟ		
breathing[28]	ܢܦܐܫ		
redeem, save	ܦܪܩ		
idol	ܦܬܟܪ		
abomination[29]	ܛܢܦܘ		
might, strength	ܚܝܠ		
look	ܚܘܪ		
sing	ܙܡܪ		
be agitated	ܙܘܥ (ܙܐܥ)		

Table 3.6: Version-specific lexemes of version A

[28] Note that the lexeme ܢܦܫ appears in version B (as a version-specific lexeme). However, it is not parallel to ܢܦܐܫ, and although the two words share the same root they are not regularly related to each other, thus justifying considering them as two different lexemes.

[29] This word occurs in the same context as ܦܬܟܪ 'idol'. According to Charlesworth, 'Prayer of Manasseh', 636, note r2, it can denote idol worship (cf. Dan 11:31). Costaz, *Dictionaire*, 129, lists 'idol' as a possible meaning.

Parallels		Pluses	
remedy	ܐܣܘܐ	**Superscription pluses**	
ask	ܫܐܠ	Israel	ܐܝܣܪܝܠ
promise	ܫܘܘܕ	Jerusalem	ܐܘܪܫܠܡ
she	ܗܝ	Babel	ܒܒܠ
they	ܗܢܘܢ	break	ܒܙ
redeem	ܙܒ (ܡܫܘܙܒ)	take captive	ܫܒܝ
indeed	ܟܝܬ	burn	ܝܩܕ
who	ܡܢ	king	ܡܠܟ
mercy	ܡܪܚܡܢܘ	harm	ܢܟܝ
inscrutable	ܡܬܒܨܝܢ (ܠܐ ܡܬܒܨܝܢܐ)	brass	ܢܚܫ
		repent	ܬܘܝ (ܐܬܬܘܝ)
infinite	ܡܬܡܫܚ (ܠܐ ܡܬܡܫܚܢܐ)	bull	ܬܘܪ
		wish	ܨܒܐ
penitent	ܡܬܬܘܝܢ	pray	ܨܠܐ
breath	ܢܦܫ	**Other pluses**	
beauty	ܦܐܝܘ	pass	ܥܒܪ
salvation	ܦܘܪܩܢ	amen	ܐܡܝܢ
praise	ܩܘܠܣ	heavenly	ܫܡܝܢ
quiver	ܪܒܠ	turn about	ܗܦܟ (ܐܬܗܦܟ)
incline	ܪܟܢ (ܡܪܟܢ)		
exaltation	ܪܘܡܪܡ	therefore	ܡܛܠ
be terrified	ܣܪܕ	number	ܡܢܝܢ
limit, border	ܬܚܘܡ	face	ܦܪܨܘܦ
readiness	ܛܘܝܒ	give praise	ܩܠܣ
strength	ܚܝܠܬܢܘ	justice	ܩܘܫܬ
will, desire	ܨܒܝܢ	under	ܬܚܝܬ
gaze	ܨܕ	debt	ܚܘܒ

Table 3.7: Version-specific lexemes of version B

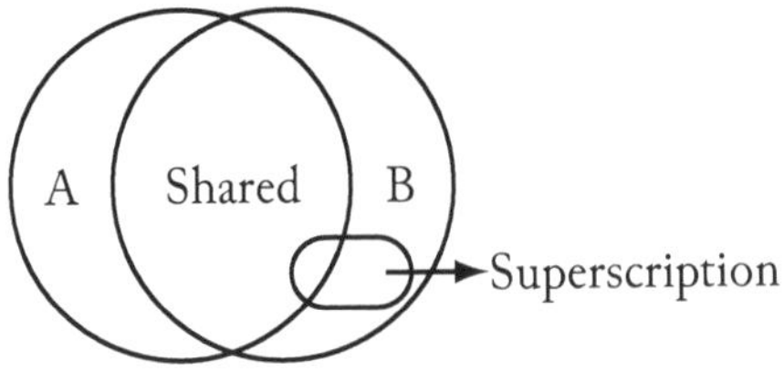

Figure 3.1: The relation of the superscription to the rest of the vocabulary

Clearly, version B has a richer lexeme inventory. This is mainly due to the superscription that does not occur in version A (see section 1.7). The treatment of the superscription as a secondary, 'external' element to the Prayer is supported by the large number of unique lexemes as well as by the appearance of three proper names, Jerusalem, Babel and Israel (in addition to Manasseh, which appears in the titles of both texts), whereas the text of the Prayer itself contains no proper names. The relationship of the vocabulary of the superscription to the other vocabulary is illustrated schematically in figure 3.1.

If we ignore the lexemes that appear in the superscription we are left with 36 version-specific lexemes which constitute then 24% of B's lexeme inventory. Thus, apart from the core vocabulary which is common to both texts, the two versions have roughly the same proportion of version-specific lexemes (18% vs. 24%). The distribution of plus-lexemes is also similar in the two versions (6% vs. 7% in B without the superscription). This is summarized in table 3.8 (all percentages are rounded down). B_0 denotes version B without the superscription. Figure 3.2 gives a graphic representation of the same data.

Ver.	Lexemes	Version-Specific	Parallels	Pluses
A	140 (100%)	25 (18%)	16 (11.5%)	9 (6.5%)
B_0	151 (100%)	36 (24%)	25 (17%)	11 (7%)
B	164 (100%)	49 (30%)	25 (15%)	24 (15%)

Table 3.8: Lexeme count results

We can turn upside down the data we have collected and look

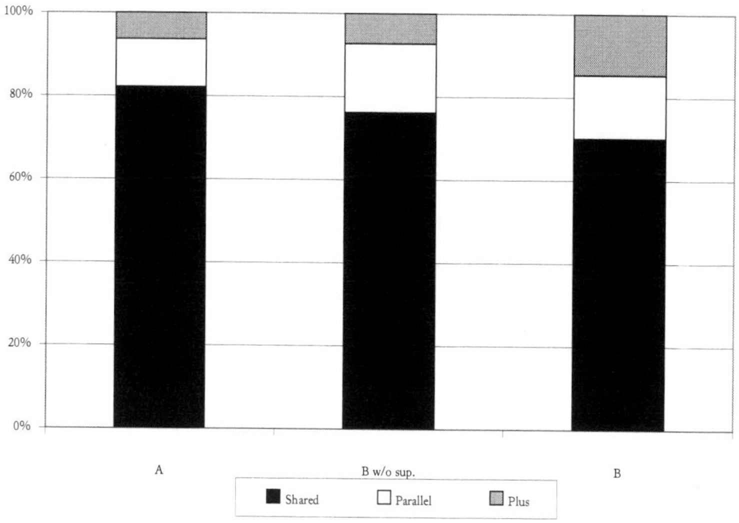

Figure 3.2: Lexeme count results

at the proportions of the shared vocabulary relative to the united vocabulary of both versions. The shared vocabulary consists of about 65% of the two versions (or 61% if we take into account the lexemes in B's introduction). The distribution of the total vocabulary of both versions is presented in figure 3.3.

So far, we have presented the results of the 'lexeme count'. Using the 'token count' approach, we obtained quite similar results, shown in table 3.8. These figures are quite similar to those of the lexeme count.[30]

From the above discussion, it can be concluded that by and large the vocabularies used, and the pattern of their usage are similar in the two texts, though version B uses a somewhat richer vocabulary. However, it should be noted that at the current state of our knowl-

[30]The somewhat greater similarity found in the token count is probably related to the large proportion of function words and suffixes in the token count. For instance, the object suffix ܗ appears 18 times in the common vocabulary use (5% of all 362 common lexemes). Since function words are frequent in both versions (as in any text) the part of the version-specific tokens is reduced. This is less marked in the lexeme count, since each function word is considered only once.

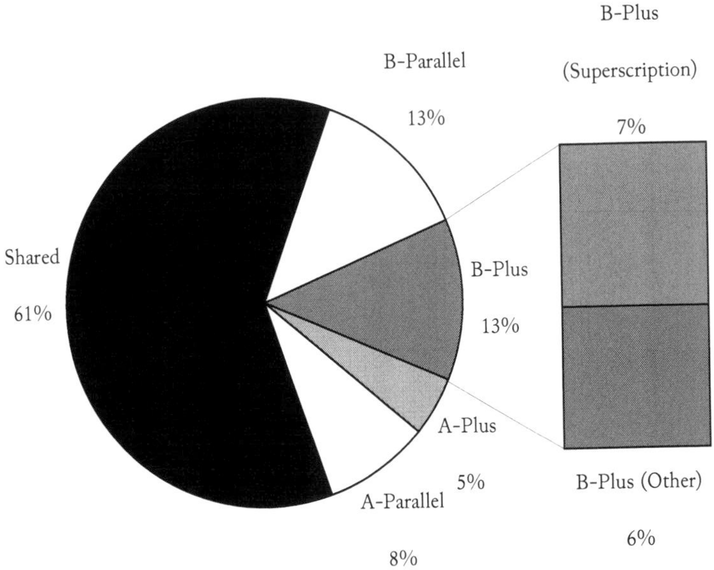

Figure 3.3: Distribution of the vocabulary of PrMan

Version	Tokens	Version-Specific
A	429 (100%)	67 (17%)
B_0	447 (100%)	89 (20%)
B	483 (100%)	121 (25%)

Table 3.9: Token count results

edge we do not have any reliable benchmark to compare these numeric results with. For instance, we do not know what is the average 'distance' measure between any two texts from the Peshiṭta, or between two arbitrary Syriac texts. Thus, although the data seem to support the intuitive notion that the two texts are quite similar, it does not provide us with a clear measure of how similar they in fact are, without further research on other Syriac texts.[31]

[31] As a preliminary comparison, we applied the above methods to the two versions of the Epistle of Baruch (=EpBar). These two texts show a much higher degree of similarity: each version has only about 5.5%–6% version-specific vocab-

ulary, and their shared vocabulary consists of almost 90% of their total vocabulary. Conversely, if we compare version A of PrMan to version A of EpBar we get, unsurprisingly, a lower degree of similarity: PrManA has 36% non-shared lexemes, while EpBarA 79%. This is not surprising, since EpBar has about three times more lexemes, being a longer text. The shared vocabulary is just above 19% of the total vocabulary. Clearly, this shows that the two versions of PrMan are more similar to each other than to another arbitrary text in the Peshiṭta, but they are not as similar as the two versions of EpBar. (On these two versions see also Bosker, *A Comparison of Parsers. Delilah, Turgama and Baruch.*)

CHAPTER 4

DISCOURSE ARRANGEMENT

4.1 METHOD OF THE TEXT HIERARCHICAL ANALYSIS

Our text hierarchical analysis concerns the determination of the relationships between clauses and the assignment of the syntactical functions of the clauses within the hierarchy of clauses. The basic assumption in our analysis is that each clause is connected to a preceding clause – which is not necessarily the immediately preceding clause – and that the relation to that clause may be either parallel or dependent. For each clause it is established which clause functions as its 'anchor'; whether the relation to that clause is parallel or dependent, and whether the syntactic function of the clause can be further specified in terms of, for example, object clause or attributive clause. A number of linguistic signals of inter-clausal relationships and other coherence markers are taken into account, such as clause opening type (syndetic or asyndetic; in the case of a conjunction: parataxis or hypotaxis); grammatical clause type (e.g. two clauses with the same pattern and verb form generally show a high degree of cohesion); grammatical and lexical correspondences; and the set of participants.

Since our method of the computer-assisted interactive text hierarchical analysis has been described extensively elsewhere,[1] we will focus in this chapter on the results of the text hierarchical analysis of PrMan, rather than repeating the description of the methodol-

[1]Van Peursen, *Language and Interpretation*, 152–153, 168–171, 385–403; Talstra–Jenner–Van Peursen, 'How to Transfer the Research Questions into Linguistic Data Types and Analytical Instruments', 45–69; Talstra, 'A Hierarchy of Clauses in Biblical Hebrew Narrative'.

ogy. Moreover, since the hierarchical analysis might be seen in some cases as an artificial analytical construct, we will concentrate here on the more clear cases. Even though one may object to details of the decisions made, it is undeniable that the two versions show several differences in the arrangement of the text and that the analysis of these differences should go beyond the clause-by-clause comparison given in chapter 2.

4.2 GENERAL OUTLINE OF THE STRUCTURE OF PRMAN

On the highest level, both versions contain elements which may be seen as external to the prayer itself – additions by the scribe, maybe (marked by *italics*) – but B uses them more extensively:[2]

Version A	Version B
Title	*Title*
	• *superscription*
• Prayer text	• Prayer text
	Closing phrase (ܐܡܝܢ)

Table 4.1: The prayer and the 'external elements'

With regard to the prayer text itself we can divide it into six main units, presented in table 4.2.[3] Both prayers begin with an invocation of the Lord, and the subsequent sections (numbered 1–5) are dependent on it.

By and large the two versions have the same structure as to the Prayer itself. However, the internal division of each section and the boundaries between the two sections are quite different, as can be seen in table 4.2.

Although we have used section labels indicating the main theme or content of the section in question, the main criterion for our divi-

[2]On the heading of the Prayer in the *Didascalia* (version B) see above, section 1.2. The closing phrase 'Amen' (version B) may have been added for liturgical use; cf. Ryle, 'The Prayer of Manasses', 525; Vegas Montaner, 'Oración de Manasés', 117, note 15.

[3]We adopt here the system presented in Charlesworth, 'Prayer of Manasseh' of dividing some verses into two parts.

Sections	Version A	Version B
Vocation of the Lord	v. 1	
1. Attributes of the Lord	vv. 2–5	
2. Mercy of the Lord	vv. 6–7a	v. 6
3. Direct addressing with ܐܢܬ	vv. 7b–11	vv. 7–8
4. Admission of sins	vv. 12–13a	vv. 9–13a
5. Asking for forgiveness	vv. 13b–15	

Table 4.2: Division of the prayer into main units

sion of the text has been the text hierarchical structure. As we shall see below, there are some cases where the syntactic division of the text does not run parallel with the thematic divisions into units that are found in scholarly literature.[4]

4.3 SECTION 1

The hierarchical structure of section 1 is determined largely by the pronouns used in it.[5] For this reason, the two versions have a different hierarchical structure, presented in table 4.3.[6]

In version A all the appositive clauses starting with the demonstrative pronoun ܗܘ have a parallel status dependent on the vocative ܡܪܝܐ 'the Lord'. In B, the change of pronominal elements disturbs this parallelism: both the first ܗܘ and the ܐܢܬ 'You' are dependent on ܡܪܝܐ but they are not parallel. The ܡܢ 'who' is subsequently dependent on ܐܢܬ and the last ܗܘ dependent on this ܡܢ.[7]

[4]This is a conclusion that turns up time and again in our computer-assisted text-hierarchical analysis of Hebrew and Syriac texts. For a Hebrew example see Talstra, 'Singers and Syntax' (on the division of Psalm 8); for Syriac examples see Van Peursen, 'Clause Hierarchy and Discourse Structure' and the references given there in notes 31 and 32.

[5]See section 2.4.1. For the significance of the 'invocation' as a structural element in the Prayer of Manasseh (in contrast to the penitential prayer in Psalm 51), see Newman, 'The Form and Settings of the Prayer of Manasseh', 108.

[6]Due to typographical considerations, we have not put translations alongside this and the following tables. Note that a full translation appears in the Appendix.

[7]The exact dependency relationships may be seen as analytical artefacts, since it is based on a hierarchy of pronominal elements: Explicit NP > Personal pronoun

Verse	Version A	Version B
1	ܡܪܝܐ ...	ܡܪܝܐ ...
2	ܗܘ ܕܥܒܕ ...	ܗܘ ܕܥܒܕܬ ...
3a	ܗܘ ܕܐܣܪ ...	ܐܢܬ ܕܐܣܪܬܝܗ̇ ...
3b	ܗܘ ܕܐܚܕ ...	ܡܢ ܕܐܚܕܬ ...
4	ܗܘ ܕܟܠܡܕܡ ...	ܗܘ ܕܟܠ ܡܕܡ ...

Table 4.3: Pronouns and hierarchical arrangement of vv. 1–4

Since the sequence of pronouns in verses 2–4 is such a strong structuring element in this section (see especially table 4.3), we prefer to take this whole sequence together as one unit of the Prayer and to consider verse 6, which starts with an asyndetic clause and introduces a new grammatical subject (ܪ̈ܚܡܐ ܕܡ̈ܘܠܟܢܝܟ 'the tenderness of your promises' in version A and ܛܘܝܒܐ ܕܫ̈ܘܘܕܝܟ 'the readiness of your declarations' in version B), as the start of a new section. Although verse 5a introduces a new subject as well, the subordination conjunction ܡܛܠ ܕ 'because' in both versions relates it to the preceding verse.[8] In this respect we differ from scholars who see a section break between verses 4 and 5.[9]

> Interrogative pronoun > Demonstrative pronoun. Consequently, a clause with a lower ranked pronoun serving as subject is taken as dependent on a clause with a higher ranked pronoun. Even if this analysis is rejected, it is obvious that in version A we have a more 'symmetrical' discourse construction than in version B.

[8]Compare the objections against considering Sirach 48:1, which begins with the preposition 'until', as the start of a new section on Elijah in Van Peursen, *Language and Interpretation*, 411–412.

[9]Thus e.g. Charlesworth, 'Prayer of Manasseh', 625, who divides these verses into verses 1–4 'invocation' and verses 5–7 'acknowledgement of the Lord's fury against sinners and of his multitudinous mercies'; similarly Newman, 'Three Contexts for Reading Manasseh's Prayer in the Didascalia', 8, who takes verses 1–4 and 5–7 as two subsections of the first main section of the Prayer, 1–7; (but contrast Newman, 'The Form and Settings of the Prayer of Manasseh', where she makes a subdivision into 1–5 and 6–7, which agrees with our division); other scholars mark neither verse 5 nor verse 6 as the start of a new section and take 1–7 as one single unit; thus e.g. Ryle, 'The Prayer of Manasses', 612, who calls verses 1–7 the 'confession of sin', and Oßwald, 'Das Gebet Manasses', 20, who calls it the 'Anrufung Gottes'.

4.4 The boundary between sections 2 and 3

The boundary between section 2 and 3 differs slightly between the two versions. In table 4.4 the end of section 2 and the beginning of section 3 are given as two different blocks in each version.

V.	version A	version B
6	...ܕܠܐ ܣܟܐ ܕܝܢ	...ܠܐ ܡܬܒܨܝܢܐ ܗܘ ܒܥܬ
7a	...ܡܛܠ ܕܐܢܬ ܗܘ ܡܪܝܐ	...ܐܢܬ ܗܘ ܓܝܪ ܡܪܝܐ
	...	...
	.ܥܠ ܒܝ̈ܫܬܗܘܢ ܕܒܢܝ̈ܢܫܐ	ܕܥܠ ܒܝ̈ܫܬܐ ܕܒܢܝ̈ܢܫܐ
7b	...ܐܢܬ	...ܐܢܬ ܗܟܝܠ

Table 4.4: Boundary between sections 2 and 3

The reason for the divergence is marked in table 4.4 by an underline: in A the clause containing the first appearance of ܐܢܬ is preceded by the subordinating compound conjunction ܡܛܠ ܕ 'because', which for that reason is considered a dependent clause. Only the subsequent ܐܢܬ 'You' is opening a new section. In B, conversely, the first ܐܢܬ appears with the connective adverb ܓܝܪ 'indeed' and thus can be seen as opening a new main section. The subsequent ܐܢܬ is seen as dependent on the first one (a relation which is reinforced by the appearance of the conjunction ܗܟܝܠ 'therefore').[10]

Here, again, the results of our text-hierarchical analysis differ from literary or thematic divisions of the text. Thus many scholars consider verse 8 as the start of a new section, for example between the 'invocation of the Deity' in verses 1–7 and the 'confession of sin' in verses 8–10,[11] or between the 'acknowledgement of the Lord's fury against sinners and of his multitudinous mercies' in verses 5–7 and the 'confession' in verses 8–10.[12] From a text-syntactical perspective,

[10]The differences in conjunctions are discussed in section 2.5.8, p. 134, where these differences are given under exapmles (48) and (49).

[11]Ryle, 'The Prayer of Manasses', 612; similarly Oßwald, 'Das Gebet Manasses', 20; Denis–Halewyck, *Introduction à la littérature religieuse judéo-hellénistique*, I, 659.

[12]Charlesworth, 'Prayer of Manasseh', 625; other scholars that take verse 8 as the start of a new section include Newman, 'Three Contexts for Reading Manasseh's Prayer in the Didascalia', 8.

however, it is rather the direct addressing with ܐܢܬ 'You' in verse 7b (version A) or 7a (version B) that marks the start of a new section. The clause-initial ܐܢܬ in verse 8 merely continues the earlier clause-initial ܐܢܬ.

4.5 THE BOUNDARY BETWEEN SECTIONS 3 AND 4

The boundary between sections 3 and 4 is very different in the two versions. This is enhanced by the fact that there is no clear linear correspondence between verses 9 and 10 in the two versions. Verses 7b and 8 are quite similar in their structure and content, as can be seen in table 4.5. However, at the beginning of verse 9 there is a marked difference between the two versions (table 4.6; note that the differences are marked by an underline and that the different clauses are presented in blocks).

V.	version A	version B
7b	ܐܢܬ ܡܪܝܐ ܐܝܟ ܒܣܝܡܘܬܐ ܕܛܝܒܘܬܟ ܐܫܬܘܕܝܬ ܫܘܒܩܢܐ	ܐܢܬ ܗܟܝܠ ܡܪܝܐ ܐܝܟ ܒܣܝܡܘܬܐ ܕܛܝܒܘܬܟ܂ ܐܫܬܘܕܝܬ ܬܝܒܘܬܐ ܕܫܘܒܩܢܐ
	ܠܟܠܡܢ ܕܬܝܒܝܢ ܡܢ ܚܛܗܝܗܘܢ܂	ܠܟܠܡܢ ܕܚܛܐ ܠܟ܂
	ܘܒܣܘܓܐ ܕܪ̈ܚܡܝܟ ܣܡܬ ܬܝܒܘܬܐ ܐܝܟ ܕܠܚܝ̈ܝܗܘܢ ܕܚܛܝ̈ܐ܂	ܘܒܣܘܓܐ ܕܪ̈ܚܡܝܟ ܬܣܡܬ ܬܝܒܘܬܐ ܠܦܘܪܩܢܐ ܕܚܛܝ̈ܐ܂
8	ܐܢܬ ܗܟܝܠ ܡܪܝܐ ܐܠܗܐ ܕܙܕܝ̈ܩܐ܂ ܠܐ ܗܘܐ ܠܙܕܝ̈ܩܐ ܣܡܬ ܬܝܒܘܬܐ ܐܝܟ ܕܠܐܒܪܗܡ ܘܠܐܝܣܚܩ ܘܠܝܥܩܘܒ	ܐܢܬ ܗܟܝܠ ܡܪܝܐ ܐܠܗܐ ܕܙܕܝ̈ܩܐ ܠܐ ܣܡܬ ܬܝܒܘܬܐ ܠܙܕܝ̈ܩܐ܂ ܠܐܒܪܗܡ ܘܠܐܝܣܚܩ ܘܠܝܥܩܘܒ
	ܗܢܘܢ ܕܐܦܠܐ ܚܛܘ ܠܟ܂	ܗܢܘܢ ܕܠܐ ܚܛܘ ܠܟ܂
	ܐܠܐ ܣܡܬ ܬܝܒܘܬܐ ܠܝ ܕܐܢܐ ܚܛܝܐ	ܐܠܐ ܣܡܬ ܬܝܒܘܬܐ ܥܠܝ ܕܐܢܐ ܚܛܝܐ܂

Table 4.5: Verses 7b–8

V.	version A	version B
9a	ܡܛܠ ܕ- ܝܬܝܪ ܡܢ ܚܠܐ ܕܝܡܐ ܣܓܝܘ ܚ̈ܛܗܝ.	ܡܛܠ ܕܚܛܝܬ ܝܬܝܪ ܡܢ ܡܫܘܚܬܐ ܕܚܠܗ ܕܝܡܐ. ܣ̈ܓܝܘ ܚ̈ܛܗܝ.

Table 4.6: Beginning of verse 9

In version A the opening clause of verse 9 is directly connected to what precedes it as an adjunct clause. It does not constitute a major break point of the section, though semantically the speaker starts talking about himself. Text-hierarchically these verses are subsumed under the section of addressing the Lord. A clear section break occurs at the start of verse 12, when the speaker places himself at the centre by using the phrase ܚܛܝܬ 'I have sinned'.

In version B, however, the addition of the verb ܚܛܝܬ in the first clause of verse 9 changes the relative position of the adjunct clause. While in version A the adjunct clause is clearly connected backwards, in B it may either be connected backwards or forwards syntactically.[13] The first reading gives:[14]

> ...ܐܠܐ ܣܡܬ ܠܬܝܒܘܬܐ ܥܠ ܕܝܠܝ ܚܛܝܐ، ܡܛܠ ܕܚܛܝܬ ܝܬܝܪ ܡܢ
> ܡܫܘܚܬܐ ܕܚܠܗ ܕܝܡܐ. ܣ̈ܓܝܘ ܚ̈ܛܗܝ، ܡܪܝܐ، ܣܓܝ̈ܘ ܥ̈ܘܠܝ ܘܚܘ̈ܒܝ.
>
> '... but You have put repentance for me, the sinner, as I have sinned more than the amount of the sand of the sea. My sins have increased, o Lord, my iniquities and debts have increased ...'

The second reading, on the other hand, yields quite a different structure:

> ...ܐܠܐ ܣܡܬ ܠܬܝܒܘܬܐ ܥܠ ܕܝܠܝ ܚܛܝܐ. ܡܛܠ ܕܚܛܝܬ ܝܬܝܪ ܡܢ
> ܡܫܘܚܬܐ ܕܚܠܗ ܕܝܡܐ، ܣ̈ܓܝܘ ܚ̈ܛܗܝ، ܡܪܝܐ، ܣܓܝ̈ܘ ܥ̈ܘܠܝ ܘܚܘ̈ܒܝ.

[13]The discussion here relates only to the syntactic dependency of the clause. From a discourse point of view, the clause relates both to the preceding and the following clause.

[14]Note that the traditional punctuation is replaced by modern punctuation, in order to facilitate the marking of the different interpretations. The traditional punctuation, a *tāḥtayā* after the first clause (ending in ܚܛܝܐ) and a *pāsoqā* after the second (ending in ܕܝܡܐ), supports the first reading.

> '... but You have put repentance for me, the sinner. Since I have sinned more than the amount of the sand of the sea, my sins have increased, o Lord, my iniquities and debts have increased ...' [15]

While both readings are plausible, the second one is preferable due to the general organization of the discourse: the ܡܛܠ ܕ 'since' phrase denotes the starting-point of a new section with several repeated ܡܛܠ ܕ phrases. The ܚܛܝܬ 'I have sinned' phrase is later repeated twice in verse 12, thus contributing to the uniformity of the section. All of this leads to seeing the beginning of verse 9 as the boundary between the two sections.

Likewise, the association of the phrase ܝܬܝܪ ܡܢ ܡܢܝܢܐ ܕܚܠܗ ܕܝܡܐ 'more than the amount of the sand of the sea' in version B is ambiguous: it can either be associated forwards to the clause ܣܓܝܘ ܚܛܗܝ 'my sins have increased' (like in version A) or it can be associated backwards to the clause ܡܛܠ ܕܚܛܝܬ 'because I have sinned'. Both readings are possible semantically and syntactically and the parallelism with version A suggests the first reading. The second interpretation, however, which is also reflected in the two alternative translations given above, is supported by the interpunction in B (which has a *pāsoqā* after this phrase and not before). In this interpretation there is a neat parallelism between the clause ܣܓ̈ܝܘ ܚܛܗ̈ܝ and the following clause ܣܓ̈ܝܘ ܥܘ̈ܠܝ ܘܚܘ̈ܒܝ 'my iniquities and debts have increased'.

Schematically, the transition between sections 3 and 4 is presented in table 4.7 (some clauses are omitted). Our division of the texts into the sections 7b–11, 12–13a (version A) and 7–8, 9–13a (version B) is different from the thematic and literary division that discerns separate sections in the 'confession' in verses 8–10 and the 'entreaty' starting in verse 11.[16] Apart from thematic considerations

[15]For the ܡܛܠ clause preceding the matrix clause compare, e.g. *Book of the Laws of the Countries* 542 (ed. Drijvers p. 8, lines 6–8) ܡܛܠ ܕܗܝܡܢܘܬܐ ܠܝܬ ܒܗܘܢ ܐܦ ܠܐ ܠܡܬܛܦܝܣܘ ܡܫܟܚܝܢ 'Because faith is not in them, they cannot be convinced'; ibid. 543 (ed. Drijvers p. 8, lines 18–19) ܘܡܛܠ ܕܐܦ ܥܠ ܐܠܗܐ ܡܬܦܠܓܘ ܡܬܦܠܓܝܢ ܐܦ ܠܐ ܕܚܠܬܗ ܐܝܬ ܒܗܘܢ 'and because they even seriously doubt about God, they also do not have the fear of God in them'. (We thank Dirk Bakker for these references.)

[16]Charlesworth, 'Prayer of Manasseh', 625; similarly Oßwald, 'Das Gebet Manasses', 20; Denis–Halewyck, *Introduction à la littérature religieuse judéo-hellénistique*,

V.	Version A	Version B
7b	ܐܢܬ	ܐܢܬ ܗܟܝܠ
	ܡܪܝܐ	ܡܪܝܐ
	ܐܝܟ ܒܣܝܡܘܬܐ...	ܐܝܟ ܒܣܝܡܘܬܐ...
8	ܐܢܬ ܗܟܝܠ	ܐܢܬ ܗܟܝܠ
	ܡܪܝܐ ܐܠܗܐ ܕܙܕܝܩܐ...	ܡܪܝܐ ܐܠܗܐ ܕܙܕܝܩܐ...
	ܐܠܐ ܣܡܬ ܬܝܒܘܬܐ...	ܐܠܐ ܣܡܬ ܬܝܒܘܬܐ...
9a	ܡܛܠ ܕܝܬܝܪ ܡܢ...	ܡܛܠ ܕܚܛܝܬ
		ܝܬܝܪ ܡܢ ܡܢܝܢܐ...
	ܣܓܝܘ ܚܛܗܝ̈	ܣܓܝܘ ܚܛܗܝ̈
9b	ܘܗܫܐ ܡܪܝܐ.	
	ܒܐܝܢܬ ܡܬܟܦܦ...	
10a		ܡܛܠ ܕܣܟܠܘܬܝ ܘܚܛܗܝ̈...
10b	ܡܛܠ ܕܐܒܐܫܬ...	ܡܛܠ ܕܚܛܝܬ ܐܦ ܐܒܐܫܬ...
11	ܘܗܫܐ...	ܘܗܫܐ...
12	ܚܛܝܬ ...	ܚܛܝܬ ܠܟ ...

Table 4.7: Transition between sections 3 and 4

for taking verse 11 as the start of a new unit, one could claim that ܘܗܫܐ 'and now' at the beginning of this verse functions as a macro-syntactic discourse marker comparable to ועתה in Hebrew,[17] of which it occurs often as a translation equivalent.[18] Nevertheless, we prefer to attach more weight to the asyndeton in verse 9 (version B) and verse 12 (version A) because we cannot automatically transpose insights about Hebrew linguistic elements to their Syriac translation equivalents, and Syriac ܘܗܫܐ still awaits a systematic investigation. If we restrict ourselves to the registration of formal characteristics,

I, 659; Newman, 'The Form and Settings of the Prayer of Manasseh', 107, takes verses 8–12 as the second main section of the Prayer ('Confession').

[17]Cf. Van der Merwe–Naudé–Kroeze, *A Biblical Hebrew Reference Grammar*, 333; Waltke–O'Connor, *An Introduction to Biblical Hebrew Syntax*, 634 (§38.1e).

[18]Cf. Borbone, Jenner *et al.*, *Concordance*, 265b. But note that there is not a one-to-one correspondence between the two particles. Other Hebrew words corresponding to ܗܫܐ in the Peshiṭta to the Pentateuch are נא (×7), הנה (×3), עוד (×2), הלא (×1), כה (×1) and על כן (×1). Six times the Hebrew ועתה is rendered with ܗܟܝܠ (ibid. 471–472; ועתה occurs in Gen 4:11; 11:16; Num 22:19; Deut 5:25 [21]; Deut 10:12; Deut 31:19).

the syndetic construction with ܘ, unlike the asyndetic constructions, suggests a relation to what precedes. Apparently, those scholars who consider verse 11 as the start of a new section do so on thematic grounds rather than because of the assumption that ܘܗܫܐ is a macro-syntactic marker, because none of them take 9b, where ܘܗܫܐ occurs as well (version A), as the start of a new section.

4.6 THE ALIGNMENT OF VERSES 9–10

4.6.1 Linear alignment and transpositions

As can be seen even from the short excerpts in the table above, in verse 9 a major mismatch occurs between the two versions. These mismatches can be analysed in two ways. A linear alignment between the two versions is presented in table 4.8. Each line in the table consists of 'clause atom' (normally a sequence of phrases containing one predication, or a vocative). If the entire clause atom is a plus, it is marked as such by a plus sign +. If part of the clause atom is added in one version, this part is underlined, and a small plus sign ₊ marks the line. The blocks mark major parallel or non-parallel passages. In total, there are 54 orthographic words which are considered as pluses in this approach.

Another option is to see the two versions as the result of transpositions of the same basic text. In table 4.9 the text in B is presented in its correct order, while in the A column the correspondences are given. Transpositions (between blocks) are marked by arrows. Again, entire clause atom pluses are marked by a big plus sign, while smaller additions are marked by an underline and a small plus sign. This approach yields 33 orthographic words, which are pluses.

The reduction of pluses from 54 to 33 graphic words (a reduction of about 40%) is done by one main transposition, transposition number 2 in table 4.9. In addition, instead of paralleling ܐܪܝܡ ܥܝܢܝ ܡܢ ܣܘܓܐܐ ܕܚܘܒܝ '(I do not have a rest that) I lift my eyes for the multitude of my iniquities' to ܐܚܙܐ ܪܘܡܗ ܕܫܡܝܐ '(I am not worthy that) I look at the height of heaven' as in the linear comparison, it is put alongside ܣܓܝܘ ܚܘܒܝ ܘܚܘܒܝ 'my iniquities and debts have increased'. The correspondence is in fact between the clause in B and the adjunct in A. Transposition number 1, on the other hand, just aligns the two vocations ܡܪܝܐ in the two versions.

A more doubtful parallelism (number 3) is between the clause ܘܠܝܬ ܠܝ ܢܝܚܐ 'and I do not have a rest' in A, which is aligned with ܘܠܝܬ ܠܝ ܡܟܝܠ ܐܣܝܘܬܐ 'and I do not have, therefore, a cure' far below in B, due to the similar construction.[19] On the other hand, transposition number 4 in the A column (between ܐܪܓܙܬ ܠܚܡܬܟ 'I provoked your fury' and ܥܒܕܬ ܒܝܫܬܐ ܩܕܡܝܟ 'I did evil before You') is a very local and obvious transposition.[20]

Consequently, it seems that these two verses are more similar to each other than appreciated at first sight. Thus ܡܪܝܐ ܣܓܝܘ ܥܘܠܝ ܘܚܘܒܝ 'Lord, my iniquities and my debts have increased' in version B, which in the first arrangement has no parallel in version A, has been put forward as evidence for the independence of version B.[21] In the second arrangement, it does have a match in the A column. Similarly, the 'repetition'[22] ܐܝܟ ܕܠܐ ܐܪܝܡ ܪܫܝ ܠܥܠ 'so I cannot lift my head upwards' in A does not have a match in B in the first alignment, but it does have one in the second alignment.

---

[19]Charlesworth has 'I do not deserve to lift up my eyes' in the main text of his translation (Charlesworth, 'Prayer of Manasseh', 636) and adds in a footnote (note k2) that the Greek text has 'and I have no relief' (καὶ οὐκ ἔστιν μοι ἄνεσις). Here, as elsewhere, what Charlesworth quotes as a difference between the Syriac and the Greek versions is in fact a difference between the Syriac version A on the one hand, and the Syriac version B and the Greek text on the other. Compare the following footnotes.

[20]The order in version B agrees with that in the Greek version. Thus, Charlesworth, 'Prayer of Manasseh', 636, note p2, refers to this as an inversion in the Greek since he translates version A.

[21]Thus e.g. Borbone, 'Preghiera di Manasseh', 548, note 5. Charlesworth, 'Prayer of Manasseh', 636, note c2, considers this an addition in the Greek (vis-à-vis the Syriac), apparently because he did not take into account version B.

[22]Borbone, 'Preghiera di Manasseh', 548, note 5.

V.		Version A	Version B	
9a		ܡܛܠ ܕ-	ܡܛܠ ܕܚܛܝܬ	+
		ܝܬܝܪ ܡܢ ܚܠܐ ܕܝܡܐ	ܝܬܝܪ ܡܢ ܡܢܝܢܐ ܕܚܠܗ ܕܝܡܐ.	+
		ܣܓܝܘ ܚܛܗ̈ܝ,	ܣܓܝܘ ܚܛܗ̈ܝ,	
			ܡܪܝܐ	+
			ܣܓܝܘ ܥܘ̈ܠܝ ܘܣܟ̈ܠܝ.	+
		ܘܠܝܬ ܠܝ ܢܦܐܫܐ	ܘܠܐ ܗܘܝܢ ܫܘܐ ܐܢܐ	
		ܕ-	ܕܐܚܝܪ	+
		ܐܪܝܡ ܚܬܝܬ	ܘܐܚܙܐ ܪܘܡܗ ܕܫܡܝܐ.	
		ܡܢ ܗܘ ܣܓܝܐܐ ܕܥܘ̈ܠܝ.	ܡܛܠ ܗܘ ܣܓܝܐܐ ܕܥܘ̈ܠܝ ܘܪܘܫܥܝ	+
9b	+	ܘܗܫܐ ܡܪܝܐ.		
	+	ܟܐܢܐܝܬ ܡܬܐܒܠܝ ܐܢܐ.		
	+	ܘܐܝܟ ܕܫܒܝܐ ܐܢܐ		
	+	ܡܬܦܪܥ ܐܢܐ. ܕܗܐ ܐܣܝܪ ܐܢܐ		
10a		ܘܟܦܝܦ ܐܢܐ	ܟܦܝܦ ܐܢܐ	
			ܕܡ ܘܪܟܝܢ ܠܬܚܬ	+
		ܒܫܘܫܠܬܐ ܕܐܣܘܪܐ ܕܦܪܙܠܐ.	ܒܫܘܫܠܬܐ ܕܐܣܘ̈ܪܐ ܕܦܪܙܠܐ.	
	+	ܐܝܟ ܕܠܐ ܐܪܝܡ ܪܫܝ ܠܥܠ.		
		ܐܦܠܐ ܓܝܪ ܫܘܐ ܐܢܐ	ܐܝܟܢ ܕܠܐ ܫܚܝܡ ܐܢܐ	
		ܕ-	ܕܐܬܗܦܟ	+
		ܐܪܝܡ ܚܬܝܬ	ܘܐܪܝܡ ܪܫܝ.	
	+	ܘܐܚܘܪ		
	+	ܘܐܚܙܐ ܪܘܡܗ ܗܘ ܕܫܡܝܐ.		
	+	ܡܛܠ ܗܘ ܣܓܝܐܐ ܕܡܟܐܒܘܬܐ ܕܪܘ̈ܫܥܝ.		
			ܡܛܠ ܕܣܟܠܘܬܝ, ܘܣܓܝܘ, ܚܛܗ̈ܝ, ܠܩܕܝ.	+
			ܘܠܝܬ ܠܝ ܡܟܝܠ ܐܣܝܘܬܐ.	+
10b		ܡܛܠ ܕ-	ܡܛܠ ܕ-	
			ܡܛܠ ܐܪܓܙܬ ܠܚܡܬܟ.	+
		ܥܒܕܬ ܒܝܫܬܐ ܩܕܡܝܟ.	ܘܟܠ ܕܒܝܫ ܩܕܡܝܟ ܥܒܕܬ.	+
	+	ܘܐܪܓܙܬ ܠܚܡܬܟ.		
		ܘܐܣܓܝܬ ܦܬܟܪ̈ܐ	ܠܐ ܓܝܪ ܥܒܕܬ ܨܒܝܢܟ	
		ܘܐܩܝܡܬ ܛܢܦܘܬܐ	ܘܠܐ ܢܛܪܬ ܦܘܩܕܢܝܟ	

Table 4.8: Verses 9–10 (linear alignment)

V.	version A	version B	V.
9	ܡܛܠ ܕ	ܡܛܠ ܕܣܠܩܬ	+ 9
	ܛܥܢܬ ܡܢ ܚܠܐ ܕܡܚܐ	ܛܥܢܬ ܡܢ ܡܚܣܢܐ ܕܚܠܗ ܕܡܚܐ.	+
	ܗܘܝܬ ܣܛܠܗܝ	ܗ̈ܘܝܬ ܣܛܠܗܝ	
+	ܘܗܫܐ		
	ܡܪܝܐ·	ܡܪܝܐ	
+	ܒܟܐܢܐܝܬ ܡܬܟܬܠܝ ܐܢܐ.		
+	ܘܐܝܟ ܕܫܘܝܐ ܐܢܐ		
+	ܡܬܦܪܥ ܐܢܐ.		
+	↕ ܕܗܐ ܐܚܝܕ ܐܢܐ		
	↕1 ⇐ (...)		
+	ܕܐܡܪܬ ܒܠܒܝ		
	ܡܢ ܗܘ ܠܟܐ ܕܟܠܒܐ.	ܗܘܝܬ ܒܟܠ ܘܣܟܪ.	+
10	ܐܦܠܐ ܒܪ ܫܘܐ ܐܢܐ	ܘܠܐ ܗܘܝܬ ܫܘܐ ܐܢܐ	
+	ܕܐܡܪܬ ܒܠܒܝ	ܕ—	
	ܘܐܣܘܪ	ܐܝܟ ܕ	
+	ܘܐܝܬܝܐ ܪܘܚܐ ܗܘ ܕܡܫܝܚܐ.	ܘܐܝܬܝܐ ܪܘܚܗ ܕܡܫܝܚܐ.	
	ܡܛܠ ܗܘ ܠܟܐ	ܡܛܠ ܗܘ ܠܟܐ	
	↕ ܕܡܬܐܢܬܐ ܕܪܘܫܡ.	ܕܒܟܠ ܘܪܘܫܡ	
	↕2 ܘܒܫܦܝ ܐܢܐ	ܒܫܦ ܐܢܐ	10
		ܕܟܝ ܘܪܒܝ ܠܗܘܬ	+
	ܒܗܘ ܠܟܐ ܕܐܘܪܚܐ ܕܦܘܪܩܢܐ.	ܒܗܘ ܠܟܐ ܕܐܘܪܚܐ ܕܦܘܪܩܢܐ.	
	ܐܝܟ ܕܠܐ	ܐܝܟܢ ܕܠܐ	
		ܡܫܒܚ ܐܢܐ ܕܐܬܦܬܚ	+
+	ܐܡܪܬ ܐܢܐ ܠܟܠ.	ܘܐܡܪܬ ܗܘܝܬ.	
		ܡܛܠ ܕܡܠܬܗ ܘܚܝܠܗ	+
		ܒܟܢ ܠܐܢܐ.	+
	⇒3 ܘܠܝܬ ܠܝ ܡܦܩܐ	ܘܠܝܬ ܠܝ ܡܫܠ ܐܫܬܘܕܥܘܬܐ.	+
	↕4 ܘܐܦ ܟܠ ܕܗܘܝܬ ܠܗܘܝܬܝ.	ܡܛܠ ܕܛܥܢܬ ܐܦ ܟܠ ܕܗܘܝܬ ܠܗܘܝܬܝ.	+
	ܡܛܠ ܕܟܒܪܬ ܒܛܥܝܬܐ ܡܕܡܝܢ.	ܘܟܠ ܕܟܒܪ ܡܕܡܝܢ ܒܟܒܪܬ.	+
	ܘܐܝܟܢܐ ܦܬܟܪܐ	ܠܐ ܒܪ ܒܟܒܪܬ ܡܥܒܕܝܢ	
	ܘܐܦܟܬܒܬ ܦܠܚܘܬܐ	ܘܠܐ ܦܠܚܬ ܦܘܠܚܢܝܢ	

Table 4.9: Verses 9–10 (alignment with transpositions)

4.6.2 Pluses unsolved by the transpositions

The transpositions do not resolve all differences between the two versions in these verses. In addition to some minor pluses in both versions that are not resolved by the transpositions, such as ܕܝܢ ܘܪܟܝܢ 'then, and reclining' in the B version, ܘܗܫܐ ܡܪܝܐ· ܒܟܐܢܘܬ ܡܬܟܐܒܠܝ ܐܢܐ. ܘܐܝܟ ܕܫܘܐ ܐܢܐ ܡܬܪܕܦ ܐܢܐ. ܕܗܐ ܐܣܝܪ ܐܢܐ 'and now, o Lord, I am justly afflicted, and as I deserve I am harassed, so that, behold, I am imprisoned' remains a substantial plus in the A version (apart from the vocation ܡܪܝܐ itself). This plus is not attested in the Greek or Latin witnesses.[23] The explanation of this plus in version A is controversial and plays a major role in the debate about the relationship between the two Syriac versions.

M. Ehrmann considers the plus a secondary element that has been added to 'correct the grammatical structure of verse 10' , because verse 10a (κατακαμπτόμενος πολλῷ δεσμῷ σιδήρου 'bowed down by many chains of iron') lacks a verb.[24] The question is, however, whether a scribe would use such a verbose way to ease the grammatical structure of verse 10. It seems to us that Ehrmann's application of the rules *lectio difficilior* and *lectio brevis* is too rigid. Moreover, the 'correction' is only needed, if at all, in the Greek version, because in Syriac ܟܦܝܦ ܐܢܐ in verse 10a is a complete clause. In other words, Ehrmann takes the plus in the Syriac as a solution of a grammatical problem in the Greek text, which implies that this reading in the Syriac goes back to a secondary reading in the Greek, although he does not make these implications explicit. Although Ehrmann's reconstruction is not impossible, to us it seems a complicated explanation for a relatively small problem.[25]

Other scholars have assumed that the plus is original and that the omission is secondary. Thus according to Charlesworth, this verse 'may be original', because 'it contains no ideas or images foreign to

[23] This means that here, again, version B agrees with the Greek text as against version A.

[24] Ehrmann, *Klagephänome im zwischentestamentlicher Literatur*, 155: 'die grammatikalische Struktur von 10a zu korrigeren'.

[25] Note that the transpositions suggested above make Ehrmann's analysis even more difficult, because they render it questionable whether the plus should be seen as immediately preceding verse 10a.

the prayer' and 'flows smoothly into the idea of being ensnared, in vs. 10'.[26] The assumption that this part of verse 9 is original, together with its absence in both the *Apostolic Constitutions* and the Greek biblical manuscripts, figures prominently in F. Nau's argument that the Greek texts of PrMan in all extant witnesses derive from the *Didascalia*.[27] Nau's analysis implies that the Syriac text of the A version is a translation from a Greek text in which this part of verse 9 was still there and which did not share the common error (omission) in all extant Greek witnesses, and that version B was translated from a Greek version that did share this error and hence did not contain the plus.[28]

4.6.3 Vocabulary counts

The transpositions in table 4.9 help us reconsider the relationship between the two versions without being bound by the order in which the elements occur in either version. It is still based, however, on a comparison of text segments rather than single words. Another approach would be to compare the vocabularies of the two versions and to apply the methods outlined in section 3.3 to these two verses. The results of the lexeme count on these two verses in given in table 4.10.[29]

Version	Lexemes	Version-Specific
A	53 (100%)	16 (30%)
B	58 (100%)	21 (36%)

Table 4.10: Lexeme count on verses 9–10

It should be borne in mind that the applicability of these measures to such short passages is problematic, and that any inference drawn from these data is tentative. Nonetheless, a comparison of the

[26]Charlesworth, 'Prayer of Manasseh', 636, note h2.

[27]Cf. above, section 1.2; Nau, 'Un extrait de la *Didascalie*', 136. See also Wilkins, 'The Prayer of Manasseh', 173.

[28]Although Nau himself does not mention version B, because his study was based on 17a6, an A-related manuscript (cf. section 1.5.4).

[29]The token count yields similar proportions: 28% version-specific lexemes in version A vs. 32% in version B.

data in table 4.10 and table 3.8 (p. 158) seems to indicate that the lexical variation in these two verses is bigger than the average lexical variation of the two versions. Conversely, the shared vocabulary (37 lexemes) is exactly 50% of the united vocabulary (74 lexemes), while the percentage for the entire texts is about 65%. In fact, these two verses account for much of the lexical diversity of the two versions: out of 25 version-specific lexemes of version A, 11 (44%) appear in these two verses. Similarly, 13 out of 36 (36%) version-specific lexemes of version B_0 (version B without the introduction) appear there.

4.6.4 Interim results

From this somewhat lengthy discussion of the verses 9–10 we can conclude that on the one hand it is possible to play down the large differences between the two versions that appear in the linear alignment, and that have played an important role in the scholarly discussion about the relationship between the various versions. The transpositions demonstrated that the two versions have more in common than is generally accepted. On the other hand, some pluses remain even after the transposition, and according to the vocabulary counts these verses account for much of the lexical diversity between the two versions. Finally, the plus in the A version remains a striking difference, but its impact on the relationship between the various versions remains disputed. If we consider it secondary (but not, as Ehrmann implies, as an addition that originated in a Greek text) it can easily be explained as an inner-Syriac addition in version A. If we consider it original (with Nau, Charlesworth), we are almost compelled to conclude that both versions go back to different Greek source texts, one with the plus (A), one without it (B).

4.7 Section 5

The fifth section has a strict parallelism between the two versions. It starts with an imperative ܫܒܘܩ 'forgive!' and develops in parallel in both versions. Here, again, our syntactic division of the text differs from some thematic divisions that can be found in the scholarly literature. The linguistic signals that in our view mark the beginning of a new paragraph are the change of the grammatical subject, the direct address by the imperative, and the asyndetic construction. Accordingly, we prefer to consider these verses as a separate unit, rather than taking verse 13 together with the two preceding verses as the 'entreaty'.[30]

The main difference between the two versions concerns the use of different conjunctions/relativizers (underlined). These differences, however, do not change dramatically the hierarchical structure. Possibly, the A version can be divided into five blocks and version B into four blocks due to these differences. This is presented in table 4.11.

The last block of B could be analysed as parallel (in the hierarchical sense) to the previous sub-block which begins in verse 14: ܘܒܝ ܬܚܘܐ ܐܢܬ 'and in me You will show' (due to the fact that both start with the conjunction ܘ). In such a case, the last block of version B would effectively be merged with the preceding one. However, we preferred the current analysis (in which verse 15 is dependent upon the initial ܫܒܘܩ ܠܝ 'forgive me'), since verse 15 clearly shows an inversion of the subject and object arguments: the 1st person is the subject while the 2nd person (the Lord) is the object.

As we have seen in our discussion of examples (22) and (23) on page 110, in the second block in both versions there is one clause that shares the negation with the preceding clause, but it is a different clause in each case.

[30] Thus e.g. Charlesworth, 'Prayer of Manasseh', 625. Oßwald, 'Das Gebet Manasses', 20, takes verses 11–14 together ('the confession of sin and the entreaty for forgiveness'). Ryle, 'The Prayer of Manasses', 612 takes verses 11–15 as one unit, which he calls the 'entreaty'.

V.	Version A	Version B
13b	ܫܒܘܩ ܠܝ ܡܪܝܐ	ܫܒܘܩ ܠܝ ܡܪܝܐ ܫܒܘܩ ܠܝ
	ܘܠܐ ܬܘܒܕܢܝ... ܘܠܐ ܠܥܠܡ ܬܪܓܙ ܥܠܝ. ܘܠܐ ܬܛܪ ܠܝ ܒ̈ܝܫܬܝ. ܘܠܐ ܬܚܝܒܢܝ ܘܬܐܣܪܢܝ ܒ̈ܬܐܚܬܝܬܗ ܕܐܪܥܐ.	ܘܠܐ ܬܘܒܕܢܝ... ܘܠܐ ܠܥܠܡ ܬܪܓܙ ܥܠܝ ܘܬܛܪ ܒ̈ܝܫܬܝ. ܘܠܐ ܬܚܝܒܢܝ ܒܬ̈ܚܬܝܬܗ ܕܐܪܥܐ.
	ܐܢܬ ܗܘ ܡܪܝ ܐܠܗܐ ܕܬ̈ܝܒܐ	ܡܛܠ ܕܐܢܬ ܗܘ ܐܠܗܐ ܕܐܝܠܝܢ ܕܬ̈ܝܒܝܢ
14	ܐܦ ܗܟܝܠ ܚܘܐ ܡܪܝ ܛܝܒܘܬܟ. ܘܟܕ ܠܐ ܫܘܐ ܐܢܐ ܦܪܘܩ ܐܢܬ ܠܝ	ܒܝ ܡܚܘܐ ܐܢܬ ܟܠܗ̇ ܛܝܒܘܬܟ. ܘܟܕ ܠܐ ܫܘܐ ܐܢܐ ܡܦܪܩ ܐܢܬ ܠܝ
15	ܡܛܠ ܗܕܐ ܐܫܒܚܟ ܒܟܠܝܘܡ.... ܡܛܠ ܕܠܟ ܡܫܒܚܝܢ... ܘܠܟ ܡܘܕܝܢ ܠܥܠܡ ܘܠܥܠܡ ܥܠܡܝܢ܀	ܘܐܫܒܚܟ ܘܐܩܠܤܟ ܒܟܠܝܘܡ... ܡܛܠ ܕܠܟ ܗܘ ܡܫ̈ܒܚܝܢ... ܘܕܠܟ ܗ̄ܝ ܬܫܒܘܚܬܐ... ܠܥܠܡ ܘܠܥܠܡ ܥܠܡܝܢ

Table 4.11: Section 5 (verses 13–15)

Chapter 5

Variant Readings

So far, we have compared the two versions that appear in the main text of the Leiden Peshiṭta edition (see section 1.6). However, the critical apparatus presents a range of variation that occur in other manuscripts, which are related to version A or B (see table 1.2). Thus in the case of version A the basis for the main text in the edition is manuscript 9a1, but other witnesses to this version include a number of biblical manuscripts and manuscripts of the *Didascalia*; in the case of version B the basis for the main text is manuscript 10t1, but this version is also attested in a number of Melkite Horologia (see table 1.2). The following sections deal with these manuscripts and the variation presented in them. These are interesting for two main reasons:

- The nature of the variation between the variant manuscripts and the main text is not very different from the nature of variation between versions A and B.
- Sometimes, the B-related manuscripts show an affinity to version A, and vice versa. In some cases, this further illuminates the nature of the grammatical difference between the two versions.[1]

These two facts, illustrated below, question the demarcation line put in the critical apparatus between the two versions and their textual witnesses, and the privileged status of the two main text versions.

[1] See footnotes 31, 50 and 112 in chapter 2.

The second point, especially, seems to hint that there was a continuous cross-influence between the two manuscript groups. This, in turn, may help us to understand better the relation between the two main text versions.

5.1 CROSS-SIMILARITIES OF MANUSCRIPTS

On several occasions, a manuscript of one 'manuscript family' (A or B) has a construction which diverges from its main text (the text of manuscript 9a1 for version A and that of 10t1 for version B) but, intriguingly, is similar to the main text of the other version. These 'cross-similarities' occur in all domains of the grammar and the lexicon. In some cases, the manuscripts use the exact wording of the other main text, but most of the times, it is only a similar grammatical construction or notion which is used. This raises the question as to whether the cross-similarities reflect influence from one version on the other, or whether the similar readings originated independently (*polygenesis*), due to the limited syntactic or lexical means of the language. (This question will be readdressed in section 6.3.1, where we discuss the question as to whether A and B are two independent translations from the Greek.)

Table 5.1 lists cases of similarity between the variant manuscripts of version A and the main text of version B. Similarly, table 5.2 lists similarities between variants of version B and the main text of version A. In both cases, syntactic variants are classified according to the section in which the difference between the main texts was discussed in chapter 2. For each case the number of the examples showing the difference between the two main texts is given. Other cases of variation are classified as pertaining to the 'lexicon' (see chapter 3) or to the domain of 'discourse arrangement' (see chapter 4).

Table 5.1: Similarities between A manuscripts and version B

Grammatical domain	Variant reading	Manuscripts	V.	See example / table
Genitive constructions	ܣܥܪܬܟ ܘܪܘܚܟ	13D1	5b	(4), p. 90[2]
	ܪܘܡܐ ܕܫܡܝܐ	14/8a1	10a	(7), p. 91
Appositions	ܡܪܝܐ ܐܚܝܕ ܟܠ	16g7	1	(16), p. 97
	ܘܕܟܠܗ ܙܒܢܘܗܝ	14/8a1	1	(16), p. 97
Mood	ܚܘܐ ܠܡܚܘܬܟ	14/8a1	14	(19), p. 107
Clause negation	ܘܬܠܝܪ	(10–19)D	13b	(22), p. 109
Verbal complements	ܠܐܒܪܗܡ	14/8a1, 16g7	8	(29), p. 116
	ܐܦ ܒ	*omnes*[3]- 17a6–9	14	(33), p. 118
Impersonal clauses	ܡܬܝܒܪ	14/8a1, 16g7	5a	(34), p. 119
Embedded clauses	ܡܥܒܕ ܕܢܡܘܣ	17a6-9, 16D2	5b	(42), p. 130
	ܘܡܬܬܘܐ ܐܝܬ ܠܟ…	16g7	7a	(43), p. 130, 3.3, p. 145
	ܘܬܐܒ ܠܟ…	14/8a1	7a	(43), p. 130
	ܐܝܟ ܕܠܐ[4] ܡܥܒܕ ܐܢܐ ܕܐܪܡ ܪܥܝ	14/8a1	10a	(44), p. 131
Conjunctions and clause connectors	ܕ̱ܐܝܬ	14/8a1	13b	(55), p. 137
	ܒ̱ܛܠܗܕܐ	All D	15	(57), p. 138
Lexicon	ܒܢܝ ܪܘܚܐ ܘܡܠܟ ܣܝܐ	16g7	7a	(59), p. 150

[2]Note that the genitive construction is the same as in the A version. Only the word order corresponds to version B.

[3]This refers to all A-family manuscripts except for 9a1. See table 1.2.

[4]This supports the alignment of A ܐܝܟ ܕܠܐ and B ܐܟܡܐ ܕܠܐ. See table 4.9, p. 175.

Table 5.1: Similarities between A manuscripts and version B (contd.)

Grammatical domain	Variant reading	Manuscripts	V.	See example / table
	ܢܓܝܪ ܪܘܚܐ ܘܡܪܚܡܢܐ	14/8a1	7a	(59), p. 150
	ܠܬܝܒܘܬܐ	14/8a1	7b	3.3, p. 145
Discourse arrangement	ܕܐܪܟܢ ܚܢܩ ܘܐܟܦܪ	14/8a1	10a	4.9, p. 175[5]
	ܕܐܪܟܢ ܚܢܩ ܘܐܟܦܐ	16g7	10a	4.9, p. 175
	ܐܡܝܢ	14/8a1	15	4.1, p. 164

Table 5.2: Similarities between B manuscripts and version A

Grammatical domain	Variant reading	Manuscripts	V.	See example / table
Genitive constructions	ܕܚܠܐ ܕܝܡܐ	*omnes*[6]	9a	(6), p. 91
Prepositional phrases	ܠܝ ܠܚܛܝܐ	*omnes*-13H5	8	(11), p. 93
Appositions	ܘܙܪܥܗܘܢ	*omnes*-13H5	1	(16), p. 97
Mood	ܫܒܘܩ ܡܪܝ	*omnes*	14	(19), p. 107[7]
Clause negation	ܘܠܐ ܬܛܪ (ܠܝ)[8]	*omnes*-13H5	13a	(22), p. 109

[5]This and the following variant, which replace the main reading of verse 10a ܕܐܪܟܢ ܚܢܩ ܘܐܟܦܪ ܘܐܟܦܐ support the transpositional alignment: the variants of the A family contain only verbs, just as their parallel in the main text of B ܕܐܓܢ ܘܐܟܦܐ (thus, the variants suppress one plus of version A). Note that according to the linear alignment we would expect to have just one verb, parallel to B ܐܪܟܢ ܢܦܫܝ (or another verb which is parallel to ܐܬܟܦܦܬ).

[6]This refers to all B-family manuscripts except for 10t1. See table 1.2.

[7]The relative order of the vocative and the imperative are different in the various manuscripts. 13H1.2 have ܡܪܝܐ as vocative. All manuscripts, however, omit the 2nd person pronoun ܐܢܬ.

[8]Only manuscript 15H1 adds the indirect object ܠܝ 'to me'. Cf. example (32), discussed on page 117.

Table 5.2: Similarities between B manuscripts and version A (contd.)

Grammatical domain	Variant reading	Manuscripts	V.	See example / table
Verbal complements	ܐܘܪܬ ܠܡܫܐ	*omnes*	3a	(25), p. 113
	ܕܠܟ ܡܘܕܝܢ	*omnes*	11	(30), p. 117
	ܫܠܝܬ ܡܪܝܐ	13H2–6, 15H2	12	(31), p. 117
	ܘܫܠܬܗܝ ܟܠܗܘܢ/ܟܠܗܝܢ ܒܥܐ ܐܢܐ	*omnes*-13H1	12	(27), p. 114
Impersonal clauses	ܡܣܬܒܪ(ܐ) ܗܘܬ	*omnes*-13H5	5a	(34), p. 119
	ܘܠܐ ܐܢܫ ܡܫܟܚ	*omnes*-13H5	5b	(35), p. 120
Clauses with an e.p.p.	ܕܠܝ ܡܫܟܚܢ	*omnes*	15	(41), p. 127
Embedded clauses	ܕܢܦܘܩ	13H4, 15H2	5b	(42), p. 130
	(ܘܦܘܫܬܐ) ܕܫܡܥ ܐܢܬ ܗܩܠܘܬܐ	*omnes*	7a	(43), p. 130
Conjunctions and clause connectors	(ܘ)ܐܦ ܟܕ	*omnes*-13H5	14	(56), p. 137
	ܐܝܟܢܐ ܕܐܘܕܐ (ܠܝ) ܘܐܫܟܚܢ	13H1–4.6, 15H1.2	15	(57), p. 138
	ܐܝܟܢܐ ܕܐܫܟܚܢ	13H5	15	(57), p. 138
Lexicon	ܘܐܪܐ/ܘܐܒ ܘܪܐܬ/ܐܪܬ	*omnes*	4	(58), p. 149
	ܡܬܡܨܐ ܐܢܐ	*omnes*	11[9]	3.4, p. 148
	ܘܐܫܟܚܢ ܟܠܟܡ	*omnes*	15	3.7, p. 157[10]

[9] The verb ܡܬܡܨܐ is added twice in most variant manuscripts. Manuscripts 13H1–5 add it in verse 11 before (or after) the verb ܒܥܐ. All manuscripts, except 13H5, add it as well in verse 13a, either instead of the verb ܫܐܠ or instead of ܒܥܐ.

[10] Note that the B version-specific verb ܐܠܨܝܢ is omitted in the variant readings.

Table 5.2: Similarities between B manuscripts and version A (contd.)

Grammatical domain	Variant reading	Manuscripts	V.	See example / table
Discourse arrangement	ܡܛܠ ܕܐܬܝܪ	13H4, 15H1	9a	4.6, p. 169
	ܕܐܪܝܡ ܚܛܗܝ (ܘ/ܕ) ܐܣܘܪ ܘܐܣܝܪܐ	*omnes*-13H5	10a	4.9, p. 175
	ܐܡܝܢ omitted	13H2	15	4.1, p. 164

5.2 OTHER VARIANTS

The previous section presented the variants that occurred whenever the two main texts were at odds regarding the text. This section, on the other hand, examines some cases of variation that occur where the main texts do not differ, or their difference is unrelated to the variant under consideration. Thus, these are variants which cannot be possibly linked to cross-influence. Again, the variants are classified according to their grammatical domain, insofar such a classification is possible. Since the main texts do not necessary differ at this point, we bring the main text of the relevant version in the table itself. Table 5.3 presents variation in the A family of manuscripts, and table 5.4 in the B family.

Table 5.3: Variation in the A family

Grammatical domain	Variant reading	Manuscript	Main text (A)	V.
Stem formation	ܕܐܣܝܪ	10D1, 16D1.2, 18D1, 19D1.2	ܕܐܣܝܪ	3b
Genitive constructions	ܕܦܘܠܚܢܝ ܕܠܝ	19D1.2, 20D2	ܕܦܘܠܚܢܝ	6
	ܒܘܪܟܝ ܠܒܝ	14/8a1, 16g7	ܒܘܪܟܘܗܝ ܕܠܒܝ	11
Prepositions	ܘܟܠܗ ܨܒܬܗܘܢ	14/8a1	ܥܡ ܟܠܗ ܨܒܬܗܘܢ	2

Table 5.3: Variation in the A family (contd.)

Grammatical domain	Variant reading	Manuscript	Main text (A)	V.
	ܩܕܡ	16D2[11]	ܡܢ ܩܕܡ	4
Appositions	ܐܒܪܗܡ	19D1.2, 20D2	ܐܒܪܗܡ	8
	ܘܠܗܘܢ	19D1.2, 20D2	ܗܘܢ	8
	ܡܪܝܐ ܐܠܗܐ	14/8a1, 16g7, 19D1.2, 20D2	ܡܪܝܐ	9b
	ܠܝ ܠܚܛܝܐ	14/8a1 , 16g7	ܠܝ ܕܝܠܝ ܚܛܝܐ	8[12]
	ܡܪܝܐ ܐܒܗܝ	14/8a1	ܡܪܝܐ	13b
Verbal Complements	ܦܪܘܩܝܢܝ	14/8a1	ܦܪܘܩ ܐܢܬ ܠܝ	14
Conjunctions	ܠܐ	18D1	ܡܛܠ ܕܠܐ	5a[13]
	ܘܕܠܐ ܣܟܐ	19D1.2, 20D2	ܕܠܐ ܣܟܐ	6
	ܘܐܢܬ ܡܪܝܐ	10D1, 16D1.2, 18D1	ܐܢܬ ܡܪܝܐ	7b
	ܘܗܐ	14/8a1, 16g7	ܕܗܐ	9b
	ܕܐܪܓܙܬ	14/8a1	ܘܐܪܓܙܬ	10b
	ܕܟܕ	All D	ܘܟܕ	14

[11]This variant was later corrected in the manuscript.

[12]Note that the same kind of variant reading occurs in the B family of manuscripts, though the main texts agree as for the appearance of ܕܝܠܝ, but not as for the prepositions (see example (11) on page 93). Whether this is a parallel development or due to influence is hard to determine.

[13]Note that this variant affects the boundary of the first section of the Prayer, presented in section 4.3.

Table 5.4: Variation in the B family

Grammatical domain	Variant reading	Manuscripts	Main text (B)	V.
Tense/aspect	ܕܚܛܝܢ ܘܬܝܒܝܢ ܠܘܬܟ	*omnes*-13H5	ܕܚܛܘ ܠܟ	7b[14]
Pronominal phrases	ܠܗܘ ܡܪܝܐ ܕܙܕܝܩܐ	15H1	ܐܢܬ ܗܟܝܠ ܡܪܝܐ ܐܠܗܐ ܕܙܕܝܩܐ	8
Genitive construction	ܕܠܝܟ ܕܚܝܠܐ	*omnes*-13H5	ܕܚܝܠܘܬܟ	4[15]
	ܕܫܘ̄ܒ ܕܠܝܟ	15H1	ܕܬܫܒܘܚܬܟ	5a
	ܟܠ ܚܝܠܘܬܐ	13H2.4.5, 15H2	ܟܠܗܘܢ ܚܝ̈ܠܘܬܐ	15
Prepositional phrases	(ܠ)ܐܒܪܗܡ ܘܐܝܣܚܩ ܘܝܥܩܘܒ	*omnes*	ܠܐܒܪܗܡ ܘܠܐܝܣܚܩ ܘܠܝܥܩܘܒ	8[16]
	ܚܝܠܘܬܐ ܫܡܝ̈ܢܐ	*omnes*-13H6	ܚܝ̈ܠܘܬܐ ܕܫܡܝܐ	15[17]
Appositions	ܡܪܝܐ ܐܠܗܐ	13H1.3.6, 15H1	ܡܪܝܐ	7b
	(ܘ)ܟܠܗܘܢ ܡܠܟܘܬܐ	*omnes*	ܒܟܠܗܘܢ ܡ̈ܠܟܘܬܐ	15[18]
Clauses with an e.p.p.	ܕܣܡܬܝܢ… ܠܚܛ̈ܐ	*omnes*	See ex. (36) and footnote 115, p. 121	6
	ܐܢܬ ܠܚܛ̈ܐ ܡܪܝܐ ܡܪܝܡܐ ܐܝܬܝܟ	*omnes*	See ex. (38), p. 122	7a

[14] Note the similarity to version A: ܕܬܝܒܝܢ.

[15] Notice the lexical similarity to version A.

[16] The first ܠ is only omitted in manuscript 15H1, making the entire phrase clearly appositive to ܠܙܕܝܩܐ.

[17] Manuscript 13H6 adds a linking ܕ yielding the possibly wrong phrase ܚܝ̈ܠܘܬܐ ܕܫܡܝ̈ܢܐ, analogous to the main text phrase of version B.

[18] All manuscripts omit the preposition ܒ, but only manuscript 13H3 adds the conjunction ܘ, effectively disturbing the apposition with ܒܟܠܗܘܢ.

Table 5.4: Variation in the B family (contd.)

Grammatical domain	Variant reading	Manuscripts	Main text (B)	V.
Conjunctions and clause connectors	ܠܒܪ	*omnes*	See ex. (36), p. 121	6
	ܘܐܝܬ ܗܟܝܠ	13H1	ܐܝܬ ܗܟܝܠ	7b
	ܐܝܬ ܠܒܪ	13H4, 15H2	ܐܝܬ ܗܟܝܠ	7b
	(ܘ)ܠܐ ܒܟܕܬ	13H1.4.5, 15H1	ܠܐ ܠܒܪ ܒܟܕܬ	10b[19]
	(ܕ)ܟܕ	*omnes*-13H2	ܘܟܕ	14[20]
Lexicon	ܣܘܪܚܢ	*omnes*	ܟܠ ܦܘܪܥܢ	9a[21]
	ܫܘܒܩܢܐ	*omnes*	ܐܣܝܘܬܐ	10a[22]

[19]Manuscripts 13H1 and 15H2 do not have the initial ܘ.
[20]Manuscripts 13H3.4 do not have the initial ܕ.
[21]Note the variant lexeme is version-specific.
[22]Manuscript 13H5 has the variant ܐܣܝܘܬܐ ܕܫܘܒܩܢܐ.

Chapter 6

Conclusions

6.1 Methodology of the comparative analysis

6.1.1 Independent analysis of the Syriac evidence

When we look at the existing studies about PrMan, or at the notes in modern annotated translations, it seems that variants in the Syriac versions are deemed worth mentioning most of all if they support variant readings in the Greek or if they are considered superior to the text preserved in the Greek version. Our aim, however, was to make an independent analysis of the Syriac text. Likewise, in the analysis of the differences between the two Syriac versions, our main concern was a comparison of the two versions in their own right, rather than evaluating the variant readings on the basis of their agreement or disagreement with the Greek version. A sound analysis of the Syriac versions of PrMan should start with the formal registration of differences, rather than a selective comparison with the Greek text. Many interesting variants between the two versions, especially the 'optional variation' between seemingly equivalent words or grammatical constructions and the non-linear vocabulary analysis would not have come to light if we had restricted ourselves to variants that have text-critical significance in relation to the Greek text.

6.1.2 Synoptic analysis and vocabulary counts

The linear synoptic analysis of parallels is appropriate to see in what places the two versions differ and how these differences can be explained. Many times this concerns cases of 'optional variation': words or grammatical constructions that are functionally or distributionally equivalent (see below, section 6.2). The non-linear word counts (section 3.3) address the question as to the relationship between the two texts at another level. They may reveal agreements between the texts that have been obscured by transpositions or other types of reorganization of the textual elements and therefore are not covered by a synoptic analysis.

The combination of these complementary approaches has played a central role in various constituents of the CALAP and Turgama projects (cf. section 2.2). In a linear alignment of two parallel texts some correspondences may remain unnoticed. If we abandon the strictly linear comparison (either by allowing for some transpositions or by non-linear vocabulary counts), it may appear that two texts have more in common than is appreciated at first sight. This was, for instance, the outcome of our comparative analysis of the story of Sennacherib's campaign against Judah in Kings and Chronicles. The computer-assisted analysis showed that the two versions had more in common than is visible in traditional synopses, such as Bendavid's *Parallels in the Bible*.[1]

The results of our analysis of PrMan were more equivocal. This appeared especially in our discussion of verses 9–10 (section 4.6), in which we combined a synoptic analysis (using both a linear alignment and a transposed alignment) with non-linear vocabulary counts: whereas the transpositional analysis showed that the two versions had more in common than usually suggested, the vocabulary counts demonstrated that in these verses A and B differ more than elsewhere in the Prayer.

In a way, these two methods – the synoptic analysis and the vocabulary counts – address two different facets of the linguistic data, which can be related to the notions of *langue* and *parole* in the structural tradition. The linear analysis deals with the texts as they appear: a sequence of linguistic signs – a syntagmatic axis – which can be paralleled to each other in order to discover syntactical paradigms – the paradigmatic axis. Thus, the analysis of the text in this form is the

[1] See Van Peursen–Talstra, 'Computer-Assisted Analysis of Parallel Texts in the Bible'.

analysis of *parole*. The vocabulary counts, on the other hand, take a holistic point of view. They approach the question of the linguistic knowledge needed to produce the texts. As such, they try to probe more directly the *langue*, or the underlying system, which lies behind the texts. For practical reasons, we have restricted our non-linear investigation to the lexical domain, but as has been argued in section 3.3 this approach can be extended to all levels of the linguistic system, taking into account morphological and syntactical constructions as well.

6.1.3 Equal treatment of the two versions

In Charlesworth's annotated translation he has the 'usual custom of following only the reading of 9a1' [i.e. our version A]. He deviates from this rule in his note to verse 13b where A has ܫܒܘܩ ܠܝ ܡܪܝܐ 'forgive me, O Lord'; and B has ܫܒܘܩ ܠܝ ܡܪܝܐ ܫܒܘܩ ܠܝ 'forgive me, O Lord, forgive me', on which he comments: 'The repetition throughout the PrMan suggests that the reading in MS 10t1 should be preferred. This choice breaks our usual custom of following only the reading of 9a1.'[2] Leaving aside the question as to whether his argument for following 10t1 [i.e. our version B] in this particular case is text-critically sound, his general custom can be challenged because there is no inherent justification for giving priority to either of the two Syriac versions.

Some of Charlesworth's observations are only valid if version B is ignored. This applies, for example, to his note to verse 4. The comment that 'this is the first occurrence of this pronoun [i.e. the suffix pronoun of the 2nd person in ܚܝܠܟ 'your might'] in Syr'[3] is imprecise, since it applies only to version A.[4] On verse 5b, in which A 'adds' ܡܣܝܒܪ 'endure', he comments: 'In Syr—but not in Gr—5a and 5b are linked by different forms of the same verb (...). The Syr. of this verse is superior to the Gr.'[5] But, again, his remark applies only to version A.[6] The same applies to some readings in verses 9–10 for

[2] Charlesworth, 'Prayer of Manasseh', 637, note z2.
[3] Charlesworth, 'Prayer of Manasseh', 635, note p.
[4] See above, section 2.4.1 (footnote 32).
[5] Charlesworth, 'Prayer of Manasseh', 635, note m.
[6] See the discussion of example (42) including footnote 139, p. 131.

which Charlesworth suggests that the Greek differs from the Syriac whereas in fact 9a1 differs from 10t1 and 10t1 agrees with the Greek.[7]

Despite these comments, Charlesworth is to be credited for the fact that he uses 9a1 and sometimes shows awareness of the readings in 10t1. Judith H. Newman, in her translation and commentary in Van der Horst–Newman, *Early Jewish Prayers in Greek*, follows always version A, without reference to version B.[8] Eva Oßwald seems to have used neither 9a1 nor 10t1, which reduces the value of her text-critical observations considerably.[9] The same applies, more justifiably, to earlier studies on PrMan, which appeared before the publication of PrMan in the Leiden Peshiṭta edition, and which show no awareness of the existence of a second version. Thus V. Ryssel refers to the Syriac verse 7b ܠܚ̈ܝܝܗܘܢ ܕܚ̈ܛܝܐ 'for the life of the sinners', which occurs in version A, as a free rendering of the Greek εις σωτηρίαν 'to salvation', but he does not mention the more literal rendering ܠܦܘܪܩܢܐ ܕܚ̈ܛܝܐ 'for the redemption of sinners' in the B version.[10]

For establishing the position of the Syriac versions within the complex textual history of PrMan, it is important to treat both versions as textual witnesses in their own right, without a priori priority to either version.

6.1.4 Importance of the Syriac versions

In the preceding paragraphs we saw some examples of scholars who refer to the Syriac versions of PrMan imprecisely or even incorrectly. Other modern translations and commentaries do not at all take into account the Syriac versions.[11] Thus the extensive discussion of the 'Metanoia-terminology' in PrMan in Von Stemm's monograph *Der betende Sünder vor Gott*, is completely based on the Greek text and

[7] See the footnotes in section 4.6. From our discussion in section 4.6 it appears that in general version B is closer to the Greek in verses 9–10.

[8] Van der Horst–Newman, *Early Jewish Prayers in Greek*, 165–180; cf. the reference to the Leiden Peshiṭta edition on p. 159; Newman is responsible for the section on PrMan in this volume (ibid. p. x).

[9] Cf. Oßwald, 'Das Gebet Manasses', 17–18.

[10] Ryssel, 'Das Gebet Manasse', 618.

[11] An exception should be made for Borbone's translation (Borbone, 'Preghiera di Manasseh'), which makes ample use of it and shows awareness of the two different versions.

therefore misses important differences between the Greek and the Syriac versions regarding the use of μετανοεῖν / μετάνοια and ܬܘܒ / ܬܝܒܘܬܐ (see section 3.1).[12] Likewise, Von Stemm's tradition-historical analysis (regarding the traditions that are based on Exod 34:6–7) should be modified if the Syriac versions are taken into account (see above, footnote 17 on page 151). We do not imply that a textual investigation cannot be restricted to a particular language (or even a particular manuscript); quite the contrary, since our research is dedicated only to the Syriac versions of PrMan. However, in such research the conclusions should be restricted to the versions under investigation. Thus, if one wants to draw any conclusions regarding PrMan *in general*, (s)he has to take into account the various ancient versions of PrMan, including the Syriac translation(s).

6.1.5 Text comparison and linguistic inquiry

So far, we have considered the various ways in which the study of the Syriac versions can enrich our knowledge of PrMan and its textual transmission. However, the study of parallel texts has another important function: enriching our knowledge of the linguistic system. As we mentioned in section 6.1.2 above, the texts are a particular instance of Syriac *parole*, of which we can extract some knowledge about the Syriac *langue*. While this is true of every linguistic corpus study, it is especially true for the study of parallel texts, since, by definition, they present us with cases of paradigmatic variation: two identical linguistic environments (clauses, phrases, words) that differ only in a restricted set of linguistic variables. The two differing linguistic expressions form a 'paradigmatic relationship', or, in other words, are 'distributionally equivalent'. Such variation is well-attested if various manuscripts of the same text have been preserved and occurs often, for example, in the critical apparatus of the Leiden Peshiṭta edition. Elsewhere we have tried to describe such variation as the text-historical counterpart of linguistic variation.[13]

[12] This is the more remarkable because it is concluded that 'im Gebet Manasses ist die Metanoia-Terminologie dominierend' (Von Stemm, *Der betende Sünder vor Gott*, 132).

[13] Van Peursen, 'Language Variation and Textual History'.

One general principle of corpus linguistics is to assume that formal variation corresponds to semantic variation. This is also true for the investigation of parallel texts; however, since we know that in many cases the two texts seek to express the same idea, it is quite probable that at least some of the formal variation is 'free variation', i.e. two differing linguistic forms expressing (exactly) the same idea. In such cases, the two expressions are 'functionally equivalent'. Nonetheless, this term must be used with caution, since, more often than not, the formal variation does establish some fine semantic nuance, be it a stylistic one or an information-structure difference. One example could be the use of the e.p.p. versus the existential copula, as described in section 2.5.6, which may have a bearing on the focus structure of the clause.

6.2 CHARACTER OF THE DIFFERENCES

In the light of the preceding discussion (section 6.1.5), it will come as no surprise that most of the variation between the two manuscripts can be classified as 'distributionally equivalent', and in some cases even 'functionally equivalent'.

In the grammatical comparison in chapter 2 we have seen the following examples of distributionally, and possibly functionally, equivalent constructions: the impersonal construction (covert generic subject) versus an overt generic subject (example (34), p. 119) and versus the passive construction (example (35), p. 120); the tripartite nominal clause versus the bipartite nominal clause (examples (39), p. 124 and (41), p. 127) and versus a clause with ܐܝܬ (example (36), p. 121); the simple direct object versus the pronominal agreement construction (example (25), p. 113) and versus the indirect object construction ('object introduced by Lamadh') (example (26), p. 114); a negated focus construction (with ܠܐ ܗܘܐ) versus an unmarked negation construction (with ܠܐ; example (24), p. 111); various conjunctions and connective adverbs (section 2.5.8, p. 134); the use of an NP with or without an accompanying apposition (section 2.4.5, p. 95); the possessive construction with suffix attached directly to a noun or to the possessive particle ܕܝܠ (examples (3), p. 90 and (4), p. 90); the genitive construction with ܕ with or without proleptic suffix (example

(5), p. 91).

The analysis of the vocabulary (chapter 3) leads to a similar conclusion, namely that most variants concern 'synonyms'. And even if we agree that a definition of 'synonyms' in the sense of 'two words with the same meaning' is problematic, the notion of 'functional equivalence' is appropriate to describe the variation of lexemes in the parallel texts.

The distributional and especially the functional equivalence raises the question as to what makes PrManA and PrManB two different versions. If the same type of variants are attested in the manuscripts of other books of the Peshiṭta Old Testament (cf. section 6.1.5), why did the editors of the Leiden Peshiṭta edition decide to present the text in two parallel columns, rather than taking one text as the main text and including the readings of the other version in the critical apparatus? Examining the different types of variants as listed in chapter 5 does not provide a clear answer, since most of the types of variation that are attested between the two main versions occur also within the A and B families (and hence are recorded in the critical apparatus of the edition), albeit in a more restricted manner. However, a closer look shows that most of the family-internal variation (tables 5.3 and 5.4) is in the domain of phrase syntax rather than clause syntax, whereas the clause syntax variations are less numerous in total and concern mostly cases of 'cross-similarities' between the manuscript families (tables 5.2 and 5.1).[14] A quick look at chapter 2 shows that there are 18 examples concerning morphology or phrase syntax, and 28 examples concerning clause syntax (not including 11 further examples regarding conjunctions in section 2.5.8). Thus, it seems that the variation between the two main texts is more 'global' in nature (i.e. it is at the clause level) while the internal variation is 'local' (phrase level).

Indeed, many verses exhibit multiple variation types when the two main versions are compared. A case in point is verse 7a: not only is the use of appositions different (see chapter 2, example (17), p. 98),

[14]With the exception, maybe, of the domain of clause connectors, which in many cases concern just a simple addition or omission of a ܘ 'and'. In any case, it should be borne in mind that tables 5.3 and 5.4 are not exhaustive, and many other 'phrase level' variants exist.

but also the lexical material differs (see chapter 3, example (59), p. 150) as well as the use of conjunctions (see chapter 2, example (48), p. 135), which affects the discourse arrangement (see chapter 4, section 4.4, p. 167). Therefore, it is not only the frequency of the variation that marks the fact that the two versions are different, but also the nature of the variation. It is true that the nature of the variation may ultimately be related to its frequency (more variation affects necessarily more linguistic domains), and there is not one type of variation that can be pin-pointed as specific to the discrepancy between the two versions (as opposed to the family-internal variation), but all in all, the decision of the editors of the Leiden Peshiṭta edition seems to be justified.[15]

6.3 THE TWO VERSIONS OF THE PRAYER OF MANASSEH

6.3.1 Text-historical conclusions

In section 1.6 we have seen that the scholarly opinions regarding the relationship between the two Syriac versions vary from 'largely different, though not wholly independent' (Baars and Schneider) to two independent translations from the Greek (Borbone). Especially Baars' and Schneider's formulation shows the difficulty of finding a way to do justice to both the differences and the agreements between the two versions. If we agree with them that 'the author of this particular version of the OrMan [i.e. our version B] is probably the same one who translated the Greek Melchite Horologion into Syriac',[16] in what sense are the two versions 'not wholly independent', and how should we account for the dependency?

Probing into the two versions, as we have done in chapter 2, shows that in fact the two versions differ almost in every clause. Indeed, a quantitative survey shows that about every second phrase differs in the two versions.[17] A closer examination shows that the large

[15] According to their introduction, two parallel texts are presented 'when two really divergent texts are available'. (*General Preface*, p. vii).

[16] Baars–Schneider, 'Prayer of Manasseh', Introduction, p. v.

[17] The exact percentage depends on the way the counting of phrases is done, and in particular if repetitions are taken into account or not (see section 3.3). The exact percentage of differing phrases varies between 40% to 60% depending on

V.	Common phrases	
2	Heaven and earth with all their ornaments	ܫܡܝܐ ܘܐܪܥܐ ܥܡ ܟܠܗ ܨܒܬܗ̈ܘܢ
7b	According to the sweetness of your grace	ܐܝܟ ܒܣܝܡܘܬܐ ܕܛܝܒܘܬܟ
7b	In the greatness of your compassion	ܘܒܣܘܓܐ ܕܪ̈ܚܡܝܟ
8	Lord, God of the righteous	ܡܪܝܐ ܐܠܗܐ ܕܙܕܝ̈ܩܐ
11	The knees of my heart	ܒܘܪ̈ܟܘܗܝ ܕܠܒܝ
13b	In the depths of earth	ܒܬܚܬܝ̈ܬܗ ܕܐܪܥܐ
15	All the heavenly powers	ܟܠܗܘܢ ܚܝ̈ܠܘܬܐ ܕܫܡܝܐ
15	Forever and ever	ܠܥܠܡ ܘܠܥܠܡ ܥܠܡܝܢ

Table 6.1: Common long phrases

majority of the phrases that are repeated identically in both versions are formed just by one lexeme (such as a verb or a conjunction) or by two lexemes (mostly a preposition followed by a pronominal suffix). The fact that such phrases are common to both versions is not surprising and does not necessarily demonstrate dependency between the two versions.

A small portion of the common phrases are longer and consist of three words or more. These are given in table 6.1. Examining these phrases reveals a striking fact: none of these are specifically linked to the prayer of Manasseh. Instead, they are phrases that are likely to appear in any liturgical context, let alone a prayer of penitence. They reflect liturgical phraseology common to both versions, rather than a genetic relationship between them.

A similar picture emerges when we examine the common 'core' of the two versions, i.e. the text that remains if we eliminate all differing phrases. The result is a prayer that is stripped of content: no more than the function words and some key phrases remain in common. Only at the end of the prayer are several passages rich in

---

these factors and the version used as baseline. In general, version B has a higher percentage of version-specific phrases.

V.	Common passages	
11	I am seeking your sweetness.	ܒܥܐ ܐܢܐ ܡܢ ܒܣܝܡܘܬܟ.
12	I have sinned, o Lord, I have sinned...	ܚܛܝܬ ܡܪܝܐ ܚܛܝܬ...
13b	forgive me, o Lord,	ܫܒܘܩ ܠܝ ܡܪܝܐ
	and do not destroy me	ܘܠܐ ܬܘܒܕܝܢܝ
	and do not be angry at me forever ...	ܘܠܐ ܠܥܠܡ ܬܪܓܙ ܥܠܝ...
	and do not condemn me to the depths of earth ...	ܘܠܐ ܬܚܝܒܝܢܝ ܒܬܚܬܝܬܗ... ܕܐܪܥܐ.
14	and although I am not worthy ...	ܘܟܕ ܠܐ ܫܘܐ ܐܢܐ...
15	I shall praise You ...	ܐܫܒܚܟ...
	Because all the heavenly powers praise You ...	ܡܛܠ ܕܠܟ ܡܫܒܚܝܢ ܟܠܗܘܢ... ܚܝܠܘܬܐ ܕܫܡܝܐ.
	forever and ever.	ܠܥܠܡ ܘܠܥܠܡ ܥܠܡܝܢ

Table 6.2: Common passages at the end of the Prayer

content, which are shared almost verbatim by the two versions,[18] as shown in table 6.2.[19]

Not surprisingly, these passages coincide with the sections we entitled as 'Admission of sins' and 'Asking for forgiveness', again reinforcing the idea that the similar wording of the two versions is related to their liturgical function rather than to any direct influence. Indeed, the rest of the similarities, being chiefly of semantic nature, can be accounted for by the assumption that the two versions are independent translations of the Greek text, without assuming any further influence between the two versions.[20]

---

[18] An exception is the passage in verse 8 ܕ(ܐܦ)ܠܐ ܚܛܘ ܠܟ. ܐܠܐ ܣܡܬ ܬܝܒܘܬܐ (ܒ)ܠܝ ܕܝܠܝ ܚܛܝܐ 'who did not sin against You, but You have put repentance for me, I who am a sinner', but note that the match is not perfect.

[19] We allow here for some marginal orthographic variation in ܬܘܒܕܝܢܝ. See section 2.3.4.

[20] The common view that the Syriac versions were translated from a Greek rather than a Hebrew original seems to be confirmed by the divergence of the two versions, since we may assume that a Hebrew original would yield more similar translations in Syriac.

Another reason to treat PrManA and PrManB as two separate and probably independent versions is the situation in verses 9–10 (section 4.6). In our synoptic analysis of these verses we saw that the answer to the question as to which lines in these verses are parallel is not so clear, because both versions express similar ideas, and there are various ways in which the parallels can be aligned in a synopsis. With some transpositions, the two versions appeared to have more in common than is generally accepted. However, the transpositions did not resolve all differences, and some striking pluses remained. Moreover, the exceptional status of verses 9–10 became clear from our vocabulary analysis, because these verses contain a disproportional number of version-specific lexemes in both A and B. This suggests that in these verses the divergence between the two versions is stronger than in the rest of the Prayer.

The divergence between the two versions in verses 9–10 may even suggest that they do not reflect the same Greek version, but rather that the respective Greek source texts of the two Syriac versions differed as well. However, as our research focuses on the Syriac versions, the question as to whether or not we can postulate intermediate stages between the original Greek version on which both versions rely and the respective Greek source texts of the two versions does not concern us here.

To conclude our discussion about the relationship between the two Syriac versions, we cannot know for sure whether the scribe or translator of the later version (presumably, version B) knew the earlier version (version A) directly or indirectly, but such an assumption is not needed in order to account for the similarities. The similarities at the content level and the outline of the prayer can be explained by the fact that both versions rely ultimately on one common Greek version, and the more specific similarities in wording can mostly, if not entirely, be explained by a shared liturgical heritage of the two scribes.

6.3.2 Two different linguistic profiles?

Looking at the linguistic variants, a general picture emerges that version B has a little more 'relief', it contains more 'emphatic' structures, and makes a broader use of the 'niceties of Syriac syntax',[21] to express certain nuances or to make the information structure more explicit. At times it seems to contain more idiomatic Syriac than version A, even though with our present state of knowledge of Syriac it is often difficult to evaluate which constructions can be considered idiomatic. Thus B uses the tripartite nominal clause where A has an ܐܝܬ clause (example (36), p. 121) or a bipartite nominal clause (example (41), p. 127). Twice it uses a focalizing ܗܘ (examples (41), p. 127 and (37), p. 122) and in one of these cases ܗܘ is preceded by ܕܝܠ as against ܠ in A (example (37), p. 122). In two other cases it uses ܕܝܠ as opposed to a normal possession construction in A (examples (3), p. 90 and (4), p. 90). It uses the pronominal agreement construction for the object (example (25), p. 113) and the genitive construction (example (5), p. 91) and it shows richer variation in the use of pronouns referring to God that provide the backbone of the first part of the Prayer (section 2.4.1, p. 87). This seems to concur with the vocabulary analysis, because B has a richer vocabulary than A. Admittedly, this general characterization describes merely a tendency. A counter example is example (24), p. 111, where A has a negated focus construction as against an unmarked construction in B.

Indeed, because so many differences between the two versions are in one way or another 'equivalent', it is hard to draw any conclusion about the linguistic profiles of the separate versions. Moreover, in the current state of research the equivalents that we encountered do not lend themselves easily to a categorization in terms of linguistic profile. The impersonal construction versus a passive construction, for example, does not lend itself to a typological, dialectal or diachronic classification.

Some of the features, however, which are related to B's linguistic 'relief', may reflect a diachronic development (assuming that version B reflects a more recent tradition of PrMan). Admittedly, in the current stage of research we lack benchmarks to evaluate the phenomena in the two versions of PrMan as they developed over time, but typologically we can postulate a tendency that constructions that

[21]This expression comes from Gideon Goldenberg; see his 'On Some Niceties of Syriac Syntax'.

start as marked constructions are gradually weakened and that in the end new devices are developed with the same function. Elsewhere we have argued that this may be the case with the tripartite nominal clause, which seems to have started as a marked construction that was used to clarify the information structure of the clause, but eventually became an unmarked construction.[22] Another example is the weakening of the emphatic state in Aramaic/Syriac from a form that marked determination to an unmarked form, which led to the use of the demonstrative as a new means to express determination. Similarly, one could argue that the more frequent use of the 'niceties of Syriac syntax' in the B version reflects a later typological stage in the development of Syriac, in which these constructions are less marked.[23]

Some differences between the two versions may be related to the contexts in which these texts may have functioned. Whether the linguistic 'relief' of B can be related to its use in liturgy as part of the Melkite Horologion is hard to tell. Apart for this 'relief' there are some version-specific elements in B that can more easily be related to its use in liturgy. Thus at the end of the prayer B has ܐܡܝܢ (cf. section 4.2; but note that there are variant readings: some Horologia do not have it, whereas some witnesses to version A do) and a more elaborate doxology (see table 6.3).

The variant readings in the B-manuscripts, which read ܡܠܟܘܬܐ 'kingdom' instead of ܩܘܠܣܐ ܘܪܘܪܒܐ 'praise and exaltation', and especially the variant of manuscript 13H6, which reads ܡܠܟܘܬܐ ܘܚܝܠܐ ܘܬܫܒܘܚܬܐ 'the kingdom and the power and the glory' make this doxology more in agreement with the doxology of the Lord's Prayer (Matthew 6:13), which can also be well accounted for in a liturgical context. Another variant reading that may reflect liturgical usage is the shift to the first person plural (although this happens only once, in one manuscript: in verse 13b manuscript 13H2 has ܥܠܝܢ '(and do not be angry) with us' instead of ܥܠܝ 'with me').[24] There are also

[22]Cf. Van Peursen, 'Three Approaches to the Tripartite Nominal Clause in Syriac', 163.

[23]This paragraph is the elaboration of a suggestion of Dr Alain Desreumaux, for which we are indebted to him.

[24]Compare the use of the plural in the main text of both A and B in verse 1 'our

V.	Version A	Version B
15	ܡܛܠ ܕܠܟ ܡܫܒܚܝܢ ܟܠܗܘܢ ܚܝܠܘܬܐ ܕܫܡܝܐ. ܘܠܟ ܡܙܡܪܝܢ ܠܥܠܡ ܘܠܥܠܡ ܥܠܡܝܢ Because all the heavenly powers praise You, and sing for You forever and ever.	ܡܛܠ ܕܠܟ ܗܘ ܡܫܒܚܝܢ ܟܠܗܘܢ ܚܝܠܘܬܐ ܕܫܡܝܐ ܘܕܝܠܟ ܗܝ ܬܫܒ̄ܘ ܘܩܘܠܣܐ ܘܪܘܡܪܡܐ ܠܥܠܡ ܘܠܥܠܡ ܥܠܡܝܢ ܐܡܝܢ Because it is You that the heavenly powers praise, and yours are the hymns and praise and exaltation forever and ever. *Amen*

Table 6.3: The doxology at the end of the prayer

some variant readings to version B that add more repetition and that put more emphasis on repentance. Obviously any attempt to relate these characteristics of version B to its liturgical usage can only be very tentative.

Can we go beyond the linguistic differences and the indications for liturgical use and identify theological differences between the two versions? Here our argumentation becomes even more tentative, but there seem to be some slight differences regarding the possibility for human beings to repent; whether they are able to repent on their own, or repentance is solely a gift attributed by God. In this vein we can understand the difference given in example (46) (p. 133, see especially footnote 145 on the same page), where in version A God promises ܫܘܒܩܢܐ 'forgiveness' to the repenters, while in version B He promises ܬܝܒܘܬܐ 'repentance' to the sinners. Similarly, the parallelism in verse 10a between A ܐܦܠܐ ܓܝܪ ܫܘܐ ܐܢܐ ܕܐܪܝܡ ܥܝܢ̈ܝ 'I am not worthy to lift my eyes' and B ܠܐ ܡܫܟܚ ܐܢܐ ܕܐܬܗܦܟ ܘܐܪܝܡ ܢܦܫܝ 'I cannot turn around and lift my soul (myself)' can be interpreted as a theological difference: in version B the (im)possibility of repentance is epistemic, having to do with the capabilities of the human being, while in version A it is deontic, having to do with God's

fathers', discussed in section 1.5.7.

evaluation of the human being.[25]

In this respect, the occurrence of the superscription concerning Manasseh's captivity in the bull[26] in the Horologia is remarkable. We would expect it rather in a narrative context (e.g. in an appendix to Chronicles) or in a context of instruction (as in the *Didascalia*), rather than in a liturgical context. However, in contrast to the *Didascalia*, where the story of Manasseh is told in length, in the Horologion there is no other reference to the alleged historical context of the Prayer. Thus, it may seem that the composer or translator of the Horologion felt a need to complete this lack of context with a short narrative passage. Indeed, in an interesting, and unexpected way, liturgical and narrative traditions flow together in the Horologion manuscripts.

[25]Note, however, that this parallelism disappears if we admit the transpositional analysis which we give in table 4.9, p. 175.

[26]See section 1.7.

Appendix A

Text and Translation of the Two Versions

The following table gives the integral text of the two versions together with their translation.[1]

The translation is as literal as possible, and attempts to reflect the Syriac grammatical differences between the two versions by parallel English 'grammatical' differences (which may not be idiomatic in English).[2] Whenever version B uses the 1st or 2nd person in the appositive clauses in verses 1–4, which is hard to translate correctly into English, this is indicated explicitly. Equivalents of the Syriac text which obscure the English meaning are put in parentheses. Following Charlesworth, we divide some verses into two units.[3]

---

[1]Note that this is not a replacement of the Leiden Peshiṭta edition, since it does not include the critical apparatus. Rather, its aim is to be used as an easy reference for the reader.

[2]For an idiomatic translation, see Charlesworth, 'Prayer of Manasseh'. Our translation bears upon Charlesworth's 'literal translation', but it differs also from it in several points, either because of different wording or interpretation, or because we choose to emphasis the difference between the two versions (necessarily leading to a very unidiomatic translation).

[3] The division of verses 5, 7 and 9 follows Charlesworth. We have further divided verses 3, 10 and 13 into smaller units. The division of verses 3 and 13 is motivated by the hierarchical structure (see sections 4.2 and 4.3), while verse 10 is divided into two units to more easily track the parallelisms between the two versions at this point (see section 4.6).

Table A.1: Text and Translation of the Two Versions

V.	Version A	Version B
S.	ܨܠܘܬܐ ܕܡܢܫܐ.	ܨܠܘܬܐ ܕܡܢܫܐ ܡܠܟܐ ܕܒܢ̈ܝ ܐܝܣܪܐܝܠ
	Prayer of Manasseh	Prayer of Manasseh, king of the Israelites
		ܟܕ ܐܫܬܒܝ ܠܒܒܠ ܘܨܒܘ ܕܢܘܩܕܘܢܝܗܝ، ܘܐܬܬܘܝ، ܟܕ ܗܘ ܒܓܘ ܬܘܪܐ ܕܢܚܫܐ ܘܨܠܝ ܘܐܬܬܒܪ ܬܘܪܐ ܕܢܚܫܐ ܘܐܫܬܟܚ ܡܟܝܠ ܕܠܐ ܢܟܝܢ ܒܐܘܪܫܠܡ
		when he was conducted in captivity in Babel, and they wanted to burn him; he felt sorry when he was inside the brazen bull, he prayed and the bull was broken into pieces, so that he found himself safe and sound in Jerusalem.
1	ܡܪܝܐ ܐܠܗܐ ܕܐܒܗ̈ܝܢ. ܐܠܗܗ ܕܐܒܪܗܡ ܘܕܐܝܣܚܩ ܘܕܝܥܩܘܒ ܘܕܙܪܥܗܘܢ ܙܕܝܩܐ.	ܡܪܝܐ ܫܡܝܢܐ ܐܚܝܕ ܟܠ. ܐܠܗܐ ܕܐܒ̈ܗܬܢ. ܕܐܒܪܗܡ ܘܕܐܝܣܚܩ ܘܕܝܥܩܘܒ ܘܕܟܠܗ ܙܪܥܗܘܢ ܙܕܝܩܐ
	O Lord, God of our fathers, God of Abraham, of Isaac and of Jacob and of all their righteous seed;	O celestial Lord, almighty, God of our fathers, of Abraham, of Isaac and of Jacob and of all their righteous seed.
2	ܗܘ ܕܥܒܕ ܫܡܝܐ ܘܐܪܥܐ ܥܡ ܟܠܗ ܨܒܬܗܘܢ.	ܗܘ ܕܥܒܕܬ ܫܡܝܐ ܘܐܪܥܐ ܥܡ ܟܠܗ ܨܒܬܗܘܢ[.]
	The one who created heaven and earth with all their ornaments;	The one who created (2nd) heaven and earth with all their ornaments.
3a	ܗܘ ܕܐܣܪ ܝܡܐ ܘܐܣܝܡܗ ܒܦܘܩܕܢܐ ܕܡܠܬܗ.	ܐܢܬ ܕܐܣܪܬܝܗܝ، ܠܝܡܐ ܒܡܠܬܐ ܕܦܘܩܕܢܟ.
	The one who bound the sea, and placed it by the commandment of his word;	You, who bound it, the sea, by the word of your commandment;

V.	Version A	Version B
3b	ܗܘ ܕܐܚܕ ܬܗܘܡܐ ܘܚܬܡܗ ܒܫܡܗ ܕܕܚܝܠܐ ܘܡܫܒܚܐ. The one who held the Abyss, and sealed it by his fearful and glorified name.	ܡܢ ܕܐܚܕܬ ܠܬܗܘܡܐ ܘܚܬܡܬܝܗ̇، ܒܫܡܐ ܕܝܠܟ ܕܕܚܝܠܐ ܘܡܫܒܚܐ. Who held (2nd) the Abyss, and sealed (2nd) it by the fearful and glorious name of yours.
4	ܗܘ ܕܟܠܡܕܡ ܕܚܠ ܘܪܬܐ ܡܢ ܩܕܡ ܚܝܠܟ. The one before whose might (2nd) everything fears and trembles.	ܗܘ ܕܟܠ ܡܕܡ ܪܥܠ ܘܡܬܒܥܬ ܡܢ ܩܕܡ ܦܪ̈ܨܘܦܐ ܕܫܠܝܛܘܬܟ. The one in whose face of might (2nd) everything quivers and is terrified.
5a	ܡܛܠ ܕܠܐ ܡܣܬܝܒܪܐ ܪܒܘܬ ܫܘܦܪܐ ܕܬܫܒܘܚܬܟ. Because the greatness of the beauty of your honour cannot be endured,	ܡܛܠ ܕܠܐ ܡܣܝܒܪ ܠܪܒܘܬ ܫܘܦܪܐ ܕܬܫܒܘܚܬܟ[.] Because one does not endure the greatness of the elegance of your honour,
5b	ܘܠܐ ܐܢܫ ܡܫܟܚ ܡܣܝܒܪ ܕܢܩܘܡ ܩܕܡ ܪܘܓܙܟ ܘܚܡܬܟ ܕܥܠ ܚܛܝܐ. And no man can endure standing in front of your rage and fury (which are) on sinners.	ܘܠܐ ܡܫܟܚ ܠܡܩܡ ܩܕܡ ܚܡܬܐ ܘܪܘܓܙܐ ܕܝܠܟ ܕܥܠ ܚܛܝܐ. And it is not possible to stand in front of the fury and rage of yours (which are) on sinners.
6	ܕܠܐ ܣܟܐ ܕܝܢ ܘܕܠܐ ܟܝܠܐ ܐܝܬܝܗܘܢ ܪܚܡܐ ܕܫܘ̈ܘܕܝܟ. Without limit, however, and without measure is the tenderness of your promises.	ܠܐ ܡܬܬܚܡܢܐ ܗܘ ܟܝܬ ܘܠܐ ܡܬܒܨܝܢܐ ܛܘܝܒܐ ܕܫܘ̈ܘܕܝܟ. Infinite, indeed, and inscrutable is the readiness of your declarations.
7a	ܡܛܠ ܕܐܢܬ ܗܘ ܡܪܝܐ ܢܓܝܪ ܪܘܚܐ. ܘܡܪܚܡܢܐ ܘܣܓܝ ܚܢܢܐ. ܘܬܐܒ ܐܢܬ ܥܠ ܒܝܫܬܗܘܢ ܕܒܢܝ̈ܢܫܐ. Because You are the Lord, long-suffering and merciful and of great compassion, and You repent on the evils of humans.	ܐܢܬ ܗܘ ܟܝܬ ܡܪܝܐ ܡܪܝܡܐ. ܚܢܢܐ ܢܓܝܪ ܪܘܚܐ. ܘܣܓܝ ܠܛܝܒܘܬܐ ܘܩܘܫܬܐ ܡܬܬܘܝܢܐ ܕܥܠ ܒܝܫܬܐ ܕܒܢܝ̈ܢܫܐ. You are, indeed, the Lord, Most High, compassionate, long-suffering and of great grace, and truly You feel sorry over the evils of humans.

V.	Version A	Version B
7b	ܐܢܬ ܡܪܝܐ ܐܝܟ ܒܣܝܡܘܬܐ ܕܛܝܒܘܬܟ ܐܫܬܘܕܝܬ ܫܘܒܩܢܐ ܠܐܝܠܝܢ ܕܬܝܒܝܢ ܡܢ ܚܛܗ̈ܝܗܘܢ܂ ܘܒܣܘܓܐ ܕܪ̈ܚܡܝܟ ܣܡܬ ܬܝܒܘܬܐ ܐܝܟ ܕܠܚ̈ܝܝܗܘܢ܂ ܕܚ̈ܛܝܐ܂ You, O Lord, according to the sweetness of your grace, promised forgiveness for those who repent of their sins. In the greatness of your compassion, You have put repentance, (as) for the life of the sinners.	ܐܢܬ ܗܟܝܠ ܡܪܝܐ ܐܝܟ ܒܣܝܡܘܬܐ ܕܛܝܒܘܬܟ܂ ܐܫܬܘܕܝܬ ܬܝܒܘܬܐ ܕܫܘܒܩܢܐ ܠܐܝܠܝܢ ܕܚܛܘ ܠܟ܂ ܘܒܣܘܓܐ ܕܪ̈ܚܡܝܟ ܬܩܢܬ ܬܝܒܘܬܐ ܠܦܘܪܩܢܐ ܕܚ̈ܛܝܐ[.] You, therefore, O Lord, according to the sweetness of your grace, promised repentance of forgiveness for those who sinned before You. In the greatness of your compassion, You have fixed repentance for the redemption of sinners.
8	ܐܢܬ ܗܟܝܠ ܡܪܝܐ ܐܠܗܐ ܕܙܕ̈ܝܩܐ܂ ܠܐ ܗܘܐ ܠܙܕ̈ܝܩܐ ܣܡܬ ܬܝܒܘܬܐ܆ ܐܝܟ ܕܠܐܒܪܗܡ ܘܠܐܝܣܚܩ ܘܠܝܥܩܘܒ ܗܢܘܢ܂ ܕܐܦܠܐ ܚܛܘ ܠܟ܂ ܐܠܐ ܣܡܬ ܬܝܒܘܬܐ ܠܝ ܕܐܢܐ ܚܛܝܐ܂ You, therefore, O Lord, God of the righteous, it is not for the righteous that You have put repentance, as for Abraham, for Isaac and as for Jacob, those who truly did not sin against You, but You have put repentance for me, I who am a sinner –	ܐܢܬ ܗܟܝܠ ܡܪܝܐ ܐܠܗܐ ܕܙܕ̈ܝܩܐ܆ ܠܐ ܣܡܬ ܬܝܒܘܬܐ ܠܙܕ̈ܝܩܐ܂ ܠܐܒܪܗܡ ܘܠܐܝܣܚܩ ܘܠܝܥܩܘܒ ܗܢܘܢ܂ ܕܠܐ ܚܛܘ ܠܟ܂ ܐܠܐ ܣܡܬ ܬܝܒܘܬܐ ܥܠܝ ܕܐܢܐ ܚܛܝܐ܂ You, therefore, O Lord, God of the righteous, You have not put repentance for the righteous, for Abraham, for Isaac, and for Jacob, they who did not sin against You, but You have put repentance for me, I who am a sinner.
9a	ܡܛܠ ܕܣܓܝ ܡܢ ܚܠܐ ܕܝܡܐ ܣܓܝܘ ܚܛܗ̈ܝ܆ ܘܠܝܬ ܠܝ ܢܦܫܐ ܕܐܪܝܡ ܥܝ̈ܢܝ ܡܢ ܣܘܓܐ ܕܥܘ̈ܠܝ܂	ܡܛܠ ܕܣܓܝܬ ܝܬܝܪ ܡܢ ܚܠܐ ܕܝܡܐ܂ ܣܓܝܘ ܚܛܗ̈ܝ܆ ܡܪܝܐ ܣܓܝܘ ܚܛܗ̈ܝ ܘܣܓܝܘ܂ ܘܠܐ ܫܘܐ ܐܢܐ ܕܐܚܪ ܘܐܚܙܐ ܪܘܡܗ ܕܫܡܝܐ܂ ܡܛܠ ܣܘܓܐ ܕܥܘ̈ܠܝ ܘܪܘܫܥܝ܂

V.	Version A	Version B
	because my sins have increased more than the sand of the sea, and I do not have a rest to lift my eyes for the multitude of my iniquities.	Since I have sinned more than the amount of the sand of the sea, my sins have increased, O Lord, my iniquities and debts have increased and I am not worthy to gaze and look at the height of heaven because of the multitude of my iniquities and wickedness.
9b	ܘܗܫܐ ܡܪܝܐ܂ ܒܟܐܢܘܬ ܡܬܐܠܨ ܐܢܐ܂ ܘܐܝܟ ܕܫܘܐ ܐܢܐ ܡܬܛܪܦ ܐܢܐ܂ ܕܗܐ ܐܣܝܪ ܐܢܐ	
	And now, O Lord, I am justly afflicted, and as I deserve I am harrassed, so that, behold, I am imprisoned.	
10a	ܘܟܦܝܦ ܐܢܐ ܒܣܘܓܐܐ ܕܐܣܘܪ̈ܐ ܕܦܪܙܠܐ܂ ܐܝܟ ܕܠܐ ܐܪܝܡ ܪܝܫܝ ܠܥܠ܂ ܐܦܠܐ ܒܪ ܫܘܐ ܐܢܐ ܕܐܪܝܡ ܥܝ̈ܢܝ ܘܐܚܘܪ ܘܐܚܙܐ ܪܘܡܐ ܗܘ ܕܫܡܝܐ܂ ܡܛܠ ܣܘܓܐܐ ܕܡܒܐܫܢܘܬܐ ܕܒܘܫܝ܂	ܟܦܝܦ ܐܢܐ ܕܝܢ ܘܪܟܝܢ ܠܬܚܬ ܣܘܓܐܐ ܕܐܣܘܪ̈ܐ ܕܦܪܙܠܐ܂ ܐܝܟ ܕܠܐ ܡܫܟܚ ܐܢܐ ܕܐܬܗܦܟ ܘܐܪܝܡ ܢܦܫܝ܂ ܡܛܠ ܕܣܟܠܘܬܝ ܘܚܛܗܝ ܥܒܪ̈ܘ ܠܪܫܝ܂ ܘܠܝܬ ܠܝ ܡܕܝܢ ܐܣܝܘܬܐ܂
	And I am bent by a multitude of iron chains, so I shall not lift my head upwards. Nor, indeed, am I worthy to lift my eyes and look and see the height, that of heaven, because of the multitude of the harm of my wickedness,	I am bent, then, and inclining under a multitude of iron chains, as one who cannot(1st) turn around and lift my soul. because my follies and my sins have passed my head, and I do not have, therefore, a cure,
10b	ܡܛܠ ܕܐܪܓܙܬ ܚܡܬܐ ܕܪܘܓܙܟ܂ ܘܥܒܕܬ ܒܝܫܬܐ ܩܕܡܝܟ܂ ܘܐܩܝܡܬ ܦܬܟܪ̈ܐ ܘܐܣܓܝܬ ܛܢܦܘܬܐ܂	ܡܛܠ ܕܐܪܓܙܬ ܐܦ ܚܡܬ ܠܪܘܓܙܟ܂ ܘܟܠ ܕܒܝܫ ܩܕܡܝܟ ܥܒܕܬ܂ ܠܐ ܓܝܪ ܥܒܕܬ ܨܒܝܢܟ ܘܠܐ ܢܛܪܬ ܦܘܩܕܢܝܟ܂

V.	Version A	Version B
	because I did evil deeds before You, and I provoked your fury, and I set up idols, and multiplied abominations.	because I provoked your fury very much, and everything which is evil before You, I did. Indeed, I did not do your will, and I did not keep your commandments.
11	ܘܗܫܐ ܗܐ ܟܦܦ ܐܢܐ ܒܘܪܟܘܗܝ، ܕܠܒܝ ܩܕܡܝܟ. ܘܒܥܐ ܐܢܐ ܡܢ ܒܣܝܡܘܬܟ.	ܘܗܫܐ ܡܪܟܢ ܐܢܐ ܒܘܪܟܘܗܝ، ܕܠܒܝ. ܟܕ ܒܥܐ ܐܢܐ ܡܢ ܒܣܝܡܘܬܟ.
	And now, behold, I am bending the knees of my heart before You, and I am seeking your sweetness.	And now I am inclining the knees of my heart, when I am seeking your sweetness.
12	ܚܛܝܬ ܡܪܝܐ ܚܛܝܬ. ܘܡܛܠ ܕܝܕܥ ܐܢܐ ܚܛܗܝ،	ܚܛܝܬ ܠܟ ܡܪܝܐ ܚܛܝܬ. ܘܠܥܘܠܝ ܝܕܥ ܐܢܐ.
	I have sinned, O Lord, I have sinned, and because I know my sins,	I have sinned to You, O Lord, I have sinned, and my iniquities I do know
13a	ܡܬܟܫܦ ܐܢܐ ܩܕܡܝܟ.	ܐܠܐ ܫܐܠ ܐܢܐ ܟܕ ܒܥܐ ܐܢܐ ܡܢܟ.
	I pray humbly before You:	but I ask You, when I seek You:
13b	ܫܒܘܩ ܠܝ ܡܪܝܐ ܘܠܐ ܬܘܒܕܢܝ ܥܡ ܣܟܠܘܬܝ، ܘܠܐ ܠܥܠܡ ܬܪܓܙ ܥܠܝ. ܘܠܐ ܬܛܪ ܠܝ ܒܝܫܬܝ، ܘܠܐ ܬܚܝܒܢܝ ܘܬܫܕܝܢܝ ܒܬܚܬܝܬܗ ܕܐܪܥܐ. ܐܢܬ ܗܘ ܓܝܪ ܐܠܗܐ ܕܬܝܒܐ.	ܫܒܘܩ ܠܝ ܡܪܝܐ ܫܒܘܩ ܠܝ ܘܠܐ ܬܘܒܕܢܝ ܒܚܛܗܝ، ܘܠܐ ܠܥܠܡ ܬܪܓܙ ܥܠܝ ܘܬܛܪ ܒܝܫܬܝ، ܘܠܐ ܬܚܝܒܢܝ ܠܬܚܬܝܬܗ ܕܐܪܥܐ. ܡܛܠ ܕܐܢܬ ܗܘ ܐܠܗܐ ܕܐܝܠܝܢ ܕܬܝܒܝܢ.
	Forgive me, O Lord, and do not destroy me with my follies, and do not be angry with me forever, and do not keep for me my evils, and do not condemn me and banish me to the depths of earth. You are, indeed, the God of the repenters.	Forgive me, O Lord, forgive me and do not destroy me for my sins, and do not be angry with me forever nor keep my evils, and do not condemn me to the depths of earth, because You are the God of those who repent.

V.	Version A	Version B
14	ܐܦ ܗܟܝܠ ܚܘܐ ܡܪܝ ܛܝܒܘܬܟ. ܘܟܕ ܠܐ ܫܘܐ ܐܢܐ ܦܪܘܩ ܐܢܬ ܠܝ ܐܝܟ ܣܘܓܐܐ ܕܪ̈ܚܡܝܟ. Truly, thus, show, my Lord, your goodness and although I am not worthy, You will redeem me, according to the greatness of your mercies.	ܘܒܝ ܚܘܝܐ ܐܢܬ ܟܠܗ ܛܝܒܘܬܟ. ܘܟܕ ܠܐ ܫܘܐ ܐܢܐ ܡܦܪܩ ܐܢܬ ܠܝ ܒܣܘܓܐܐ ܕܡܪܚܡܢܘܬܟ. And in me You will show all your goodness, and although I am not worthy, You will deliver me with the greatness of your mercy.
15	ܡܛܠ ܗܕܐ ܐܫܒܚܟ ܒܟܠܙܒܢ. ܘܒܟܠܗܘܢ ܝܘ̈ܡܬܐ ܕܚܝ̈ܝ. ܡܛܠ ܕܠܟ ܡܫܒܚܝܢ ܟܠܗܘܢ ܚܝ̈ܠܘܬܐ ܕܫܡܝܐ. ܘܠܟ ܡܙܡܪܝܢ ܠܥܠܡ ܘܠܥܠܡ ܥܠܡܝܢ.❖ Because of this, I shall praise You at all times and at all days of my life; Because all the heavenly powers praise You, and sing for You forever and ever.	ܘܐܫܒܚܟ ܘܐܥܠܝܟ ܒܟܠܙܒܢ. ܒܟܠܗܘܢ ܝܘ̈ܡܬܐ ܕܚܝ̈ܝ. ܡܛܠ ܕܠܟ ܗܘ ܡܫܒ̈ܚܝܢ ܟܠܗܘܢ ܚܝ̈ܠܘܬܐ ܕܫܡܝܐ ܘܕܝܠܟ ܗܝ ܬܫܒ̈ܚܬܐ ܘܩܘܠܣܐ ܘܪܘܡܪܡܐ ܠܥܠܡ ܘܠܥܠܡ ܥܠܡܝܢ And I shall praise and extol You at all times, at all days of my life; Because it is You that the heavenly powers praise, and yours are the hymns and praise and exaltation forever and ever. ܐܡܝܢ[.] Amen

Appendix B

Transcription and Glossing of the Two Versions

The following sections give the entire transcribed text of the two versions together with glosses, following the notation given on page xvii. Note that some verses are divided into two parts as explained in footnote 3, p. 207.

B.1 Version A

ṣlotā da-mnaššе
prayer LNK-Manasseh

(1) māryā ˀalāhā d-ˀabāhay-n. ˀalāh-ēh
Lord God LNK-father.PL-POSS.1PL God-POSS.3
d-ˀabrāhām wa-d-ˀisḥāq wa-d-yaˁqob
LNK-Abraham and-LNK-Isaac and-LNK-Jacob
wa-d-zarˁ-hon zaddiqā.
and-LNK-seed-POSS.3PL righteous

(2) haw da-ˁbad šmayyā w-ˀarˁā ˁam koll-ēh
DEM LNK-do:PRF.3 heaven and-earth with all-POSS.3
ṣbat-hon.
ornament-POSS.3PL

(3) a. haw d-ˀesar yammā
DEM LNK-bind:PRF.3 sea
w-ˀaqim-ēh b-puqdānā
and-stand.CAUS:PRF.3-OBJ.3 in-commandment
d-mellt-ēh
LNK-word-POSS.3

b. haw d-ˀeḥad thomā w-ḥatm-ēh
DEM LNK-hold:PRF.3 Abyss and-seal:PRF.3-OBJ.3
ba-šm-ēh dḥilā wa-mšabbḥā
in-name-POSS.3 fear:PP and-glorify.INT:PP

(4) haw d-kol-meddem dāḥel w-zāˀaˁ men qdām
DEM LNK-all.CST-thing fear:AP and-tremble:AP from before
ḥayl-āk.
might-POSS.2

(5) a. meṭṭol d-lā mestaybrā
because LNK-NEG endure.INT.REFL:AP.3.EMPH
rabbut yāyutā d-tešboḥt-āk
greatness.CST beauty LNK-honour-POSS.2

b. w-lā (ˀ)nāš meškaḥ msaybar
and-NEG man.ABS can.CAUS:AP endure.INT:AP
da-nqum qdām rugz-āk w-ḥemt-āk
LNK-stand:IMPF.3 before rage-POSS.2 and-fury-POSS.2
d-ˁal ḥaṭṭāyē
LNK-on sinner.PL

(6) d-lā sākā dēn wa-d-lā kaylā ˀitay-hon
LNK-NEG limit however and-LNK-NEG measure EXP-POSS.3PL
raḥmē d-mulkānay-k.
mercy.PL LNK-promise.PL-POSS.2

(7) a. meṭṭol d-ˀa(n)t =(h)u māryā ngir ruḥā
because LNK-2 =3 Lord long.CST spirit
wa-mraḥmānā w-saggi ḥnānā.
and-merciful and-great.CST compassion.
w-tāˀeb =ˀa(n)t ˁal bišāt-hon
and-repent:AP =2 on evil.F.PL-POSS.3PL
da-bnay-nāšā.
LNK-son.CST.PL-man

b. ˀa(n)t māryā ˀa(y)k bassimutā d-ṭaybut-āk
2 Lord as sweetness LNK-grace-POSS.2
ˀeštawdit šubqānā l-ˀaylēn
promise.REFL:PRF.2 forgiveness to-Q.PL
d-tāybin men ḥṭāhay-hon.
LNK-repent:AP.PL from sin.PL-POSS.3PL
wa-b-sog(ˀ)ā d-raḥmay-k
and-in-multitude LNK-compassion.PL-POSS.2
sāmt tyābutā ˀa(y)k da-l-ḥayyay-hon
put:PRF.2 repentance as LNK-to-life.PL-POSS.3PL
d-ḥaṭṭāyē.
LNK-sinner.PL

(8) ˀa(n)t hākēl māryā ˀalāhā d-zaddiqē lā
2 therefore Lord God LNK-righteous.PL NEG
=(h)wā l-zaddiqē sāmt tyābutā ˀa(y)k
=be:PRF.3 to-righteous.PL put:PRF.2 repentance as
da-l-ˀabrāhām wa-l-ˀisḥāq wa-l-yaˁqob hānnon
LNK-to-Abraham and-to-Isaac and-to-Jacob DEM.PL
d-ˀāp-lā ḥṭaw l-āk. ˀellā sāmt
LNK-even-NEG sin:PRF.3PL to-POSS.2 but put:PRF.2
tyābutā l-i dil-(y) ḥaṭṭāyā.
repentance to-POSS.1 LNK-POSS.1 sinner

(9) a. meṭṭol d-yattir men ḥālā d-yammā
because LNK-more.ABS from sand LNK-sea
sgiw ḥṭāh-ay. w-la-(ˀ)yt l-i
increase:PRF.3PL sin.pl-POSS.1 and-NEG-EXP to-POSS.1
npēšā d-ˀarim ˁayn-ay men
rest LNK-lift.CAUS:IMPF.1 eye.PL-POSS.1 from
sog(ˀ)ā̄ d-ˁawl-ay
multitude LNK-iniquity.PL-POSS.1

b. w-hāšā māryā, kē(ˀ)nāˀit metˀalleṣ =(ˀ)nā.
and-now Lord justly afflict.REFL:AP =1
w-ˀa(y)k d-šāwē =(ˀ)nā metṭarrep
and-as LNK-be_worth:AP =1 harass.INT.REFL:AP
=(ˀ)nā. d-hā ˀasir =(ˀ)nā.
=1 LNK-behold imprison:PP =1

(10) a. wa-kpip =(ˀ)nā b-sog(ˀ)ā̄ d-ˀasurē
and-bend:PP =1 in-multitude LNK-chain.PL
d-parzlā. ˀa(y)k d-lā ˀarim
LNK-iron as LNK-NEG rise.CAUS:IMPF.1
rēš-(y) l-ˁel. ˀāp-lā gēr šāwē
head-POSS.1 to-up even-NEG indeed be_worth:AP
=(ˀ)nā d-ˀarim ˁayn-ay
=1 LNK-raise.CAUS:IMPF.1 eye.PL-POSS.1
w-ˀaḥur w-ˀeḥzē rawmā haw
and-look:IMPF.1 and-see:IMPF.1 height DEM
da-šmayyā. meṭṭol sog(ˀ)ā̄ d-mabē(ˀ)šānutā
LNK-heaven because multitude LNK-harm
d-rušˁ-ay,
LNK-wickedness.PL-POSS.1

b. meṭṭol d-ˁebdet bišātā qdāmay-k,
because LNK-do:PRF.1 evil.F.PL before-POSS.2
w-ˀargzet l-ḥemt-āk
and-be_angry.CAUS:PRF.1 to-fury.POSS.2
w-ˀaqimet ptakrē
and-stand.CAUS:PRF.1 idol.PL

w-ˀasgit ṭanputā.
and-multiply.CAUS:PRF.1 abomination

(11) w-hāšā hā kāˀep =(ˀ)nā burkaw-(hy)
and-now behold bend:AP =1 knee.PL-POSS.3
d-leb-(y) qdāmay-k, w-bāˁē =(ˀ)nā men
LNK-heart-POSS.1 before-POSS.2 and-seek:AP =1 from
bassimut-āk.
sweetness-POSS.2

(12) ḥṭēt māryā ḥṭēt. w-meṭṭol d-yādaˁ
sin:PRF.1 Lord sin:PRF.1 and-because LNK-know:AP
=(ˀ)nā ḥtāh-ay
=1 sin.PL-POSS.1

(13) a. metkaššep =(ˀ)nā qdāmay-k.
pray_humbly.INT.REFL:AP =1 before-POSS.2
b. šboq l-i māryā w-lā
forgive:IMPT.SG to-POSS.1 Lord and-NEG
tawbd-ayn(y) ˁam saklwāt-(y).
perish.CAUS:IMPF.2-OBJ.1 with folly.PL-POSS.1
w-lā l-ˁālam tergaz ˁl-ay,
and-NEG to-eternity.ABS be_angry:IMPF.2 on-POSS.1
w-lā teṭṭar l-i bišāt-(y).
and-NEG keep:IMPF.2 to-POSS.1 evil.F.PL-POSS.1
w-lā tḥayyb-an(y)
and-NEG owe.INT:IMPF.2-OBJ.1
w-tē(ˀ)šd-an(y) b-ta(ˀ)ḥtāyāt-āh
and-pour_out:IMPF.2-OBJ.1 in-lower_part.PL-POSS.3F
d-ˀarˁā. ˀa(n)t =(h)u gēr ˀalāhā
LNK-earth 2 =3 indeed God
d-tāybē.
LNK-repent:AP.3PL.EMPH

(14) ˀāp hākēl ḥawwā mār-(y) ṭaybut-āk.
even therefore show.INT:IMPT Lord-POSS.1 grace-POSS.2
w-kad lā šāwē =(ˀ)nā pāreq =ˀa(n)t
and-when NEG worth:AP =1 redeem:AP =2
l-i ˀa(y)k sog(ˀ)ā d-raḥmay-k.
to-POSS.1 as multitude LNK-mercy.PL-POSS.2

(15) meṭṭol-hādē ˀeššabbḥ-āk b-kol-zban,
because-DEM.F praise.INT:IMPF-OBJ.1 in-all.CST-time
wa-b-kol-hon yawmātā d-ḥayy-ay. meṭṭol
and-in-all-POSS.3PL day.PL LNK-life.PL-POSS.1 because
d-l-āk mšabbḥin kol-hon ḥaylwātā
LNK-to-POSS.2 praise.INT:AP.PL all-POSS.3PL power.PL
da-šmayyā. w-l-āk mzammrin l-ˁālam
LNK-heaven and-to-POSS.2 sing.INT:AP.PL to-eternity.ABS
wa-l-ˁālam ˁālmin.
and-to-eternity.CST eternity.PL.ABS

B.2 Version B

ṣlotā da-mnašše, malkā da-bnay ˀisraˀil kad
prayer LNK-Manasseh king LNK-son.CST.PL Israel when
ˀeštbi l-babel wa-ṣbaw
capture.REFL:PRF.3 to-Babel and-want:PRF.3PL
d-nawqdun-āy(hy) w-ˀettawwi kad hu
LNK-burn.CAUS:IMPF.3PL-OBJ.3 and-pray.INT:PRF.3 when 3
b-tawrā da-nḥāšā w-ṣalli w-ˀetbazzaˁ
in-mule LNK-bronze and-pray.INT:PRF.3 and-shatter.INT.REFL:PRF.3
tawrā da-nḥāšā w-ˀeštkaḥ qāˀem d-lā
mule LNK-bronze and-find.REFL:PRF.3 stand:AP.3 LNK-NEG
nekkin b-ˀurišlem.
harm.ABS in-Jerusalem

(1) māryā šamminā ˀāḥid kol. ˀalāhā
Lord heavenly hold:AP all.ABS God
d-ˀabāhāt-an. d-ˀabrāhām wa-d-ˀisḥāq
LNK-father.PL-POSS.1PL LNK-Abraham and-LNK-Isaac
wa-d-yaˁqob wa-d-koll-ēh zarˁ-hon
and-LNK-Jacob and-LNK-all-POSS.3 seed-POSS.3PL
zaddiqē.
righteous.PL

(2) haw da-ˁbadt šmayyā w-ˀarˁā ˁam koll-āh
DEM LNK-do:PRF.2 heaven and-earth with all-POSS.3F
ṣbat-hon.
ornament-POSS.3PL

(3) a. ˀa(n)t d-ˀesart-āy(hy) l-yammā b-melltā
2 LNK-bind:PRF.2-OBJ.3 to-sea in-word
d-puqdān-āk.
LNK-commadment-POSS.2
b. man d-ˀeḥadt la-thomā w-ḥtamt-āy(hy)
Q LNK-hold:PRF.3 to-Abyss and-seal:PRF.2-OBJ.3
ba-šmā dil-āk dḥilā wa-šbiḥā.
in-name LNK-POSS.2 fear:PP and-glorify:PP

(4) haw d-kol-meddem rāˁel w-mestarrad
DEM LNK-all.CST-thing quiver:AP and-terrify.INT.REFL:AP
men qdām parṣopā d-ḥayltānut-āk.
from before face LNK-might-POSS.2

(5) a. meṭṭol d-lā msaybar l-rabbut
because LNK-NEG endure.INT:AP.3 to-greatness.CST
pāyutā d-tešboḥt-āk.
elegance LNK-honour-POSS.2

b. w-lā meškaḥ la-mqām qdām ḥemtā
and-NEG can.CAUS:AP to-stand:INF before fury
w-rugzā dil-āk d-ˁal ḥaṭṭāyē.
and-rage LNK-POSS.2 LNK-on sinner.PL.

(6) lā metmašḥānā =(h)u kit w-lā metˁaqbānā
NEG finite =3 indeed and-NEG scrutable.abs
ṭuyābā d-šuwiday-k.
readiness LNK-promise.PL-POSS.2

(7) a. ˀa(n)t =(h)u gēr māryā mrimā. ḥannānā
2 =3 indeed Lord high compassionate
ngir ruḥā. w-saggi ṭaybutā w-quštā
long.CST spirit and-great.CST grace and-true
mettawyānā d-ˁal bišātā
feeling_sorry.EMPH LNK-on evil.F.PL
da-bnay-nāšā.
LNK-son.CST.PL-man
b. ˀa(n)t hākē(y)l māryā ˀa(y)k bassimutā
2 therefore Lord as sweetness
d-ṭaybut-āk. ˀeštawdit tyābutā
LNK-grace-POSS.2 promise.REFL:PRF.2 repentance
d-šubqānā l-ˀaylēn d-ḥṭaw l-āk.
LNK-forgiveness to-Q.PL LNK-sin:PRF.3PL to-POSS.2
wa-b-sog(ˀ)ā d-raḥmay-k tḥamt
and-in-multitude LNK-compassion.PL-POSS.2 fix:PRF.2
tyābutā l-purqānā d-ḥaṭṭāyē.
repentance to-redemption LNK-sinner.PL

(8) ˀa(n)t hākē(y)l māryā ˀalāhā d-zaddiqē, lā
2 therefore Lord God LNK-righteous.PL NEG
sāmt tyābutā l-zaddiqē. l-ˀabrāhām
put:PRF.2 repentance to-rigtheous.PL to-Abraham
wa-l-ˀisḥāq wa-l-yaˁqob hennon d-lā ḥṭaw
and-to-Isaac and-to-Jacob DEM.PL LNK-NEG sin:PRF.3PL

l-āk. ˀellā sāmt tyābutā ˁl-ay dil-(y)
to-POSS.2 but put:PRF.2 repentance on-POSS.1 LNK-POSS.1
ḥaṭṭāyā.
sinner

(9) a. meṭṭol da-ḥṭēt yattir men menyānā
because LNK-sin:PRF.1 more.ABS from number
d-ḥāl-ēh d-yammā. sgiw
LNK-sand-POSS.3 LNK-sea increase:PRF.3PL
ḥṭāh-ay māryā sgiw
sin.PL-POSS.1 Lord increase:PRF.3PL
ˁawl-ay w-ḥawb-ay. w-lā
iniquity.PL-POSS.1 and-debt.PL-POSS.1 and-NEG
sāk šāwē =(ˀ)nā d-ˀeṣad
limit.ABS be_worth:AP =1 LNK-gaze:IMPF.1
w-ˀeḥzē rāwmā-h da-šmayyā. meṭṭol
and-look:IMPF.1 height-POSS.3F LNK-heaven because
sog(ˀ)ā d-ˁawl-ay
multitdue LNK-iniquity.PL-POSS.1
w-rušˁ-(y).
and-wickedness-POSS.1

(10) a. kpip =(ˀ)nā dēn wa-rkin l-taḥt
bend:PP =1 however and-incline:PP to-under
b-sog(ˀ)ā d-ˀasurē d-parzlā. ˀak-man
in-multitude LNK-chain.PL LNK-iron as-Q
d-lā meškaḥ =(ˀ)nā
LNK-NEG can.CAUS:AP =1
d-ˀethpek w-ˀarim
LNK-turn_around.REFL:IMPF.1 and-rise.CAUS:IMPF.1
napš-(y). meṭṭol d-saklwāt-(y)
soul-POSS.1 because LNK-folly.PL-POSS.1
wa-ḥṭāh-ay ˁbar(y) l-rēš-(y).
and-sin.PL-POSS.1 pass:PRF.3F.PL to-head-POSS.1

w-la-(ʔ)yt l-i mekkēl ʔāsyutā.
and-NEG-EXP to-POSS.1 therefore cure

b. meṭṭol d-yattir ʔargzet
because LNK-more.ABS be_angry.CAUS:PRF.1
l-ḥemt-āk. w-kol d-biš
to-fury-POSS.2 and-all.ABS LNK-evil.M.ABS
qdāmay-k ʕebdet. lā gēr ʕebdet
before-POSS.2 do:PRF.1 NEG indeed do:PRF.1
ṣebyān-āk w-lā neṭret
will-POSS.2 and-NEG keep:PRF.1
puqdānay-k.
commandment.PL-POSS.2

(11) w-hāšā marken =(ʔ)nā burkaw(hy) d-leb-(y).
and-now incline:AP =1 knee.CST.PL LNK-heart-POSS.1
kad bāʕē =(ʔ)nā men bassimut-āk.
when seek:AP from sweetness-POSS.2

(12) ḥṭēt l-ak māryā ḥṭēt,
sin:PRF.1 to-POSS.2 Lord sin:PRF.1
w-l-ʕawl-ay (ʔ)nā yādaʕ =(ʔ)nā
and-to-iniquity.PL-POSS.1 1 know:AP =1

(13) a. ʔellā šāʔel =(ʔ)nā kad bāʕē =(ʔ)nā
but ask:AP =1 when seek:AP from-POSS.2
men-āk.

b. šboq l-i māryā šboq
forgive:IMPT.SG to-POSS.1 Lord forgive:IMPT.SG
l-i w-lā tawbd-an(y)
to-POSS.1 and-NEG perish.CAUS:IMPF.2-OBJ.1
b-ḥṭāh-ay. w-lā l-ʕālam
in-sin.PL-POSS.1 and-NEG to-eternity.ABS
tergaz ʕl-ay w-teṭṭar
be_angry:IMPF.2 on-POSS.1 and-keep:IMPF.2

bišāt-(y). w-lā tḥayyb-an(y)
evil.F.PL-POSS.1 and-NEG owe.INT:IMPF.2-OBJ.1
b-taḥtāyāt-āh d-ˀarˁā. meṭṭol d-ˀa(n)t
in-lower_part.PL-POSS.3F LNK-earth because LNK-2
=(h)u ˀalāhā d-ˀāylēn d-tāybin.
=3 God LNK-Q.PL LNK-repent:AP.PL

(14) w-b-i mḥawwē =ˀa(n)t koll-āh ṭaybut-āk.
and-in-POSS.1 show.INT:AP =2 all-POSS.3F grace-POSS.2
w-kad lā šāwē =(ˀ)nā mšawzeb
and-when NEG be_worth:AP =1 deliver.INT:AP=2
=ˀa(n)t l-i b-sog(ˀ)ā
to-POSS.1 in-multitude LNK-mercy-POSS.2
da-mraḥmānut-āk.

(15) w-ˀeššabbḥ-āk w-ˀeqalls-āk
and-praise.INT:IMPF.1-obj.2 and-extol.INT:IMPF.1-OBJ.2
b-kol-zban. b-kol-hon yawmātā
in-all.CST-time in-all-POSS.3PL day.PL
d-ḥayy-ay. meṭṭol d-l-āk =(h)u
LNK-life.PL-POSS.1 because LNK-to-POSS.2 =3
mšabbḥin kol-hon ḥaylwātā da-šmayyā
praise.INT:AP.PL all-POSS.3PL power.PL LNK-heaven
w-dil-āk =(h)i tešbo[ḥtā] w-qulāsā w-rumrāmā
and-LNK-POSS.2 =3F hymn and-praise and-exaltation
l-ˁālam wa-l-ˁālam ˁālmin ˀamin.
to-eternity.ABS and-to-eternity.CST eternity.PL.ABS Amen

Index of Verses

Index of Authors

Bibliography

Achelis, H., 1897. *Hippolytstudien*. Hinrichs, Leipzig.

Acuña-Farina, Juan Carlos, 1999. On apposition. *English Language and Linguistics* 3 (1), 59–81.

Albayrak, İsmail, 2002. Isrā'īliyyāt and classical exegetes' comments on the calf with a hollow sound Q20: 83–98 / 7: 147–155 with special reference to Ibn 'Aṭiyya. *Journal of Semitic Studies* 47, 39–65.

Alikin, V. A., 2009. *The Earliest History of the Christian Gathering. Origin, Development and Content of the Christian Gathering in the First to Third Centuries*. Ph.D. thesis, Leiden University.

Anastasius Sinaiticus, 1865. *Oratio in Sextum Psalmum*. Edited by H. Canisius. In: *Patrologia Graeca*. Vol. 89. Migne, Paris, pp. 1077–1144.

Anderson, S. R., 2005. *Aspects of the Theory of Clitics*. Oxford University Press.

Anonymous, 1916. *Chronicle to the Year 1234. Chronicon ad annum Christi 1234 pertinens edidit I.-B. Chabot II*. Vol. 82 of *Corpus Scriptorum Christianorum Orientalium; Scriptores Syri* 37 / III, 15. E typographeo Reipublicae J. Gabalde, Bibliopola, Paris, [=II, Text].

Anonymous, 1920. *Chronicle to the Year 1234. Chronicon ad annum Christi 1234 pertinens edidit I.-B. Chabot I. Praemissum est Chronicon Anonymum ad A. D. 819 pertinens curante Aphram Barsaum*. Vol. 81 of *Corpus Scriptorum Christianorum Orientalium; Scriptores*

Syri 36/ III, 14. E typographeo Reipublicae J. Gabalde, Bibliopola, Paris, [=I, Text].

Anonymous, 1952. *Chronicle to the Year 1234. Anonymi Auctoris Chronicon ad annum Christi 1234 pertinens I, Praemissum est Chronicon anonymum ad A. D. 819 pertinens interpretatus est I.-B. Chabot*. Vol. 109 of *Corpus Scriptorum Christianorum Orientalium; Scriptores Syri* 56. Durbecq, Leuven, [=I, Translation].

Anonymous, 1974. *Chronicle to the Year 1234. Anonymi Auctoris Chronicon Ad A.C. [sic!] 1234 pertinens II traduit par Albert Abouna. Introduction, notes et index de J.-M. Fiey*. Vol. 354 of *Corpus Scriptorum Christianorum Orientalium; Scriptores Syri* 154. Secrétariat du CorpusSCO, Leuven, [=II, Translation].

Aronoff, Mark, 1994. *Morphology by Itself: Stems and Inflectional Classes*. Vol. 24 of *Linguistic Inquiry Monographs*. The MIT Press, Cambridge (MA)-London.

Azar, Moshe, 1976. The emphatic sentence in Modern Hebrew. In: Cole, Peter (Ed.), *Studies in Modern Hebrew Syntax and Semantics: The Transformational-Generative Approach*. Vol. 32 of *North-Holland Linguistic Series*. North-Holland Publishing Company, Amsterdam etc., pp. 209–230.

Baars, W., 1961. An additional fragment of the Syriac version of the Psalms of Solomon. *Vetus Testamentum* 11, 222–223.

Baars, W., and Koster, M.D., 1961. *List of the Old Testament Peshitta Manuscripts*. Brill, Leiden, preliminary issue, edited by the Peshitta Institute, Leiden University.

Baars, W., and Schneider, H., 1972. Prayer of Manasseh. In: *The Old Testament in Syriac according to the Peshitta Version*. Vol. IV/6 *Canticles or Odes, Prayer of Manasseh, Apocryphal Psalms, Psalms of Solomon, Tobit, I (3) Esdras*. Brill, Leiden.

Baasten, Martin F. J., 2006. *The Non-Verbal Clause in Qumran Hebrew*. Ph.D. thesis, Leiden University.

Bacher, W., 1902. Le taureau de Phalaris dans l'Agada. *Revue des Études Juives* 45, 291–295.

Bakker, Dirk, 2008. Lemma and lexeme: The case of third-Alaph and third-Yodh verbs. In: Dyk and Peursen, van (2008), Vol. 4 of *Perspectives on Syriac Linguistics*, pp. 11–25.

Bakker, Dirk, 2011. *Bardaisan's Book of the Laws of the Countries: A computer-assisted linguistic analysis*. Ph.D. thesis, Leiden University.

Bar Hebraeus, 1890. *Chronicon Syriacum. Gregorii Barhebræi Chronicon Syriacum e codd. mss. emendatum ac punctis vocalibus adnotationibusque locupletatum a Paulo Bedjan*. Paris.

Bartlet, J. V., 1917. Fragments of the Didascalia Apostolorum in Greek. *Journal of Theological Studies* 18, 301–309.

Bauer, W., 1988. *Griechisch-deutsches Wörterbuch zu den Schriften des Neuen Testaments und der frühchristlichen Literatur*. Edited by K. Aland and B. Aland, sixth Edition. De Gruyter, Berlin.

Baumstark, A., 1958. *Comparative Liturgy*. Mowbray, London, English edition by F. L. Cross. Revised by Bernard Botte.

Bazzana, G. B., 2005-2006. L'*Oratio Manasse* a Hierapolis. Osservazioni di una storia testuale. In: *Rendiconti. Atti della Pontificia Accademia Romana di Archeologia (Serie III)*. Vol. 78. pp. 434–442.

Bendavid, Abba, 1972. מקבילות במקרא *(Parallels in the Bible)*. Carta, Jerusalem.

Bertholdt, L., 1968. *Historischkritische Einleitung in sämmtliche kanonische und apokryphische Schriften des alten und neuen Testaments 5/2*. Palm, Erlangen.

Black, M., 1954. *A Christian Palestinian Syriac Horologion (Berlin MS. Or Oct. 1019)*. Cambridge University Press, Cambridge.

Bogaert, P., 1969. *Apocalypse de Baruch. Introduction, traduction du syriaque et commentaire*. Vol. 144–145 of *Sources Chrétiennes*. Les éditions du Cerf, Paris, 2 volumes.

Borbone, P. G., 1995. Correspondances lexicales entre Peshitta et TM du Pentateuque. Les racines verbales. In: Dirksen and Kooij, van der (1995), pp. 1–16.

Borbone, P. G., 1999. Preghiera di Manasseh. In: Sacchi, Paolo (Ed.), *Apocrifi dell'Antico Testamento.* Vol. III. Paideia, Brescia, pp. 539—549.

Borbone, P. G., and Jenner, K.D., 1997. *The Old Testament in Syriac according to the Peshitta Version* V. *Concordance* 1. *The Pentateuch.* Brill, Leiden.

Bosker, H. R., 2008. A comparison of parsers. Delilah, Turgama and Baruch, BA thesis, Leiden University.

Brock, S. P., 1984. East Syrian liturgical fragments from the Cairo Genizah. *Oriens Christianus* 68, 58–79.

Brock, Sebastian P., 1989. Some observations on the use of Classical Syriac in the late twentieth century. *Journal of Semitic Studies* 34/2, 363–375.

Brock, Sebastian P., 1990a. Diachronic aspects of Syriac word formation: An aid for dating anonymous texts. In: Lavenant (1990), pp. 321–330.

Brock, S. P., 1990b. Some further East Syrian liturgical fragments from the Cairo Genizah. *Oriens Christianus* 74, 44–61.

Brock, Sebastian P., 1997. *A Brief Outline of Syriac Literature.* Vol. 9 of *Mōrān ʔEthʔō.* St. Ephrem Ecumenical Research Institute.

Brock, Sebastian P., 2006a. *An Introduction to Syriac Studies.* Vol. 4 of *Gorgias Handbooks.* Gorgias, Piscataway, NJ.

Brock, S. P., 2006b. Manuscrits liturgiques en syriaque. In: Cassingena-Trévedy, F., and Jurasz, I. (Eds.), *Les liturgies syriaques.* Vol. 3 of *Études Syriaques.* Geuthner, Paris, pp. 267–283.

Brock, S. P., and Witakowski, W., 2001. *The Hidden Pearl. The Syrian Orthodox Church and Its Ancient Aramaic Heritage* 3. *At the Turn of the Third Millennium; The Syrian Orthodox Witnesses*. Gorgias, Piscataway, NJ.

Brockelmann, Carl, 1976. *Syrische Grammatik*, twelfth Edition. Verlag Enzyklopädie, Leipzig.

Buberl, Paul, 1917. *Die Minaturenhandschriften der Nationalbibliothek in Athen*. Hölder.

Buth, Randall John, 1987. *Word Order in Aramaic from the Perspectives of Functional Grammar and Discourse Analysis*. Ph.D. thesis, University of California, Los Angeles.

Carbajosa, Ignacio, 2008. *The Character of the Syriac Version of Psalms. A Study of Psalms 90–150 in the Peshitta*. Vol. 17 of *Monographs of the Peshitta Institute Leiden*. Brill, Leiden, translated by Paul Stevenson.

Caron, Bernard, 2000. Assertion et préconstruit: topicalisation et focalisation dans les langues africaines. In: Caron, Bernard (Ed.), *Topicalisation et focalisation dans les langues africaines*. Vol. 1 of *Afrique et langage*. Peeters, Louvain-Paris, pp. 7–42.

Charlesworth, J. H. (Ed.), 1983–1985a. *The Old Testament Pseudepigrapha*. 2 volumes. Darton, Longmann and Todd, London.

Charlesworth, James H., 1983–1985b. Prayer of Manasseh. In: Charlesworth (1983–1985a), pp. 2.625–637.

Cohen, D., 1975. Phrase nominale et verbalisation en sémitique. In: Bader, Françoise (Ed.), *Mélanges Linguistiques Offerts à Émile Benveniste*. Vol. 70 of *Collection linguistique*. Peeters, Leuven, pp. 87–98.

Cohen, David, 1984. *La phrase nominale et l'évolution du système verbal en sémitique: études de syntaxe historique*. Vol. 72 of *Collection linguistique*. Peeters, Leuven [etc.].

Comrie, Bernard, 1989. *Language Universals and Linguistic Typology*, 2nd Edition. Basil Blackwell, Oxford.

Connolly, R. H. (Ed.), 1929. *Didascalia Apostolorum. The Syriac Version Translated and Accompanied by the Verona Latin Fragments.* Clarendon, Oxford.

Conybeare, F. C., 1905. *Rituale Armenorum.* Oxford.

Costaz, L., 1955. *Grammaire syriaque.* Librairie orientale, Beirut.

Costaz, Louis, 1963. *Dictionnaire syriaque-français: Syriac-English Dictionary:* قاموس سرياني عربي. Imprimerie catholique, Beirut.

Cutler, Antony, 1984. *The Aristocratic Psalters in Byzantium.* Vol. 13 of *Bibliothèque des Cahiers Archéologiques.* Picard, Paris.

Dancy, J. C., 1972. *The Shorter Books of the Apocrypha.* Cambridge University Press, Cambridge, with contributions by W. J. Fuerst and R. J. Hammer.

D'Andria, F., Zaccaria Ruggiu, A., Ritti, T., Bazzana, G. B., and Caccitti, R., 2005–2006. L'iscrizione dipinta con la *Preghiera di Manasse* a Hierapolis di Frigia (Turchia). In: *Rendiconti. Atti della Pontificia Accademia Romana di Archeologia (Serie III).* Vol. 78. pp. 349–449.

David, Joseph, 1911. L'église Sainte-Marie-Antique dans son état originaire. Étude hagiographique et liturgique suivie d'un catalogue raisonné des saints de cette église. In: Grüneisen, W. de (Ed.), *Sainte Marie Antique.* Max Betschneider, Rome, pp. 449–560.

Davila, James R., 2005. *The Provenance of the Pseudepigrapha: Jewish, Christian, or Other.* Vol. 105 of *Supplements to the Journal for the Study of Judaism.* Brill, Leiden.

Davila, James R., 2007. Is the Prayer of Manasseh a Jewish work? In: LiDonnici, Lynn, and Lieber, Andrea (Eds.), *Heavenly Tablets. Interpretation, Identity and Tradition in Ancient Judaism.* Vol. 119 of *Supplements to the Journal for the Study of Judaism.* Brill, pp. 75–85.

Denis, A.-M., and Haelewyck, J.-C., 2000. *Introduction à la littérature religieuse judéo-hellénistique (pseudépigraphes de l'Ancien Testament)*. Brepols, Turnhout, 2 volumes.

Dionysius of Tell-Mahre, Pseudo-, 1927a. *Chronicon anonymum pseudo-Dionysianum vulgo dictum interpretatus est J.-B. Chabot*. Vol. 91 of *Corpus Scriptorum Christianorum Orientalium; Scriptores Syri* 61 / III, 1 Textus. Durbeck, Leuven, [=I, Text].

Dionysius of Tell-Mahre, Pseudo-, 1927b. *Incerti auctoris Chronicon anonymum pseudo-Dionysianum vulgo dictum I interpretatus est J.-B. Chabot*. Vol. 121 of *Corpus Scriptorum Christianorum Orientalium; Scriptores Syri* 61 / III, 1 Versio. Durbeck, Leuven, [=I, Translation].

Dionysius of Tell-Mahre, Pseudo-, 1933. *Chronicon anonymum pseudo-Dionysianum vulgo dictum editit J.-B. Chabot II. Accedunt Iohannis Ephesini Fragmenta curante E.-W. Brooks*. Vol. 104 of *Corpus Scriptorum Christianorum Orientalium; Scriptores Syri* 53 / III, 2 Textus. E Typographeo Reipublicae, Paris, [=II, Text].

Dionysius of Tell-Mahre, Pseudo-, 1989. *Chronicon Anonymum pseudo-Dionysianum vulgo dictum II gallice vertit Robert Hespel*. Vol. 507 of *Corpus Scriptorum Christianorum Orientalium; Scriptores Syri* 213 Versio. Peeters, Leuven, [=II, Translation].

Dirksen, P. B., and Kooij, A. van der (Eds.), 1995. *The Peshitta as a Translation: Papers Read at the II Peshitta Symposium Held at Leiden 19–21 August 1993*. Vol. 8 of *Monographs of the Peshitta Institute Leiden*. Brill, Leiden.

Drijvers, H. J. W., 1965. *The Book of the Laws of the Countries. Dialogue on Fate of Bardaisan of Edessa*. Van Gorcum and Comp., Assen.

Duchaussoy, J., 1972. *Le bestiaire divin ou la symbolique des animaux*, 2nd Edition. Le Courrier du Livre, Paris.

Dyk, J. W., 2006a. 1 Kings 2:1–9: Some results of a structured hierarchical approach. In: Keulen, van and Peursen, van (2006), Vol. 48 of *Studia Semitica Neerlandica*, pp. 277–309.

Dyk, J. W., 2006b. Lexical correspondence and translation equivalents: Building an electronic concordance. In: Keulen, van and Peursen, van (2006), Vol. 48 of *Studia Semitica Neerlandica*, pp. 311–326.

Dyk, J. W., 2008. A synopsis-based translation concordance as a tool for lexical and text-critical exploration. In: Dyk and Peursen, van (2008), Vol. 4 of *Perspectives on Syriac Linguistics*, pp. 161–179.

Dyk, J. W., and Keulen, P. S. F. van, forthcoming. *Language System, Translation Technique and Textual Tradition in the Peshitta of Kings. Monographs of the Peshitta Institute Leiden*. Brill, Leiden.

Dyk, J. W., and Peursen, W. Th. van (Eds.), 2008. *Foundations for Syriac Lexicography III. Colloquia of the International Syriac Language Project*. Vol. 4 of *Perspectives on Syriac Linguistics*. Gorgias, Piscataway, NJ.

Edmonds, Philip, and Hirst, Graeme, 2002. Near-synonymy and lexical choice. *Computational Linguistics* 28 (2), 105–144. URL `http://www.mitpressjournals.org/doi/abs/10.1162/089120102760173625`

Ehrmann, Michael, 1996. *Klagephänomene im zwischentestamentlicher Literatur*. Vol. 41 of *Beiträge zur Erforschung des Alten Testaments und des Antiken Judentums*. Peter Lang, Frankfurt am Main.

Eissfeldt, Otto, 1934. *Einleitung in das Alte Testament unter Einschluß der Apokryphen und Pseudepigraphen*. Mohr–Siebeck, Tübingen.

Elias bar Sinaya, 1910a. *Chronography. Eliae Metropolitae Nisibeni Opus Chronologium (pars prior) edidit E. W. Brooks*. Vol. 62 of *Corpus Scriptorum Christianorum Orientalium; Scriptores Syri* III, 7. Rome: Excudebat Karolus de Luigi; Parisiis Carolus Poussielgue Bibliopola; Lipsiae: Otto Harrassowitz, [=I, Text].

Elias bar Sinaya, 1910b. *Chronography. Eliae Metropolitae Nisibeni Opus Chronologium (pars prior) interpretatus est E. W. Brooks*. Vol. 63 of *Corpus Scriptorum Christianorum Orientalium; Scriptores Syri* III, 7. Rome: Excudebat Karolus de Luigi; Parisiis Carolus

Poussielgue Bibliopola; Lipsiae: Otto Harrassowitz, [=I, Translation].

Elliot, J. K., 2006. *A Synopsis of the Apocryphal Nativity and Infancy Narratives*. Vol. 34 of *New Testament Tools and Studies*. Brill, Leiden.

Ephrem, 1955. *Hymns on Faith. Des heiligen Ephraem des Syrers Hymnen de Fide herausgegeben und übersetzt von Edmund Beck*. Vol. 154–155 of *Corpus Scriptorum Christianorum Orientalium; Scriptores Syri* 73–74. Durbecq, Leuven.

Eutychius, 1863. *Annales. Translated by J. Selden and E. Pococke*. Vol. 111 of *Patrologia Graeca*. J.-P. Migne, Paris.

Eutychius, 1906. *Annales. Eutychii Patriarchae Alexandrini Annales (pars prior) editit et interpretatus est L. Cheikho*. Vol. 471–472 of *Corpus Scriptorum Christianorum Orientalium; Scriptores Arabici* 6-7. E Typographeo Catholico; Pariis Carolus Poussielgue, Bibliopola, Beryti.

Eutychius, 1985. *Annales. Das Annalenwerk des Eutychios von Alexandrien. Ausgewählte Geschichten und Legenden kompiliert von Saʿid ibn Baṭrīq um 935 A.D., herausgegeben und übersetzt von Michael Breydy*. Vol. 471–472 of *Corpus Scriptorum Christianorum Orientalium; Scriptores Arabici* 44–45. Peeters, Leuven.

Eutychius, 1987. *Annales. Eutichio Patriarca di Alessandria (877–940), Gli Annali. Introduzione traduzione e note a cura di Bartolomeo Pirone*. Vol. 1 of *Studia Orientalia Christiana Monographiae*. Franciscan Centre of Christian Oriental Studies, Cairo.

Ewald, Georg Heinrich August, 1832. Über das syrische Punctationssystem, nach syrischen Handschriften. In: Ewald, Georg Heinrich August (Ed.), *Abhandlungen zur orientalischen und biblischen Literatur I*. Dieterich, Göttingen, pp. 53–129.

Falla, T. C., 2005. A conceptual framework for a new comprehensive Syriac-English lexicon. In: Forbes, A. Dean, and Taylor, David G.K. (Eds.), *Foundations for Syriac Lexicography I. Colloquia of the International Syriac Language Project*. Vol. 1 of *Perspectives on Syriac Linguistics*. Gorgias, Piscataway, NJ, pp. 1–79.

Farina, Margherita, 2009. *An Outline of Middle Voice in Syriac. Evidence of a Linguistic Category*. Ph.D. thesis, Scuola Normale Superiore, Pisa.

Fiensy, David Arthur, 1985. *Prayers Alleged to Be Jewish: An Examination of the Constitutiones Apostolorum*. Vol. 65 of *Brown Judaic Studies*. Scholars Press, Chico, Calif.

Fiensy, D. A., and Darnell, D. R., 1983–1985. Hellenistic Synagogal Prayers. In: Charlesworth (1983–1985a), pp. 2.671–697.

Funk, Franciscus Xaverius, 1905. *Didadascalia et Constitutiones Apostolorum*. Schoeningh, Paderborn, 2 volumes.

Gardner, Stephen, 1973. 47. Psalter. In: Vikan, Gary (Ed.), *Illuminated Greek Manuscripts from American Collections. An Exhibition in Honor of Kurt Weitzmann*. The Art Museum, Princeton University; distributed by Princeton University Press, Princeton, N.J., pp. 168–171.

Geirnaert, Dirk, and Smith, Paul J., 1999. The sources of the emblematic fable book *De warachtighe fabulen der dieren* (1567). In: Manning, John, Porteman, Karel, and Vaeck, Marc van (Eds.), *The Emblem Tradition in the Low Countries. Selected Papers of the Leuven International Emblem Conference, 18–23 August, 1996*. Vol. 1b of *Imago Figurata*. Brepols, Turnhout, pp. 23–38.

Georgius Syncellus, 1984. *Chronography. Georgii Syncelli Ecologa Chronographica edidit Alden A. Mosshammer*. Bibliotheca Scriptorum Graecorum et Romanorum Teubneriana. Teubner, Leipzig.

Gibson, Margaret Dunlop, 1903a. *The Didascalia Apostolorum in English. Translated from the Syriac by Margaret Dunlop Gibson*. Vol. I of *Horae Semiticae*. Clay and Sons, London.

Gibson, Margaret Dunlop, 1903b. *The Didascalia Apostolorum in Syriac. Edited from a Mesopotamian Manuscript with various readings and collations of other MSS*. Vol. I of *Horae Semiticae*. Clay and Sons, London.

Ginzberg, Louis, 1909–1938. *The Legends of the Jews*. The Jewish Publication Society, Philadelphia, 7 volumes.

Goldenberg, Gideon, 1977. Imperfectly-transformed cleft sentences. In: *Proceedings of the Sixth World Congress of Jewish Studies*. Vol. I. Jerusalem, pp. 127–133, (=idem, *Studies in Semitic Linguistics*, 116–122).

Goldenberg, Gideon, 1983. On Syriac sentence structure. In: Sokoloff, M. (Ed.), *Arameans, Aramaic and the Aramaic Literary Tradition*. Bar-Ilan University Press, Ramat-Gan, pp. 97–140, (=idem, *Studies in Semitic Linguistics*, 525–568).

Goldenberg, Gideon, 1985. On verbal structure and the Hebrew verb. *Language Studies* I (xl–xlii), 295–348, (=idem, *Studies in Semitic Linguistics*, 148–196).

Goldenberg, Gideon, 1990. On some niceties of Syriac syntax. In: Lavenant (1990), pp. 335–344, (=idem, *Studies in Semitic Linguistics*, 569–578).

Goldenberg, Gideon, 1995a. Attribution in Semitic languages. *Langues Orientales Anciennes: Philologie et Linguistique* 5-6, 1–20, (=idem, *Studies in Semitic Linguistics*, 46–55).

Goldenberg, Gideon, 1995b. Bible translations and Syriac idiom. In: Dirksen and Kooij, van der (1995), pp. 25–40, (=idem, *Studies in Semitic Linguistics*, 591–604).

Goldenberg, Gideon, 2006. Comments on 'Three approaches to the tripartite nominal clause in Syriac' by Wido van Peursen. In: Keulen, van and Peursen, van (2006), Vol. 48 of *Studia Semitica Neerlandica*, pp. 175–184.

Graf, Georg, 1944. *Die Übersetzungen*. Vol. I of *Geschichte der christlichen arabischen Literatur*. Bibliotheca Apostolica Vaticana, Vatican City, studi e Testi 118.

Greenberg, Gillian, 2008. Sin, iniquity, wickedness and rebellion in the Peshitta to Isaiah and Jeremiah. *Aramaic Studies* 6, 195–206.

Gry, Léon, 1945. Le roi Manassé, d'après les légends midrashiques (exposé et critique des sources). In: *Mélanges E. Podechard. Études des sciences religieuses offertes pour son éméritat au doyen honoraire de la Faculté de Théologie de Lyon*. Facultés Catholiques, Lyon, pp. 147–157.

Gzella, Holger, and Folmer, Margaretha L. (Eds.), 2008. *Aramaic in its Historical and Linguistic Setting*. Vol. 50 of *Veröffentlichungen der Orientalischen Kommission*. Harrassowitz, Wiesbaden.

Hauler, Edmund (Ed.), 1900. *Didascaliae Apostolorum Fragmenta Ueronensia Latina*. Teubner, Leipzig.

Healey, John F., 2007. The Edessan milieu and the birth of Syriac. *Hugoye* 10 (2).
URL `http://syrcom.cua.edu/Hugoye/Vol10No2/HV10N2Healey.html`

Hoftijzer, J., 1991. A preliminary remark on the study of the verbal system in Classical Hebrew. In: Kaye, A. S. (Ed.), *Semitic Studies in Honor of Wolf Leslau on the Occasion of his Eighty-Fifth Birthday, November 14th, 1991*. Vol. I. Harrassowitz, Wiesbaden, pp. 645–651, 2 volumes.

Hollander, H.W., and Jonge, M. de, 1985. *The Testaments of the Twelve Patriarchs. A Commentary*. Vol. 8 of *Studia in Veteris Testamenti Pseudepigrapha*. Brill, Leiden / New York / Köln.

Hollander, H. W., 1985. The Testaments of the Twelve Patriarchs. In: Jonge, M. de (Ed.), *Outside the Old Testament*. Vol. 4 of *Cambridge Commentaries on Writings of the Jewish and Christian World 200 BC to AD 200*. Cambridge University Press, Cambridge, pp. 71–91.

Horst, Pieter W. van der, and Newman, Judith H., 2008. *Early Jewish Prayers in Greek*. Commentaries on Early Jewish Literature. Walter de Gruyter, Berlin and New York.

Ishodad of Merv, 1962. *Commentary on the Beth Mawtbe. Commentaire d'Išodad de Merv sur l'Ancien Testament*. III. *Livre des Sessions. Édité et traduit par Ceslas Van den Eynde*. Vol. 229–230 of *Corpus Scriptorum Christianorum Orientalium; Scriptores Syri* 96–97. Secretariat du CorpusSCO, Leuven.

Jenner, Konrad D., 1993. A review of the methods by which Syriac biblical and related manuscripts have been described and analysed: Some preliminary remarks. *Aram* 5, 255–266, a Festschrift for Dr. Sebastian P. Brock.

Jenner, Konrad D., 1994. *De perikopentitels van de geïllustreerde Syrische kanselbijbel van Parijs (MS Paris, Bibliothèque Nationale, Syriaque 341): een vergelijkend onderzoek naar de oudste Syrische perikopenstelsels*. Ph.D. thesis, Leiden University.

Jerome, Pseudo-, 1883. *Quastiones hebraicae in libros Regum et Paralipomenon*. Vol. 23 of *Patrologia Latina*. J.-P. Migne, Paris.

Jervell, Jacob, 1998. *Die Apostelgeschichte*, seventeenth Edition. Vol. 3 of *Kritisch-exegetischer Kommentar über das Neue Testament*. Vandenhoeck und Ruprecht, Göttingen.

Jonge, M. de, 1975. *The Testaments of the Twelve Patriarchs. A Study of their Text Composition and Origin*. Van Gorcum, Assen.

Jonge, M. de, 2003. *Pseudepigrapha of the Old Testament as Part of Christian Literature*. Vol. 18 of *Studia in Veteris Testamenti Pseudepigrapha*. Brill.

Joosten, J., 1996. *The Syriac Language of the Peshitta and Old Syriac Versions of Matthew: Syntactic Structure, Translation Technique and Inner Syriac Developments*. Vol. 22 of *Studies in Semitic Languages and Linguistics*. Brill, Leiden.

Joosten, Jan, 2006. Comments on 'Three approaches to the tripartite nominal clause in Syriac' by Wido van Peursen. In: Keulen, van and Peursen, van (2006), Vol. 48 of *Studia Semitica Neerlandica*, pp. 185–188.

Justin Martyr, 2003. *Dialogue avec Tryphon. Édition critique, traduction, commentaire par P. Bobichon*. Vol. 47/1–2 of *Paradosis: Études de littérature et de théologie anciennes*. Academic Press, Fribourg, 2 volumes.

Kemmer, Suzanne, 1993. *The Middle Voice*. Vol. 23 of *Typological Studies in Language*. John Benjamins Publishing Company, Amsterdam.

Keulen, P. S. F. van, 1996. *Manasseh through the Eyes of the Deuteronomists. The Manasseh Account (2 Kings 21:1–18) and the Final Chapters of the Deuteronomistic History*. Vol. 38 of *Oudtestamentische Studiën*. Brill, Leiden.

Keulen, P. S. F. van, and Peursen, W. Th. van (Eds.), 2006. *Corpus Linguistics and Textual History. A Computer-Assisted Interdisciplinary Approach to the Peshitta*. Vol. 48 of *Studia Semitica Neerlandica*. Van Gorcum, Assen.

Khalifeh, Elia N., 2006. A project on the Antiochian Chalcedonian Orthodox manuscripts: Syriac, Arabic, CPA and Greek. *Parole d'Orient* 31, 1–9.

Khalil, Samir, 1978. Le codex Kacmarcik et sa version arabe de la liturgie alexandrine. *Orientalia Christiana Periodica* 44, 74–106.

Khan, Geoffrey, 1984. Object markers and agreement pronouns in Semitic languages. *Bulletin of the School of Oriental and African Studies* 47, 468–500.

Khan, Geoffrey, 1988. *Studies in Semitic Syntax*. Vol. 38 of *London Oriental Series*. Oxford University Press, Oxford.

Klavans, Judith L., 1985. The independence of syntax and phonology in cliticization. *Language* 61 (1), 95–120.

Kohler, Kaufmann, 1901–1906. Didascalia. In: Adler, C., and Singer, I. (Eds.), *The Jewish Encyclopedia*. Funk and Wagnalis, New York, pp. 4.588–594, 12 volumes.

Koster, M.D., 1977. *The Peshiṭta of Exodus. The Development of its Text in the Course of Fifteen Centuries.* Van Gorcum, Assen–Amsterdam.

Kraft, Robert A, 1994. The Pseudepigrapha in Christianity. In: Reeves, John C. (Ed.), *Tracing the Threads: Studies in the Vitality of Jewish Pseudepigrapha.* Vol. 6 of *Society of Biblical Literature Early Judaism and Literature.* Scholars Press, Atlanta, pp. 55–86.

Krauss, Samuel, 1903. Die Legende des Königs Manasse. *Zeitschrift für die alttestamentliche Wissenschaft* 23, 326–336.

Kubińska, Jadwiga, 1981. Une pierre funéraire chrétienne au Musée National de Varsovie. *Revue Archéologique* 1, 74–76.

Kuty, Renaud J., 2008. *Studies in the Syntax of Targum Jonathan to Samuel.* Ph.D. thesis, Leiden University.

Lagarde, P. de (Ed.), 1854. *Didascalia Apostolorum Syriace.* Teubner, Leipzig.

Lagarde, Paul de, 1867. *Materialien zur Kritik und Geschichte des Pentateuchs.* Vol. I. Teubner, Leipzig.

Łajtar, Adam, 1992. Notes on Greek Christian inscriptions from the Nile valley. *Zeitschrift für Papyrologie und Epigraphik* 93, 137–141.

Łajtar, Adam, 2003. 100. Épitaphe de Kollouthos. In: Łajtar, Adam, and Twardecki, Alfred (Eds.), *Catalogue des inscriptions grecques du Musée National de Varsovie.* Vol. 2 of *The Journal for Juristic Papyrology Supplements.* The Raphael Taubenschlag Foundation, Warsaw, pp. 256–259.

Lambert, Pierre-Yves, 1998. L'impersonnel. In: Feuillet, Jack (Ed.), *Actance et valence dans les langues de L'Europe.* Vol. 20/2 of *Empirical Approaches to Language Typology.* Mouton de Gruyter, Berlin/New York, pp. 295–345.

Lambrecht, Knud, 1994. *Information Structure and Semantic Form: Topic, Focus, and the Mental Representations of Discourse Referents.*

Cambridge Studies in Linguistics. Cambridge University Press, Cambridge.

Lane, David J., 1994. *The Peshitta of Leviticus*. Vol. 6 of *Monographs of the Peshitta Institute Leiden*. Brill, Leiden.

Lavenant, R. (Ed.), 1990. *V Symposium Syriacum, 1988: Katholieke Universiteit, Leuven, 29-31 août 1988*. Vol. 236 of *Orientalia Christiana Analecta*. Pont. Institutum Studiorum Orientalium.

Leclercq, Henri, 1907–1953. Manassé. In: Cabrol, Fernand, and Leclerq, Henri (Eds.), *Dictionaire d'archéologie chrétienne et de liturgie*. Vol. 10. Letouzey et Ané, Paris, p. 1361.

Lehmann, W. P., March 1973. A structural principle of language and its implications. *Language* 49 (1).
URL `http://www.jstor.org/stable/412102`

Leicht, Reimund, 1996. A newly discovered Hebrew version of the apocryphal "Prayer of Manasseh". *Jewish Studies Quarterly* 3, 359–373.

Lenschau, Th., 1938. Phalaris. In: *Paulys Real-Encyclopädie der Classischen Altertumswissenschaft*. Vol. 19/2 (38). Metzler, Stuttgart, pp. 1649–1652, neue Bearbeitung begonnen von Georg Wissowa under Mitwirkung zahlreicher Fachgenossen herausgegeben von Wilhem Kroll.

Macomber, William F., 1975. The Kacmarcik Codex. A 14th century Greek-Arabic manuscript of the Coptic Mass. *Le Muséon* 88, 391–395.

Macomber, William F., 1977. The Greek text of the Coptic Mass and the Anaphoras of Basil and Gregory according to the Kacmarcik Codex. *Orientalia Christiana Periodica* 43, 308–344.

Macomber, William F., 1979. The Anaphora of Saint Mark according to the Kacmarcik Codex. *Orientalia Christiana Periodica* 45, 75–98.

Marquardt, Joachim, 1886. *Das Privatleben der Römer*. Vol. 7 of *Handbuch der Römischen Alterthümer*. Hirzel, Leipzig, 2 volumes.

McEngery, Tony, and Wilson, Andrew, 1996. *Corpus Linguistics. Edinburgh Textbooks in Empirical Linguistics*. Edinburgh University Press.

McIvor, J. Stanley, 1994. The Targum to Chronicles. Translated with introduction, apparatus, and notes. In: Beattie, D.R.G., and McIvor, J. Stanley (Eds.), *The Targum of Ruth. The Targum of Chronicles*. Vol. 19 of *The Aramaic Bible*. T&T Clark, Edinburgh.

Merwe, C. H. J. van der, Naudé, J. A., and Kroeze, J. H., 1999. *A Biblical Hebrew Reference Grammar*. Sheffield Academic Press, Sheffield.

Metzger, Bruce M., 1977. *Apocrypha of the Old Testament*. Oxford University Press, Oxford.

Metzger, Marcel, 1985. *Les Constitutions Apostoliques. Introdcution, texte critique, traduction et notes*. Vol. 320, 329, 336 of *Sources Chrétiennes*. Les éditions du Cerf, Paris, 3 volumes.

Michael Glycas, 1836. *Annales. Michaelis Glycae Annales recognovit Immanuel Bekkerus*. Corpus Scriptorum Historiae Byzantinae. Weber, Bonn, also edited in Patrologia Graeca 158 (Michaelis Glycae Opera Omnia; Paris, 1866).

Michael the Syrian, 1899–1910. *Chronicle. Chronique de Michel de Syrien Patriarche jacobite d'Antioche (1166–1199) éditée pour la première fois et traduite en français par J.-B. Chabot*. Leroux, Paris, 4 volumes.

Migne, J. P., 1856–1858. *Dictionnaire des Apocryphes*. Migne, Paris, 2 volumes, reprint Turnhout: Brepols, 1989.

Mingana, A., 1933. *Catalogue of the Mingana Collection of Manuscripts now in the Possession of the Trustees of the Woodbrooke Settlement, Selly Oak, Birmingham* 1. *Syriac and Garshūni Manuscripts*. W. Heffer and Sons, Cambridge, 3 volumes.

Muraoka, Takamitsu, 1987. *Classical Syriac for Hebraists.* Harrassowitz, Wiesbaden.

Muraoka, Takamitsu, 1995. Response to G. Goldenberg, 'Bible translations and Syriac idiom'. In: Dirksen and Kooij, van der (1995), Vol. 8 of *Monographs of the Peshitta Institute Leiden*, pp. 41–46.

Muraoka, Takamitsu, 2005. *Classical Syriac: A Basic Grammar With a Chrestomathy*, 2nd Edition. Vol. 19 of *Porta Linguarum Orientalium (Neue Serie)*. Harrassowitz Verlag.

Muraoka, Takamitsu, 2006. A response to 'Three approaches to the tripartite nominal clause in Syriac' by Wido van Peursen and a bit more. In: Keulen, van and Peursen, van (2006), Vol. 48 of *Studia Semitica Neerlandica*, pp. 189–196.

Murre-van den Berg, Heleen, 2008. Classical Syriac, Neo-Aramaic, and Arabic in the Church of the East and the Chaldean Church between 1500 and 1800. In: Gzella and Folmer (2008), Vol. 50 of *Veröffentlichungen der Orientalischen Kommission*, p. 335–351.

Nau, F., 1908. Un extrait de la *Didascalie*: la prière de Manassé (avec une édition de la version syriaque). *Revue de l'Orient Chrétien* 13, 134–141.

Nestle, Eberhard, 1899. *Septuagintastudien III.* Vereins-Buchdrukerei, Stuttgart, wissenschaftliche Beilage zum Programm des Königlich Württembergischen Evangelisch-Theologischen Seminars Maulbronn.

Nestle, Eb., 1902. Miscellen. *Zeitschrift für die Alttestamentliche Wissenschaft* 22, 309–312.

Newman, J. H., 2007a. The form and settings of the Prayer of Manasseh. In: Boda, Mark J., Falk, Daniel K., and Werline, Rodney A. (Eds.), *Seeking the Favor of God 2. The Development of Penitential Prayer in Second Temple Judaism.* Vol. 22/2 of *Society of Biblical Literature Early Judaism and Literature.* Brill, Leiden, pp. 105–125.

Newman, J. H., 2007b. Three contexts for reading Manasseh's Prayer in the Didascalia. *Journal of the Canadian Society for Syriac Studies* 7, 3–17.

Nickelsburg, George W., 2001. Prayer of Manasseh. In: Barton, John, and Muddiman, John (Eds.), *The Oxford Bible Commentary*. Oxford University Press, Oxford, pp. 770–773.

Nikonanos, Nikos, 1989. *Meteora. A Complete Guide to the Monasteries and their History*. Athenon, Athens.

Nir, Rivka, 2003. *The Destruction of Jerusalem and the Idea of Redemption in the Syriac Apocalypse of Baruch*. Vol. 20 of *Society of Biblical Literature Early Judaism and Literature*. Society of Biblical Literature, Atlanta.

Nöldeke, Th., 1898. *Kurzgefasste syrische Grammatik*, 2nd Edition. Tauchnitz, Leipzig, reprint with additional materials: Wissenschaftliche Buchgesellschaft, Darmstadt, 1966.

Omont, Henri, 1929. *Miniatures des plus anciens manuscripts grecs de la Bibliothèque Nationale du VIe au XIVe siècle*. Librairie Ancienne Honoré Champion, Paris.

Oßwald, Eva, 1974–1983. Das Gebet Manasses. In: Lichtenberger, Hermann, and Oegema, Gerbern S. (Eds.), *Jüdische Schriften aus hellenistisch-römischer Zeit*. Vol. IV/1-3. Gütersloher Verlagshaus Gerd Mohn, pp. 17–27.

Pat-El, Na'ama, 2006. Syntactical aspects of negation in Syriac. *Journal of Semitic Studies* 51/2, 329–348.

Payne Smith, J., 1903. *A Compendious Syriac Dictionary Founded upon the Thesaurus Syriacus by R. Payne Smith*. Oxford, reprint Winona Lake, 1998.

Pérez Fernández, Miguel, 1997. *An Introductory Grammar of Rabbinic Hebrew*. Brill, Leiden, translated by John Elwolde.

Peursen, Wido van, and Talstra, Eep, 2007. Computer-assisted analysis of parallel texts in the Bible. the case of 2 Kings xviii-xix and its parallels in Isaiah and Chronicles. *Vetus Testamentum* 57, 45–72.

Peursen, W. Th. van, 2004. The Peshitta of Ben Sira: Jewish and/or Christian? *Aramaic Studies* 2, 243–262.

Peursen, W. Th. van, 2006a. Clause hierarchy and discourse structure in the Syriac text of Sirach 14:20–27. In: Peursen, W. Th. van, and Haar Romeny, R. B. ter (Eds.), *Text, Translation, and Tradition. Studies on the Peshitta and its Use in the Syriac Tradition Presented to Konrad D. Jenner on the Occasion of his Sixty-Fifth Birthday*. Vol. 14 of *Monographs of the Peshitta Institute*. Brill, Leiden, pp. 135–148.

Peursen, W. Th. van, 2006b. Response to the responses. In: Keulen, van and Peursen, van (2006), Vol. 48 of *Studia Semitica Neerlandica*, pp. 197–204.

Peursen, W. Th. van, 2006c. Three approaches to the tripartite nominal clause in Classical Syriac. In: Keulen, van and Peursen, van (2006), Vol. 48 of *Studia Semitica Neerlandica*, pp. 157–173.

Peursen, W. Th. van, 2007. *Language and Interpretation in the Syriac Text of Ben Sira. A Comparative Linguistic and Literary Study*. Vol. 16 of *Monographs of the Peshitta Institute Leiden*. Brill, Leiden.

Peursen, W. Th. van, 2008a. La diffusion des manuscrits bibliques conservés: typologie, organisation, nombre et époques de copie. In: Briquel-Chatonnet, F., and Moigne, Ph. Le (Eds.), *L'Ancient Testament en syriaque*. Vol. 5 of *Études Syriaques*. Geuthner, Paris, pp. 193–214.

Peursen, W. Th. van, 2008b. Language variation, language development and the textual history of the Peshitta. In: Gzella and Folmer (2008), Vol. 50 of *Veröffentlichungen der Orientalischen Kommission*, pp. 231–256.

Peursen, W. Th. van, 2009a. How to establish a verbal paradigm on the basis of ancient Syriac manuscripts. In: Rosner, M., and Wintner, S. (Eds.), *Proceedings of the EACL 2009 Workshop on Computational Approaches to Semitic Languages, 31 March 2009, Megaron*

Athens International Conference Centre, Athens, Greece. pp. 1–9. URL `http://staff.um.edu.mt/mros1/casl09`

Peursen, W. Th. van, 2009b. Plagiaatbestrijding en analyse van oude bijbelvertalingen. Computationele tekstvergelijking in onderwijs en onderzoek. *Nederlandsch Theologisch Tijdschrift* 63 (1), 22–36.

Peursen, W. Th. van, and Falla, T. C., 2009. The particles ܟܝܬ and ܓܝܪ in Classical Syriac. In: Williams, P. J. (Ed.), *Foundations for Syriac Lexicography II. Colloquia of the International Syriac Language Project*. Vol. 3 of *Perspectives on Syriac Linguistics*. Gorgias, pp. 63–98.

Phillips, David, 2006. The reception of Peshitta Chronicles: Some elements for investigation. In: Haar Romeny, R. B. ter (Ed.), *The Peshitta: Its Use in Literature and Liturgy. Papers Read at the Third Peshitta Symposium*. Vol. 15 of *Monographs of the Peshitta Institute Leiden*. Brill, Leiden, pp. 259–295.

Pigoulewski, N., 1937. Manuscrits syriaques bibliques de Léningrad. *Revue biblique* 46, 83–92.

Platt, Thomas Pell (Ed.), 1834. *The Ethiopic Didascalia or The Ethiopic Version of the Apostolic Constitutions, received in the Church of Abyssinia*. Published for the Oriental Translation Fund of Great Britain and Ireland by Richard Bentley, London.

Raes, A., 1951. Les complies dans les rites orientaux. *Orientalia Christiana Periodica* 17, 133–145.

Rahlfs, Alfred (Ed.), 1967. *Psalmi cum Odis*. Vol. 10 of *Septuaginta*. Vandenhoeck und Ruprecht, Göttingen.

Reiling, J., and Swellengiebel, J. L., 1971. *A Translator's Handbook on the Gospel of Luke*. Vol. 10 of *Helps for Translators*. Brill, Leiden, published for the United Bible Societies.

Rodrigue-Scharzwald, Ora, and Sokoloff, Michael, 1992. מילון למונחי בלשנות ודקדוק (*A Hebrew Dictionary of Linguistics and Philology*). Reches, Even-Yehuda.

Ryle, Herbert E., 1913. The Prayer of Manasses. In: Charles, R.H. (Ed.), *The Apocrypha and Pseudepigrapha of the Old Testament in English with Introductions and Critical and Explanatory Notes to the Several Books* 1. *Apocrypha*. Clarendon, Oxford, pp. 612–614.

Ryssel, V, 1900. Das Gebet Manasse. In: Kautzsch, E. (Ed.), *Die Apokrypen und Pseudepigraphen des Alten Testament*. Mohr–Siebeck, Tübingen, pp. 165–171, 2 volumes.

Sabar, Yona, 1976. *Pəšaṭ Wayəhî Bəšallaḥ: A Neo-Aramaic Midrash on Beshallaḥ*. Harrssowitz, Wiesbaden.

Schäfer, Peter, and Shaked, Shaul, 1997. *Magische Texte aus der Kairoer Geniza 2*. Vol. 64 of *Texte und Studien zum Antiken Judentum*. Mohr Siebeck, Tübingen.

Schneider, Heinrich, 1949a. Die biblischen Oden im christlichen Altertum. *Biblica* 30, 239–272.

Schneider, Heinrich, 1949b. Die biblischen Oden seit dem sechsten Jahrhundert. *Biblica* 30, 239–272.

Schneider, Heinrich, 1960. Der Vulgata-Text der Oratio Manasseh. *Biblische Zeitschrift* 4, 27–82.

Schneider, Heinrich, 1972. Canticles or Odes. In: *The Old Testament in Syriac according to the Peshitta Version*. Vol. IV/6 *Canticles or Odes, Prayer of Manasseh, Apocryphal Psalms, Psalms of Solomon, Tobit, I (3) Esdras*. Brill, Leiden.

Schniedewind, W. M., 1996. A Qumran fragment of the ancient Prayer of Manasseh? *Zeitschrift für die Alttestamentliche Wissenschaft* 108, 105–107.

Schuller, Eileen, 1992. 4Q380 and 4Q381: Non-canonical Psalms from Qumran. In: *The Dead Sea Scrolls. Forty Years of Research*. Vol. 10 of *Studies of the Texts of the Desert of Judah*. Brill, Leiden, pp. 90–99.

Schuller, Eileen, 1998. Non-canonical Psalms. In: Ester Eshel et al. (Ed.), *Qumran Cave 4 6. Poetical and Liturgical Texts, Part 1.*

Vol. 11 of *Discoveries in the Judaean Desert*. Clarendon, Oxford, pp. 75–172.

Segal, J. B., 1953. *The Diacritical Point and the Accents in Syriac*. Vol. 2 of *London Oriental Series*. Oxford University Press, London (etc.).

Sikkel, Constantijn J., 2008. Lexeme status of pronominal suffixes. In: Dyk and Peursen, van (2008), Vol. 4 of *Perspectives on Syriac Linguistics*, pp. 59–67.

Simon, Uriel, 1994. *Jona. Ein jüdischer Kommentar*. Vol. 157 of *Stuttgarter Bibelstudien*. Verlag Katholisches Bibelwerk GmbH, Stuttgart, mit einem Geleitwort von Erich Zenger.

Simonsohn, Uriel, forthcoming. The biblical narrative in the *Annales* of Saʿīd b. Baṭrīq and the question of medieval Byzantine-Orthodox identity. In: Thomas, David (Ed.), *Cross-Fertilisation and Cooperation in the Islamic Milieu*. Brill, Leiden.

Smith, Paul J., 1997. The viper and the file: Metamorphoses of an emblematic fable (from Corrozet to Barlow). In: Westerweel, Bart (Ed.), *Anglo-Dutch Relations in the Field of the Emblem*. Vol. 8 of *Symbola et Eblemata*. Brill, Leiden, pp. 63–86.

Smith, Paul J., 2001. Het dronken hert. Een emblematische fabel bij De Dene en Vondel. In: Bostoen, Karel, Kolfin, Elmer, and Smith, Paul J. (Eds.), *'Tweelinge eener dragt'. Woord en beeld in de Nederlanden (1500–1750)*. Verloren, Hilversum, pp. 13–40.

Smith, Paul J., 2003. Arnold Freitag's *Mythologia Ethica* (1579) and the tradition of the emblematic fable. In: Enenkel, Karl A. E., and Visser, Arnoud S. Q. (Eds.), *Mundus emblematicus. Studies in Neo-Latin Emblem Books*. Vol. 4 of *Imago Figurata*. Brepols, Turnhout, pp. 172–200.

Solomon of Akhlat, 1886. *The Book of the Bee: the Syriac Text Edited from the Manuscripts in London, Oxford, and Munich with an English Translation by Ernest A. Wallis Budge*. Vol. 2 of *Anecdota Oxoniensia Semitic Series*. Clarendon, Oxford.

Sperber, Alexander, 1959-1974. *The Bible in Aramaic*. Brill, Leiden, 5 volumes.

Stadler, Johann Evangelist, and Ginal, J. N., 1975. *Völlständiges Heiligen-Lexicon*. Olms, Hildesheim/New York, 5 volumes.

Stanley Jones, F., 1998. Early Syriac pointing in and behind British Museum additional manuscript 12,150. In: Lavenant, René (Ed.), *Symposium Syriacum VII*. Vol. 256 of *Orientalia Christiana Analecta*. Pontificio Istituto Orientale, Rome, pp. 429–444.

Stemm, Sönke von, 1999. *Der betende Sünder vor Gott. Studien zu Vergebungsvorstellungen in urchristlichen und frühjüdischen Texten*. Vol. 45 of *Arbeiten zur Geschichte des Antiken Judentums und des Urchristentums*. Brill, Leiden.

Strack, Hermann Leberecht, and Billerbeck, Paul, 1978. *Kommentar zum Neuen Testament aus Talmud und Midrasch*. Beck, München, 6 volumes.

Talstra, Eep, 1996. Singers and syntax. On the balance of grammar and poetry in Psalm 8. In: Dyk, J. W. (Ed.), *Give Ear to My Words. Psalms and other Poetry in and around the Hebrew Bible. Essays in Honour of Professor N.A. van Uchelen*. Societas Hebraica, Amsterdam, pp. 11–22.

Talstra, Eep, 1997. A hierarchy of clauses in Biblical Hebrew narrative. In: Wolde, Ellen van (Ed.), *Narrative Syntax and the Hebrew Bible: Papers of the Tilburg Conference 1996*. Vol. 29 of *Biblical Interpretation Series*. Leiden, pp. 85–118.

Talstra, E., Jenner, K. D., and Peursen, W. Th., 2006. How to transfer the research questions into linguistic data types and analytical instruments. In: Keulen, van and Peursen, van (2006), Vol. 48 of *Studia Semitica Neerlandica*, pp. 45–83.

Tidner, Erik (Ed.), 1983. *Didascalia Apostolorum Canonum Ecclesiasticorum Traditionis Apostolicae Versiones Latinae*. Vol. 75 of *Texte und Untersuchungen zur Geschichte der Altchristlichen Literatur*. Akademie-Verlag, Berlin.

Till, Walter, and Sanz, Peter, 1939. *Eine griechisch-koptische Odenhandschrift (Papyrus C. Vindob. K. 8706)*. Vol. 5 of *Monumenta Biblica et Ecclesiastica*. Päpstliches Bibelinstitut, Rome.

Tosco, Mauro, 2002. A whole lotta focusin' goin' on: Information packaging in Somali texts. *Studies in African Linguistics* 31 (1/2), 27–53.

Tromp, Johannes, 2002. *Het Leven van Adam en Eva. Een joods-christelijke vertelling over het menselijk bestaan*. Ten Have, Baarn.

Tromp, Johannes, 2004. The story of our lives. the *qz*-text of the *Life of Adam and Eve*, the Apostle Paul, and the Jewish-Christian oral tradition concerning Adam and Eve. *New Testament Studies* 50, 205–223.

Tromp, Johannes, 2005. *The Life of Adam and Eve in Greek. A Critical Edition*. Vol. 6 of *Pseudepigrapha Veteris Testamenti Graece*. Brill, Leiden.

Tromp, Johannes, 2008. Review of J. Herzer, *4 Baruch (Paraleipomena Jeremiou)*. *Journal for the Study of Judaism* 39, 104–106.

Vegas Montaner, L., 1982. Oración de Manasés. In: Macho, Alejandro Díez (Ed.), *Apocrifos del Antiguo Testamento III*. Ediciones Cristiandad, Madrid, pp. 103–197.

Vliet, W. M. van, 1991. Deuteronomy. In: *The Old Testament in Syriac according to the Peshitta Version*. Vol. I/2 and II/1b *Leviticus, Numbers, Deuteronomy, Joshua*. Brill, Leiden, prepared by W. M. van Vliet on the basis of material collected and studied by J. H. Hospers and H. J. W. Drijvers.

Volz, Hans, 1959. Zur Überlieferung des Gebetes Manasse. *Zeitschrift für Kirchengeschichte* 70, 293–307.

Vööbus, Arthur, 1979. *Didascalia: The Didascalia Apostolorum in Syriac I: Chapters I-X*. Vol. 401-402 of *Corpus Scriptorum Christianorum Orientalium; Scriptores Syri* 175–176. Secrétariat du CorpusSCO, Leuven.

Waard, Jan de, 1998. The Ethiopic Didascalia. Introduction, text and Harden's translation. Master's thesis, Leiden University.

Walter, Donald M., 2008. *Studies in the Peshitta of Kings. The Transmission and Revision of the Text, Relations with other Texts, and Translation Features*. Vol. 7 of *Texts and Studies, Third Series*. Gorgias, Piscataway, NJ.

Waltke, B. K., and O'Connor, M., 1990. *An Introduction to Biblical Hebrew Syntax*. Eisenbrauns, Winona Lake, Indiana.

Weiss, Theodor, 1933. *Zur ostsyrischen Laut- und Akzentlehre auf Grund der Ostsyrischen Massorah-Handschrift des British Museum mit Facsimiles von 50 Seiten der Londoner Handschrift*. Vol. 5 of *Bonner Orientalische Studien*. Kohlhammer, Stuttgart.

Weitzman, M.P., 1999. *The Syriac version of the Old Testament. An Introduction*. Vol. 56 of *University of Cambridge Oriental Publications*. Cambridge University Press, Cambridge.

Weitzmann, Kurt, 1970. *Illustrations in Roll and Codex. A Study of the Origin and Method of Text Illustration*. Vol. 2 of *Studies in Manuscript Illumination*. Princeton University Press, Princeton, N.J.

Weitzmann, Kurt, 1975. The study of byzantine book illumination: Past, present and future. In: Weitzmann, Kurt, Loerke, William C. Kitzinger, Ernst, and Buchthal, Hugo (Eds.), *The Place of Book Illumination in Byzantine Art*. Princeton University Press, Princeton, N.J., pp. 1–60.

Weitzmann, Kurt, 1976. The Ode pictures of the aristocratic Psalter recension. *Dumbarton Oaks Papers* 30, 65–84.

Weitzmann, Kurt, 1979. *The Miniatures of the Sacra Parallela Parisinus Graecus 923*. Vol. 8 of *Studies in Manuscript Illumination*. Princeton University Press, Princeton N.J.

Wertheimer, Ada, January 2001. עיונים נוספים במשפטים מבוקעים (More thoughts about cleft sentences). בלשנות עברית (*Hebrew Linguistics*) 49, 21–34.

Wilkins, George, 1911. The Prayer of Manasseh. *Hermathema* 16, 167–178.

Williams, P.J., 2001. *Studies in the Syntax of the Peshitta of 1 Kings*. Vol. 12 of *Monographs of the Peshitta Institute Leiden*. Brill, Leiden.

Wright, William, 1894. *A Short History of Syriac Literature*. Adam and Charles Black, London, reprint Piscataway, NJ: Gorgias, 2001.

Wright, William, 1901. *A Catalogue of the Syriac Manuscripts Preserved in the Library of the University of Cambridge*. Cambridge University Press, Cambridge, 2 volumes. With an Introduction and Appendix by Stanley Arthur Cook.

Yazıcıoğlu, Ahmed Bican, 2007. *Dürr-i Meknûn*. Kritische Edition mit Kommentar von Laban Kaptein. Herausgegeben im Selbstverlag, Asch.

Zotenberg, H., 1874. *Catalogues des manuscrits syriaques et sabéens (mandaïtes) de la Bibliothèque Nationale*. Imprimerie Nationale, Paris.